Then They Started Shooting

Then They Started Shooting

GROWING UP IN WARTIME BOSNIA

LYNNE JONES

HARVARD UNIVERSITY PRESS

Cambridge, Massachusetts, and London, England

2004

Library of Congress Cataloging-in-Publication Data

Jones, Lynne.
Then they started shooting : growing up in wartime Bosnia / Lynne Jones.
p. cm.
Includes bibliographical references and index.
ISBN 0-674-01561-4 (alk. paper)
1. Children and war—Bosnia and Hercegovina.   2. Yugoslav War, 1991–1995—
Children—Bosnia and Hercegovina.   3. Post-traumatic stress disorder—Bosnia and
Hercegovina.   4. Yugoslav War, 1991–1995—Psychological aspects.   I. Title.

HQ784.W3J66 2004
305.23′09497′09049—dc22
2004047382

For my father

Contents

part three **Psychosocial Consequences**

The Balkans, 1990

The Balkans, 2003

CROATIA

Vojvodina
Novi Sad •

Republika Srpska
• Banja Luka   Brcko •   **Belgrade** ⊚

BOSNIA-
HERZEGOVINA

Inter-entity
Boundary

Srebrenica •   Serbia

Federation of   Sarajevo •
Bosnia and   ⊚ • Pale
Herzegovina   Gorazde •
                                 Drina
                    Foca •

Mostar •   FEDERAL
         Republika   REPUBLIC OF
         Srpska   YUGOSLAVIA

                    Montenegro

Adriatic Sea   Kosovo
         Dubrovnik •

0   80 miles   ALBANIA
0   80 km

Bosnia-Herzegovina, 1998

Federation of
Bosnia and
Herzegovina

Inter-entity
Boundary

Srebrenica •

Drina

Republika
Srpska

Serbia

Sarajevo ⊙

Pale •

Rogatica
•

• Visegrad

TRESKAVICA

Gorazde • Kopaci
GREBAK •
• Vitkovici

Ustikolina •
Josanice •
Foca •

Cehotina

Republika
Srpska

Montenegro

0   30 miles

Tara

0   30 km

The Drina Valley, 1998

Abbreviations

BIH   Bosnia and Herzegovina
ICTY   International Criminal Tribunal for the Former Yugoslavia
JNA   Yugoslav People's Army
NGO   Non-governmental organization
RS   Republika Srpska
SDA   Party for Democratic Action
SDS   Serb Democratic Party
SFOR   United Nations Stabilization Force
SRS   Serb Radical Party
VRS   Army of Republika Srpska

Then They Started Shooting

Introduction

It is the river that catches your heart. I would wake to it every morning, stretched like a small sea below my bedroom window, reflecting the light of the sky and the mood of the town. My flat was upstairs in a comfortable villa overlooking the Drina, three minutes' walk from the center of Gorazde. This had been what Nerma, my landlord's fourteen-year-old daughter, called *the first front line* during the war. The house was neatly positioned under the line of hills to the south, from which Serbian troops could bombard the town with impunity. Nerma and her family had escaped for a few months to the town center and then returned to live downstairs. When they offered me the upstairs flat it had a large shell hole through the bedroom ceiling, broken floorboards, shrapnel scars over all the walls, and no windows. Nerma's father took my rent money and repaired the damage in a week, putting in a new stove and helping me order wood for the winter. Beyond the front garden was an unpaved road, followed by a stretch of reed bed and water meadow where old people walked their single cows in the evening, or sat on the path for a smoke, watching the light fade on the newly reconstructed dome of the mosque across the river.

Gorazde is a small place. It has two main streets, one on each side of the Drina, connected by three bridges. Before 1992 it was one of the more prosperous towns in the area, with two industrial suburbs, Kopaci and Vitkovici, and an armaments factory in town. There were

clusters of communist-style apartment blocks and increasing numbers of private houses built with wages hard earned in Germany. It
had two primary schools and three high schools and a large health
center, with a hospital in the neighboring town of Foca. A quarter of
Gorazde's population was Serb, the rest Muslim. The different ethnic
communities got along well.

Then war came. For Gorazde this meant four years of siege and
bombardment, followed by a peace settlement that divided Bosnia
between two political Entities: the Federation belonging to Muslims
and Croats, and Republika Srpska belonging to Serbs. Gorazde became an island of Federation territory entirely surrounded by
Republika Srpska, connected to the Federation's capital, Sarajevo, by
a yet-to-be-built road.

I arrived in late 1996, appointed by an aid agency to work as the
municipality's sole psychiatrist; there had been none for the previous
four years. The war had been over for a year, but the town was still
half destroyed, with roofless houses and shattered public buildings.
Electricity had only come on that month, and there was still no running water. A continuing reminder of war was that non-Serbs who
had been displaced from what was now Republika Srpska could not
return to live there because local Serbs, particularly those in the town
of Foca and the Gorazde suburb of Kopaci, were against it.

By the summer of 1998 the mood had changed. Many houses had
been rebuilt and repainted in vivid colors. Around the corner from
my flat was a new sports hall donated by the Dutch government,
where Nerma would drag me to pop concerts and handball matches
against visiting teams. Farther down the road was a street of cafés
and small boutiques packed full of young people on warm nights.
Displaced families were still living in crowded collective centers.
Otherwise the only obvious signs of war were the scaffolding walk-
way clinging to the underside of the central bridge, built to protect
pedestrians from snipers, and the ring of burned, unoccupied houses

on the edge of the town, whose Serb owners had still not reclaimed them after the war.

There were two completely gutted buildings next door to ours, where Serb families had lived. They had the appearance of having been burned from the inside, not hit by bombs. These Serbs had been good friends with Nerma's family and their other neighbors. One day Nerma's family heard gunfire. Thinking it must be coming from the hills, they climbed out the windows to escape. Then they saw that their Serb neighbors were shooting from their house. A short time later the Serb family took to the hills, leaving large piles of weapons and a short-wave radio in their living room. Not long before I moved in, one of the Serb women came back to visit her former best friend. *We asked why she didn't warn us,* Nerma told me, *and she said she wasn't responsible. Then she asked for a spade. We lent her one and she went and dug up some gold from her garden and left again.*

There was something striking about Nerma. It was not simply that she was intelligent and attractive. It was that in spite of having had her home, school, and community shelled from the surrounding hills for four years, and in spite of having lost friends and relatives, she was completely well. She told funny stories when she showed me where her family got spring water during the war. She said she would not mind if her Serb neighbors came back to live near her again. In break time and after school she sat with her girlfriends under the cherry trees on a low stone wall beside the river outside the primary school. They gossiped, giggled, ate hamburgers, and ignored the admiring groups of boys. She was happy and full of plans for the future: exchange holidays in Spain, high school, medical school in Sarajevo. The war had begun when Nerma was nine and ended when she was thirteen. Yet there was no evidence here of the war-traumatized child so often portrayed by the media. Nor in six months of psychiatric practice in the town did I see very many others.

The war had come suddenly when I was living in Slovenia in the summer of 1991. Since that time I had divided my life between aid work in the Balkans and training in child psychiatry in Britain. As the war moved south and gained ferocity, I had moved with it. I worked with adolescent refugees from Croatia and Bosnia in the summers of 1991 and 1992, worked in Sarajevo while it was under siege in 1994 and 1995, and arrived in Gorazde a year later. It was never difficult to find work. "War-traumatized children" attract public attention and funds, and any number of humanitarian agencies were looking for staff.

Yet through meetings with children like Nerma and her school friends I came to believe that humanitarian programs and mental health professionals were approaching the subject of war trauma and children from the wrong direction. The largely unquestioned assumption was that large numbers of children would be traumatized—that is, made medically unwell—by war and would need psychological assistance. Such children were identified by means of questionnaires (filled out by the children themselves or their mothers) that established whether they had symptoms, and the symptomatic children then received psychological treatment. Regardless of whether they were Croat, Muslim, or Serb, regardless of their particular experiences—bombing, rape, or ethnic cleansing—it was assumed that "traumatized" children would manifest their problems in similar ways, and that the Western treatment methods adopted by most humanitarian agencies would help them. Other assumptions were that war was necessarily brutalizing and damaging to children's moral development, and that today's traumatized and untreated children were tomorrow's terrorists, hence the need for "treatment." Underlying this approach was a belief that individuals' psychological worlds existed in a vacuum, completely separate from political and social realities.

But the majority of the children with whom I worked did not fit this picture. Some teenagers in Gorazde did have "symptoms," poor concentration in school or nightmares, but often they did not see their symptoms as illness requiring treatment, but rather as normal reactions to horrifying events. They were angry, unhappy, grieving, bewildered, but not, in most cases, psychologically disturbed. They had complex and sometimes discomfiting moral and political perspectives, but certainly not stunted ones. Moreover, the most significant factors affecting their mental health seemed to be rooted in the immediate environment in which they lived, rather than in the amount of trauma they had witnessed.

As I explored the academic literature I found much that supported my view. In conflicts studied around the world, 60–80 percent of children showed no psychological ill effects. Furthermore, their well-being was not necessarily related to the amount of violence they had suffered, but it was related to the way they made sense of their experiences, their subjective view of events. However, most of the large body of work exploring the effects of war on children focused on rates of illness and the identification of symptom clusters and "vulnerability" and "protective factors"; no one appeared to be examining the experience of war from the child's perspective. For all the children I had encountered, war had been a life-changing event, but it had not necessarily made them ill. If I wanted to understand the true impact of war on childhood, I had to step away from a medical model and the search for psychopathology and start to listen to children describing their experiences and their own understandings of the ways such experiences had affected them.

What happens if you are nine years old and you see your neighbors and school friends being forcibly evicted and half the town burned down? How does it make you feel, and how do you feel if those neighbors come back? What if your father or brother is killed on the front line? How do you make sense of that? Whom do you hold responsible? What happens if you are trapped in a city where the safest place for months on end is the basement? How does it feel to be imprisoned in your home by your neighbors? What is it like to fight over food parcels or to walk across mountains in the snow? How do children who have had such experiences view the future? After four years of war, how do they adjust to peace? Is there an enduring effect on their psychological health? I set out to learn from Bosnian teenagers themselves how they experienced war, how they made sense of it, and how it affected them. I did not want to confine myself to one side of the conflict: I would talk with Muslim young people in Gorazde and with their Serb contemporaries in Foca.

Foca is half an hour from Gorazde by road. Before the war it was another provincial town on the Drina, rather similar to Gorazde. It had industry centered on timber; 55 percent of the population was Muslim and some 45 percent Serb, with good relations between communities and frequent movement, for work and other reasons, between the two cities. In April 1992, in the first three weeks of the war, Bosnian Serb forces, with the assistance of paramilitary groups from Serbia, took control of the city, and the Muslim residents fled, were forcibly expelled, or were imprisoned. Many of the detainees were tortured and killed, while Muslim shops, homes, and mosques were destroyed. In the following three years the Serb residents lived in considerable hardship, although there was no direct assault on the town until NATO bombing destroyed its three bridges in September 1995. Since the end of the war, Foca had remained relatively isolated from the outside world, and had received relatively little in humanitarian assistance because its authorities refused to comply with the Dayton Peace Agreement of December 1995: they did not wish non-Serb residents to return to their homes, and a number of indicted war criminals lived in the town.

I visited Foca for the first time in the early summer of 1997. One of the local school psychologists had visited Gorazde for a seminar organized by some international aid organizations and had told me I would be welcome to visit her school to see how the students felt about talking to me. The weather that day was terrible, rain and wind dragging plum blossom off the trees and whipping the Drina into brown foam. The road follows the river. After Ustikolina the valley narrows, the rounded hills acquire more forceful and dramatic outlines. The only indication that we were crossing into another Entity was the sudden dearth of traffic and an orange stick with a round disk like a lollipop stuck beside the road marking the Inter-Entity Boundary Line. This was closely followed by a large sign in Cyrillic announcing that we were in Republika Srpska.

We crossed into town on a Bailey bridge built by SFOR (the United Nations Stabilization Force) to replace one of those destroyed by NATO, and bumped along a cobbled street past a hillside covered with gutted houses. There was little sign of the shell damage so evident in Gorazde, but the town had a dilapidated, uncared-for appearance. The school looked much like its counterpart in Gorazde, one of those buildings that say public school the world over, with wide drafty corridors stretching in three directions, dirty paintwork, and unmarked doors. We opened one into a bare classroom where the children, sitting at double desks, rose politely to greet us.

I had been worried that because I had worked in Gorazde, teachers and pupils in Foca would not want to talk to me. I was completely mistaken. They were pleased that I wanted to talk to children on both sides, and one boy, Mladen, volunteered to be interviewed that day as a pilot for my study. We sat in the small library. He was a pleasant, articulate child who felt well and happy with his life, and like Nerma he wanted to be a doctor. The fighting in town had scared him, as had the NATO bombing, but it appeared to have had no lasting effects. He told me unequivocally that ethnic cleansing—a term he used without embarrassment—had made Foca safe for Serbs to live in, because without it, he believed, all the Serbs, including old people and babies, would have been in danger of being killed in their beds by Muslim fanatics. Ethnic cleansing was not a crime but a defensive necessity, and ethnic separation was essential for Serb survival.

In a short journey up the Drina valley I had stepped through a mirror reversing all my previous understandings of the conflict. It was becoming clear to me that the lasting legacies of the war were not the psychopathological effects on young people, but their profoundly different understandings of why it had happened, what it had achieved, and what should be the relations between ethnic groups. These understandings resulted in quite different and incompatible wishes for the future. If I wanted to understand the war's impact on Mladen and Nerma, I would have to immerse myself in both their worlds.

That is what I did for the following year. For security reasons I could not live full time in Foca. However, I spent three to four full days of every week there, and as in Gorazde I interviewed young teenagers and their families at length about their experiences, their under-standings of the war, and their psychological well-being. I spent time with the children, at school and at home, participating in the normal life of both communities, shopping, watching TV, going on trips and to parties and various festivals.

This book is the result. In it I recount my exploration of the way children in the Drina valley, from both sides of the conflict, experi-enced and made sense of the Bosnian war. I set their experiences in the context of other wars and suggest implications for our under-standing of how children survive and develop in wartime. The book is not a history of the war, though it includes a chronology of key events to guide the reader through the political context in which these children lived. History is written looking backward. Hindsight and the passage of time allow a broader and supposedly more objec-tive view. Yet history is lived forward. All of us have a limited, partial, and subjective view of what we witness and experience. We grasp at selected events that have personal meaning, and we interpret them in the frameworks available to us at that moment. We create new stories which determine the way we remember and explain the past. It is the beliefs, attitudes, and feelings arising from these fragmentary perspectives that drive the future and that need to be understood.

The book is divided into three parts. In Part One I describe the war through the children's eyes. I interviewed forty children and many of their parents, but for this part I have interwoven the stories of eight children whose experiences are particularly representative of the conflict on both sides. Children's perceptions of what happened, their concerns, fears, and preoccupations, are often startlingly different from those of adults. Their concerns focus on the domestic environment as much as the external one. The stories are presented exactly as the children told them to me, in their own (translated) words. I have not extrapolated upon their experiences or guessed at feelings they did not share with me.

In Part Two the focus shifts to the children's understanding of the issues raised by the conflict. I explore the way parents made sense of the conflict to give some idea of the world in which the children lived. I then examine the manner in which war has crystallized ethnic identity and altered children's perceptions of themselves, their neighbors, their communities, and their country. These chapters show that the war in Bosnia did not arise out of deep-rooted ethnic animosities. On the contrary, these communities had spent most of the last half-millennium living harmoniously together. However, this last war, and in particular the settlement that brought it to an end, has had an enduring impact on these young people's sense of themselves and their neighbors, which has significant consequences for the future stability of the region.

Part Three concerns the war's impact on the children's psychological and social well-being two years after its end. I begin by summarizing changes, over the past half-century, in professional beliefs about the psychological impact of war on children, and how the changes have framed their assessment and treatment. I then explore the children's own perceptions of their psychological health, looking at the diverse responses to particular events such as the loss of a parent, or being bombed, or losing one's home; and the relationship between the children's well-being and the way they made sense of events. I discovered that in this war the specific interpretation of an event mattered less than whether or not a child chose to look for meaning. Children who avoided searching for explanations for past events appeared to have better individual psychological health than those who did not. Distancing oneself from the past could be protective, but in some contexts it has costs for the community as a whole.

My intention was to come home in mid-1998 and spend the following year analyzing my findings and writing this book. Events overtook me. In Kosovo, a province of Serbia, Albanians had lived under a form of apartheid for the previous decade, although they were the majority. They had learned from their exclusion from the Dayton peace process that nonviolent protest does not get the world's attention. By 1998 the province was at war. I was asked by an aid organization to go to Kosovo to set up mobile clinics and an emergency mental health program. A three-month commitment extended into three years, setting up a child and family mental health service in what had become a UN-administered area. The book had to be put aside.

The delay created an opportunity. In four years my young teenagers had grown into young adults and their world had changed. Milosevic had fallen from power and been indicted for genocide in Kosovo, Croatia, and Bosnia at the International Criminal Tribunal for the Former Yugoslavia (ICTY) at The Hague. At the request of the United Nations, Kofi Annan had produced his report on the town of Srebrenica, where despite its designation as a United Nations Safe Area, Serb forces had killed approximately seven thousand non-Serb civilians and expelled twenty-five thousand. The report criticized both the UN and the international community for failing to recognize what the war was about and to take action to stop it. He wrote: "Srebrenica crystallized a truth understood only too late by the

United Nations and the world at large: that Bosnia was as much a moral cause as a military conflict."[1]

Was that how young people in the Drina valley saw it? Had they recovered from the stresses and miseries of those years? What did they think now of all the crimes of the past and the possibilities of the future? I went back to find out, and the story of that return makes the final chapter of this book.

There are some points to note about the text. Most of the interviews were conducted through translators. The children spoke an almost identical language which they identified as Bosnian in Gorazde and Serbian in Foca. (In communist Yugoslavia Bosnian and Serbian were considered to be separate dialects of Serbo-Croatian. The linguistic differences have been emphasized on both sides since the war.) My experience of working both in refugee mental health clinics and in the field is that the presence of a good interpreter from the local community (one who understands the work and has a few years' experience of speaking English) often leads to better interviews than those conducted in my own language in Britain. The presence of someone friendly from their own town seemed to increase the children's ease and confidence with me and freed me to pay attention to nonverbal language as well as verbal. Also, the interpreter could explain to me many cultural references the children took for granted. Perhaps most important, common language can give the illusion of comprehension when there is none. Not speaking the language made me take the time and trouble to clarify, to make sure I understood.

Quotations from my interviews and conversations with people in Bosnia, and from the children's written stories, are given in italic type without quotation marks. In these quotations, three unadorned ellipsis points mark the speaker's or writer's own pauses, while ellipsis points enclosed in brackets indicate places where I have omitted words or sentences.

I use the term "Muslim" rather than the now officially sanctioned

"Bosniak" for references to the Muslim population in Bosnia. It is the term all the Muslims I spoke to in Gorazde, adults and children, used (with the exception of some politicians). More important, young people made clear that it was their preferred choice on my second visit, by which time they had become aware of the official terminology and rejected it.

The names of almost all my respondents and their relatives and friends have been altered along with personal details such as parental occupation to provide anonymity. In a couple of cases children asked me to use their own names and I have done so. They know who they are.

As I write, Milosevic's trial has begun its second year and the name Yugoslavia has disappeared from the map of Europe. Biljana Plavsic, one of the architects of the ethnic cleansing of Republika Srpska, has pleaded guilty to crimes against humanity at The Hague. At her sentencing hearing she acknowledged the terrible suffering of Muslims and Croats caused by organized ethnic cleansing and condemned the current Serb leadership that "without shame, continues to seek the loyalty and support of our people . . . by provoking fear and speaking half-truths." She pointed out that Serbian people continued to pay "a terrible price for our leadership . . . graves, refugees, isolation, and bitterness against the whole world, which spurns us because of these very leaders." She called on "others, especially leaders, on any side of the conflict, to examine themselves and their own conduct."[2] This unprecedented action opens up the possibility of genuine reconciliation in Bosnia-Herzegovina, based on truth rather than denial. Meanwhile a group of Western allies have again gone to war to depose a dictatorial leader of a multinational state, whom at one time they built up as an ally and friend. Now the West again wrestles with the issues of how to heal the cumulative damage caused by dictatorship, sanctions, and invasion; how to reconcile differences in a multi-ethnic state; how to balance competing needs for "justice" and "order"; how to help a country and its youth emerge from a long period of tyranny and establish a truly indigenous democracy.

Thus the issues raised in this book are as pertinent now as ever, and the youth of Gorazde and Foca have much to teach us. They bore no responsibility for the Balkan conflict but they suffered its consequences: the wasteful loss of their childhoods, the deaths of friends and relatives, and the complete disruption of their common community. Their stories confront our stereotypes about war, trauma, identity, and justice. For example, Bosnian young people challenge the monolithic and negative image of what it means to be a Muslim and the prejudices this has created. They demonstrate that it is possible to grow up in the shadow of genocide and destruction and retain vitality and spirit. They all debate how to deal with the past in order to live in the present and ensure a better future. Their stories also show that interventions of any kind, whether military, political, or judicial, that are ill thought out and halfheartedly applied may prolong conflict rather than resolve it. As always, it is young people who will pay the price.

part one

Children in Wartime

1

Fighting Begins

Foca, April 1992

Stojan knew something was wrong when he found his father's gun. His father was a teacher and had nothing to do with guns. He felt very frightened. When he thought about it, he realized that he had been frightened for quite a while. He was eight years old and had enjoyed his life. He and his family had a nice apartment not far from the river, and he liked his teachers at school. He had wanted to be a football player when he grew up, but he had just discovered basketball and decided it was much more interesting.

Now there was fighting on TV, not movie fighting, real fighting. The army had been sent to a town called Vukovar in Croatia. The Muslims had had a big meeting here in Foca, with people waving flags. The Muslims were fighting—well, not actually fighting, but wanting an independent Bosnia—and there was a Serb meeting too. He didn't understand. There was a Serb party, maybe they had given his father the gun, but his father wasn't interested in politics. Stojan decided to pretend he hadn't seen it. Maybe things would get better.

Over the next few days he became even more worried. There was more shooting on TV. Then without any warning or explanation he and his mother were sent to Montenegro. That was fun. They could swim and he didn't have to go to school. He could still see things on TV, but it didn't seem so bad. He thought he understood what was happening. The Muslims wanted to be in control of Bosnia, and there was fighting in Sarajevo. But he didn't want to think about war anymore. They were going to stay with his grandparents in Belgrade.

Svetlana wished she could be in Belgrade. That was where her father was. Things were always better when her father was there, but he was usually away. Her mother said he was always away when things went wrong. Like the time Svetlana was really sick with her throat and had to go to the hospital. But it wasn't her father's fault. He was a builder and he had to work. If he went away he got a lot of money. Sometimes he went to places like Iraq and Libya. Recently he had been home more, which was good because he could help with the work in their fields, but bad because everyone was worried about money. That's why he had gone to Belgrade, to see if he could find more work. Now her mother was worrying all the time about "war" coming.

Her mother was the kind of person who worried if there was a thunderstorm, but Svetlana was a little worried herself. She loved her home. There were three houses connected, belonging to her father, her uncle's family, and her grandfather, so she was never lonely. She was nine, had been in the village school one year, and had lots of friends, and the teacher was very kind. But now things were different. Her mother had started to worry and walk halfway to school with her, and then she had stopped her from going to school, so she had to stay home, and she couldn't see her friends, or talk to them as her family had no phone.

People were talking about "Muslims" and "Serbs." She knew that both Muslims and Serbs lived in her village. Muslims had a holiday called Bajram and played music outside and made cakes. She had cried once because her mother hadn't made cakes too. But her family had Christmas, and their neighbors came to them. She was still not really sure who was a Muslim and who was a Serb because they all lived mixed up together. Now everyone together was "guarding" against any "outsiders" coming in. People were getting more and more frightened, she could tell. A neighbor had come round one night crying, asking what was going to happen, as if her mother would know.

They had the TV news on all the time. She didn't understand it, she was sick of it. Sometimes her mother was so nervous she just insisted they lie on the bed together. Then one day there was a football match on TV. Red Star, the Belgrade team, won, and immediately afterward they heard shooting outside. Her mother was really scared and said *Come on, get dressed, we have to go, the war has begun*—but it hadn't. People had been shooting in the air, as they always did after football matches and weddings.

Then her mother said they were going to Belgrade. Just like that. Lots of other women and children from the town were leaving, and her mother had decided they should leave too. Svetlana was glad because now she would see her father.

Ivana lived in a large house that her parents were building themselves. The family had moved around a lot in her life, and it had taken time to get used to the new house, but she was just beginning to feel that Foca was home.

It was a morning in early April. She had started school that year, but was still at home because she was in the afternoon shift. Her parents had just left for work. Then the shooting started. Ivana had no idea where it was coming from or who was doing it. Luckily, her mother came home quickly and seemed quite calm. She just said they should stay inside. Then her father telephoned and said he was coming home too.

I went to the clinic, her father said. *I thought I'd better get a sick note for the next few days, in case I can't get to work. Don't want to lose the job.* Ivana's father worked in a business in Gorazde; he had been at the bus station when the shooting started. *They wouldn't let me into the clinic at first, it was all locked up, and I think they thought I had come to shoot them! Then Dr. Mehmed saw it was me, and let me in. No problem giving me a note.*

The family spent most of the next ten days in the basement. There was not so much shooting in their part of town, so Ivana was allowed outside in the evenings. Not many people were out, and those who were behaved oddly. For one thing, Ivana had noticed that Muslim people were not coming out of their houses at all, but Serb people could move around freely. Then one day she and a group of Serb friends saw the police go into a Muslim house and take the men out. The children stood and watched as the men were marched by. Someone said they were being taken to the prison to work.

Ivana's friend Asra lived in an apartment in the neighborhood. Ivana had not seen her for two weeks, so she decided to visit. Asra was really glad to see her. She told Ivana that no one in her family had left the house for fifteen days. They began to play, and then Asra started crying. Ivana didn't know what to say. Asra was mumbling about the police coming the day before and taking her father to prison, and that she wanted to see him, and she was going to see him. Ivana thought about the men she had seen being marched off in the street.

Suddenly there was a terrible banging on the door. The whole family leapt to their feet. Everyone looked terrified. Asra was still crying. Someone opened the door and all these police came in. They started shouting something about looking for weapons. Ivana was really scared; no one seemed to be paying attention to her, so she ran out of the apartment and into the street. She felt bad for Asra, but what could she do?

Nothing was the same anymore. She was afraid to go back to Asra's. Anyway it seemed that Muslim families were leaving town, some by themselves, some sent away by the police. She saw people going into the empty houses and turning everything upside down, taking some things, ruining others. There were some empty shops and people were stealing from those too. She didn't feel scared for herself so much, but she felt sorry for all the people who had left their homes.

One night she couldn't sleep. There was a bright light across the river, so she got up to have a look. Her fourteen-year-old brother was up as well. They could see what it was: houses on fire. Her mother came and said *Don't watch! It's not good to watch, go back to bed.* She was crying. *Maybe our house will burn like that someday.* Ivana felt scared again. Why would anyone want to burn their house? She did what she was told and went back to bed. In the morning the houses were completely destroyed; only the walls remained.

A few days later her mother told her she had to go to Belgrade. *It's not safe here. People are getting shot. You could be killed.* Ivana cried all that night, she didn't want to be sent away, but her mother insisted.

Gorazde, April–May 1992

Serb children were leaving Gorazde, and Amela was jealous. She was nine and lived with her younger brother, parents, and grandmother in a Serb part of town, on the same side of the river as the health center and the post office. That spring it seemed as if all her friends had left at the same time. When she asked their fathers, who had mostly stayed behind, they said *Oh they are just away for the weekend,* but it did seem odd that they would all go away on the same weekend. She was bored. There was no one to play with. She had asked her mother if she could go away for the weekend too.

But even before they left, her Serb friends had been somehow different. They all stayed together and didn't want to talk to other children. They seemed angry without any reason, and when she phoned them to ask if they could come over to play as usual, their parents would say they didn't have time.

She loved school. Her dad hadn't wanted her to go. He said it was a waste of time and that she would be better off in the village. This second year he had refused to buy her schoolbooks. Sometimes if he saw her struggling with homework he yelled at her, *Why are you wasting time in school when you don't know anything?* Sometimes her mum tried to help. But he shouted at her mum, and sometimes he got drunk and beat her. Sometimes he hit Amela and her brother as well. When he was drunk and they were fighting, she wished she were dead. Sometimes she felt so frustrated she just banged her head against the wall until she couldn't feel anything at all. Once she ran off into the woods and hid there, just to be by herself and be quiet, then her mother came to find her. She really loved her mum and her little brother, so she came home.

Then one day she had another fight with her dad. Only he was not drunk, he was really angry. She had gone outside and found a strange sign on their door. It was like a cross, and then there were four Cs around it. She wondered if this was a new game: maybe some children were playing hide-and-seek and this was "home." They might have asked her first, she was a bit cross, so she started to shout *Why are you writing on my door?* Then her dad came out on his way to work. He saw the sign and got mad and told her to go in and look after her brother. He told her she was never to phone her Serb friends again, and she was not to see them—not that any were around anyway—and did she understand that if she was with them, she could get killed. Then he went off and she felt terrible. It didn't make any sense. She didn't think her friends were stronger than she was, or could do her any harm.[1]

She wondered if it was because he was angry with the fathers of her friends. They never spoke to one another anymore. Last year, even a few months ago, they were always inviting her dad for drinks. Now they never did. And they looked different. The father of one close friend had changed a lot since his daughter had gone. He suddenly had a beard and a hat called a "subaru." He had had a beard before, but now he didn't cut it and it was long and dirty. He smelled so bad that she could hardly bear to talk to him. Almost all the men in the neighborhood were growing beards.

There was one old Serb lady who was still friendly, but she was a little crazy. Once she had called Amela's grandmother to come over and give her a hand with something heavy. When her grandmother got there she saw it was weapons! There were guns on all the couches. The old lady said they belonged to her two sons. Grandma was terrified and ran home as soon as possible to tell them all about it. Grandma talked a lot about war. She wanted to explain everything to Amela. She kept saying she understood it all, because she had lived through one war, and they should get ready for another. Amela told her she would hit her if she didn't shut up about war.

Nina was ten and doing very well in third grade. She had noticed that her Serb classmates were leaving. Every day there was a different reason: *I have to go to the village. We are going to the seaside for a picnic. Please can I leave the class.* She wasn't bothered, although things were a bit strange. Around her apartment block people had started guarding at night, she didn't know why. Then they had seen all these tanks go by on the train. She thought they might be going to Slovenia, or Croatia. She knew there was a war there. She had seen pictures of houses burning and felt so sorry for those people, when everything was so nice here. She had been a little worried and asked if it could happen here; but her mother promised it could not.

Only now everyone had gone from the apartment block except the two or three Muslim families who lived there. Then her mother's best friend phoned from Belgrade and said *You should leave, there is going to be a war.* Her mother didn't believe her. So Nina was determined not to worry.

Narcisa's parents had decided they would leave even though they both had good jobs at the factory. Narcisa felt very upset. She didn't want to go. She loved Gorazde, she loved her house, which her parents had built themselves, and she didn't want to leave her parrot and her dog. A lot of people seemed to be coming and going. She was in second grade, and when the spring term started half the class had gone. Then all these new people came into town. Then there were barricades in the street, and she had to stop going to school. Her parents said it was dangerous and they were going to a friend's house in Visegrad. The Yugoslav Army had promised it was safe to go there. They would travel on to Czechoslovakia.

Narcisa was standing in the living room when she heard a strange noise, a sort of droning like a large insect, only louder. It felt really close and everything began to shake. She was terrified. She ran outside just in time to see an airplane flying really low over the town. Maybe it would be better to go. *You see,* her mother said. *Fighting has started; if we don't leave we'll be killed.*

The friend's house was big, but it had too many people staying in it: her grandparents, her aunt, uncle, and cousins, her parents, and her older brother. It was much more frightening in Visegrad than in Gorazde. A few days ago she had nearly been killed. She and her brother were playing in a field and he got hot and hung his sweater in a tree. On the way home he realized he had forgotten it, so because she adored her brother and would do anything for him, she offered to go and get it. She was just untying it when she heard something whiz past her head really close, then a small branch fell off and hit her on the head. She suddenly realized that someone was actually shooting at her. She felt sick with fear and ran home as fast as she could, clutching the sweater.

Since then she hadn't been out so much. But home wasn't pleasant either. You could sit on the balcony at night and hear shooting in the town. People said it was on the bridge. It was the old bridge, the famous one in a novel. She believed them because you would hear screams, and then a sound like a body falling in the water. It was horrible. Her father, grandfather, and uncle mostly stayed away from the house. They were hiding because Chetniks, that's what everyone called Serbs now, were looking for Muslim men to put them in prison. Her mother said they might have to move again.

So they moved, all of them, but it was no better in the new house. The Chetniks came around almost every day, sometimes five or six, sometimes more. They wore uniforms and they had guns, so the family had to open the door. Sometimes they said they were looking for weapons, or they just came in and demanded gold and money and took anything they could find. They came one night and tried to kill the landlady. Narcisa was awake and saw them come in and point a gun right in her eye and say they would kill her. They kept asking where her husband was. All the men were hiding or they would have been killed. Narcisa had been really scared, but nothing had happened. Then they came back in the daytime and pushed the landlady into a room by herself. Narcisa couldn't see what was happening, but after the soldiers left the landlady was crying and went to take a bath right away. Narcisa thought they had searched her and made her take off her clothes. She knew her mother and her aunt hid some money in their clothes, probably the soldiers knew that too. But she didn't think she should ask. The landlady was too upset.

Then the Chetniks came again. Her mother was in town, and all the men were hiding somewhere outside, and Narcisa was terrified. They were screaming at the landlady: *Where is your husband, where is he hiding? Where is your son?* They got the Koran down from a shelf and started kicking it around the room. Narcisa had studied the Koran with her grandmother and knew it should be treated with respect. She wished her mother were there. Then it seemed the soldiers were bored, they were leaving. She watched them go down the street, but they met her mother coming home, so they all came back and it started all over again, just like before. Except that this time they told all the women that if they stayed in the house it would be set on fire. So they spent the night in the field. Thank goodness it was summer and not too cold. She wished she could see her father.

The next morning there was no sign of the soldiers, so they went back to the house. No one knew what to do. People were coming into town all the time; they said the Chetniks had set fire to all the villages. Some people were gathering at the fire station but her family didn't want to go there. Narcisa thought they might get locked in. They decided to spend another night in the field, as the house didn't feel safe anymore, so many houses were burning. Narcisa was more and more terrified. She wondered if they would be killed just like those people on the bridge. Her father and uncle and all the other men were hiding and preparing to go into the mountains, to try and get back to Gorazde. Then some Serb men, including a priest, came over and read from bits of paper. They told all the people sitting outside that they had to go and wait in a certain place, and there would be trucks to take them to their own side. It was true, there were trucks, and people were being pushed on as if they were cattle. Narcisa got on with her family and the trucks set off. She wasn't sure where they were going. She was still scared to death.

She saw a road sign saying Foca, then some forests. Then the trucks stopped. Men yelled *Get out, get down, be quick,* and pushed them onto the road. Narcisa could see woods ahead; someone said their own soldiers were there. They kept walking. The road curved and they couldn't see the trucks anymore, but suddenly there was shooting. Narcisa wondered if the Muslim soldiers would think they were Serbs and shoot them by mistake. She was so tired. Everything seemed confused.

All of a sudden there were lots of people and they were being told to go to a school. Then her mother said she must go and get some water, but Narcisa didn't want to let her go. It was dark now and there was always a curfew, it was dangerous, there were Chetniks. *Narcisa, there are no Chetniks anymore, these are our own soldiers, there isn't a curfew here. You are safe.* Narcisa looked around. Her mother looked exhausted but she was smiling. So were the soldiers. Narcisa sat down at a table, buried her head in her arms, and burst into tears. She could hear the soldiers asking her mother what was the matter. They sounded very kind, but she wanted her father, she wanted her uncle and her grandfather. She missed them so much she could not speak.

Back in Gorazde, Nina had stopped going to school. Her mother thought it was too dangerous. After talking with some other relatives about the telephone call from Belgrade, they had decided to leave. So everyone had to get photos and passports, then they planned to meet at the family's house in the countryside. Twenty minutes after they got there, Nina's mother was making coffee in the kitchen and Nina was playing outside when she heard shots in the hills quite near. She rushed into the house calling for her mother. *What is it? What is it?* Her father went outside to listen. Everyone panicked and started talking at once. They decided to get in the car. Her parents said the greatest danger would be in the direction of Foca, and they should go toward Pale, so they drove up into the hills.

Amela's first feeling when she heard all the noise was curiosity. She had never seen grenades before, and although she was a little scared, she wanted to go out and see. But her grandmother told her to watch out because she might be killed. Then just after she and her brother went to bed, Dragan, their next-door neighbor, arrived. She liked him. He had always given her and her brother presents at Christmas, and he had not changed like the other neighbors.

She listened through the door. He was talking with her parents. He kept saying *I am not going to hurt you or your children but I don't know about others. You should go, take the children and go.* Then her mother came in and got them out of bed and made them get in the car with her father and her grandmother, with just their pyjamas and their slippers on, nothing else. Grandma was going on again about how they shouldn't worry because they would get through this. They had to leave their home and *resign themselves to fate,* and Grandma knew all about it because she had lived through one war. Only this

time Amela didn't feel like hitting her. Dragan hugged her mother
and he hugged Amela and her brother as well. He said *Don't tell anyone I helped you,* and they drove across the river to her aunt's house.

The house was cold and completely empty, because her aunt had
gone away to Germany ages ago, but you could see across the river to
their own house. Amela went upstairs to have a look. It was strange;
she could see a little fire. Maybe someone had started a fire next to
the house. Why would they do that? She hoped her toys would be
all right, and her bicycle and her harmonica. Her grandmother
came and got her. *Don't watch,* she said. *It's better not to watch houses
burning.*

Samir was playing outside when the shooting began—alone, because
his best friend, Milan, had gone away some time before. He saw the
shells in the air and bolted into the house. After that, none of the
family was able to go out again. First of all his father came home and
locked the door. He seemed very nervous and worried. Then some
neighbors came around and said *Why lock the house? You are free,* so
Father stopped locking it. The shooting was still going on, and they
had hardly any food. Father wanted to go into town to buy food, but
these neighbors, who were all Serbs according to his father, stopped
him. They said *Stay at home, because this won't take long. We just have
to deal with these extremists from Foca and Visegrad. It's not safe going
into town. Your Muslim friends might mistake you for a Serb and kill
you.*

Samir didn't really understand what it meant to be a Serb or a
Muslim. The names were different. His friend Milan was Serb and so
were most of their neighbors apparently. He had thought they were
all friends, but when his father asked one of them to get food for him,
this man said he didn't even have any for himself. His father said this
was not true, because they were taking it from some of the shops.
Then one of them shouted *Get Alija to give you food! You voted for
him.*[2]

Now these friends came around whenever they liked, and his parents were always polite and treated them as guests. His mother made coffee. He and his two sisters sat on the floor, keeping very quiet. But the Serbs were not polite at all, they had really changed. They carried rifles. They hadn't hurt anyone, but they shouted *Bring me the water! Shut up!* and other impolite things. They stayed for hours, drinking rakia and having long discussions with Father. Not real discussions, because Father never said anything, he just listened while they went on and on about history. Samir couldn't understand it. It was all about what things were like six hundred years ago, how everyone was Serb before and then Turkish people came and somehow, some of them, the ones who were Muslim now, got Turkished. They said that all Muslims were originally Serb. His father told him later that it wasn't true, but anyway it didn't matter because they weren't religious. He never went to mosque. But it seemed to matter to the neighbors a lot, as if they wanted to prove something. It felt as if the family were in prison in their own house. It was weeks since they had been allowed out.

Then the Serbs began to get more aggressive. Once a neighbor, one of Father's old school friends, came and shouted at Father to come outside, and when he did, the neighbor yelled at him, accusing him of shooting at the neighbor's brother. Father said he had no weapons and would never do such a thing. Then the old friend shouted *You stay here and you have to obey us, and if something happens to my brother, I will kill you all.*

They came every few days. They said *If you have any kind of weapons you'd better give them to us,* and when his parents said they had none, they would go through the cupboards and throw things around. Sometimes one of them would go out on the balcony and start shooting toward the hill. Samir knew that was where the Muslim soldiers were. Then they would shout at the family not to leave the house or they would shoot them. Sometimes they said they were going to kill them the next day anyway. Samir was more and more terrified. But his parents went on being very polite and offering coffee.

One afternoon two Serbs came to visit again. Samir knew them. They always pretended to be friendly, but he didn't believe them and neither did his father. Once one of them had said he would help them escape, but he offered to take them to Rogatica, which was a town in Serb territory. Father said if they went there they might be put in a camp or killed, so they should stay here. Samir and his two sisters sat on the sofa together. His mother brought in the coffee. The other Serb was telling his father about the war in Croatia. He had spent a year there and was boasting that he had killed forty Muslims. Samir could see that his mother and father were unhappy, but they just sipped their coffee without speaking.

So, what do you think, what kind of weapon did I use to kill those guys? Father looked at the floor and stayed silent. Samir could see he didn't want to answer, but the Serb man insisted. *Come on, what do you think?*

Father lifted his head and looked at the man's stomach. There were two guns stuck in holsters; he pointed at one. The man laughed. *No, it's not this gun.* Father pointed at the other gun, and the man laughed again. He was enjoying himself. *No, it's not this one either.*

Father shrugged. *I really don't know what kind of weapon you used to kill them.*

Come on, I insist. Samir wondered if Father had seen the knife on the man's belt. He was scared; it didn't feel like a game.

With that knife?

No, not with this knife. The man looked really pleased with himself. With a flourish, he pulled a small knife out of his pocket, the kind some men use as a razor. *This is what did the job, forty Balija, with this little knife.*

Samir felt sick. The men gulped their coffee, then the one who had said he would rescue them stood up. He looked straight at Samir and his sisters. *You better choose three knives yourself and kill these children of yours. Better to kill your children yourself than watch while some Serb does the job for you. Kill the boy first and then the others, they're just Balija.*[3]

The men left. Samir and his sisters sat frozen on the couch. Samir didn't want to speak, he was too scared. What would his father do? What was Balija? After what seemed like hours, he heard his older sister whisper *Oh Father, it's not true is it . . . you won't kill us.* Immediately Father hugged them and told them not to be silly. He would never do such a thing, he was there to help and protect them, he would always be with them, and never leave them.

Samir had lost count of the days they had been in the house. He was nervous all the time, about everything. He wished they could go away but he was scared to go anywhere. Now it seemed they had to go. More Serbs in army uniforms had arrived. They kicked in the door and started shouting *Come out! Get out! Take your things with you, and come with us!* They shoved the family onto a truck with a whole lot of other people. Samir's mother tried to reassure the children, but he heard her say something to his father about camps and he could see she was crying. He thought maybe now the Serbs would take them somewhere and kill them. He was not going to cry. He would just keep quiet and try not to think about whether it was going to be good or bad.

The truck stopped and someone shouted at them to get out. They had to wait all night, then a bus came and they all got on, and a Chetnik explained that when the bus stopped they should get out and run. Samir was sitting near a fat guy called Edo. The Chetnik didn't like Edo, and threatened him with a knife. Then the bus started and drove an hour, with Samir keyed up, ready to run at any moment. Finally it stopped. The Chetnik wanted to keep hold of Edo but he got away, and they all just ran and ran. Edo kept telling Samir to go faster, but he couldn't, he had a pain in his leg. So he ran toward a small stream. If anyone was shooting, maybe they wouldn't notice him.

No one was shooting. They all spent the night by the stream. Someone said there were Chetniks on another hill, but it seemed all right here. Samir slept.

2

The War Goes On

Foca, 1992–1993

Stojan's father phoned when they had been away a little more than a month. He told them they could come back because *Everything is finished.* Stojan was glad, even though he liked being in Belgrade. He had heard that their apartment had been robbed and had felt very upset at the thought of robbers sitting in his home drinking and having fun.

When he got back things were both better and worse than he expected. The apartment had not actually been destroyed, but a lot of things were missing. So many houses were burned around the town. It seemed to be mostly Muslim houses, although some Serb houses were burned too. He felt awful when he saw the damage. He knew that the town had been liberated very fast, and that most of those Muslim people had gone away on buses to Croatia or wherever they wanted to go; but what if they wanted to come back someday and found their houses burned down? He didn't think that could be right.

Even though there was no fighting in town, things still felt rather frightening. A lot of people were going off to fight, and some said there might be more fighting. At least his father was at home. He had a job in the army, but it was in town, so Stojan saw him every day. They stayed at his grandmother's house now. Sometimes there was no electricity, but they had water all the time because she had her own well.

In Dusan's house there was no electricity or water. It was an old house, large enough for his whole family including grandparents and uncles and aunts to live together. He hadn't seen any fighting because they had left Foca before it began and gone to their house in the village. But it had been very tense. Everyone talked about Muslims attacking. His older brother, Vlado, had been very angry. He had not wanted to leave and had argued with their father. He had been doing so for months. Vlado had known there was going to be a war. Once he had told their mother *All Muslims should be killed.* She was completely shocked and asked him *Who put so much hate inside you? What about your Muslim friends?*

Mother, you have no idea, you don't go into town and you don't know anything, he had replied. *There are cafés where only Muslims go and the others where only Serbs go. That's how it is now.*

Dusan was eight and thought his older brother was one of the cleverest and bravest people in the world. His parents had told him not to worry, it was just some extremists. Those who wanted to fight could go out on the bridge and fight there, and it would be over in a few days. Then the shooting had begun, and the family decided they would go to Serbia, but Vlado had refused, he wanted to be with his friends. Father told him he was too young, and threatened to tell the authorities he was only seventeen. But Vlado had somehow got a ride back on a truck and lied about his age. So now he was on the line, along with his father and uncle. After a month Father had told the rest of them to come back to their house. He said the war would be over very soon.

Dusan's neighborhood had completely changed. Nothing was there anymore except their house and their neighbor's house. Almost everything else was burned down. They saw another neighbor, who told them that Muslim Green Berets [SDA militia] had been burning houses. Dusan's next-door neighbors were Muslim. They had stopped Dusan's house being burned because theirs was connected to it and would have burned as well. Then Serbs came and started burning Muslim houses, but some Serbs had saved the neighbor's house to stop Dusan's from being burned. The only damage he could find was two bullet holes: one in the bedroom by the bed and another in the TV. He was glad his family had come back. When he looked out the window he could see people going into the empty houses that were still standing and just taking anything they could carry: televisions, doors, windows. When there was nothing left to take, they threw a hand grenade and burned down that house too. Once Dusan saw some children running in and out of the empty houses and wondered if it would be fun to go with them. But his parents and his grandparents told him *You never take things that don't belong to you.*

Dusan's Muslim next-door neighbors were gone. He didn't know where. They had not been very close friends. Actually, his father said that just before the war began, before they left for Serbia, he and Dusan's uncle had looked out the window and had seen the neighbor with a gun. He hadn't been shooting, just standing in his yard. At the beginning of the war those same neighbors had asked his aunt *Who sleeps in which room?* Looking back, everyone thought that was a strange question, especially after they heard that some lists had been found in some Muslim houses. Everyone said these were lists of the people they had planned to kill.

Dusan's family didn't have much food. Just before the war his grandfather had told them to store food for the hard times coming and his parents had laughed and told him he was being silly. Fortunately, they had home-grown vegetables, and flour given out by the Red Cross. He was a bit bored. There was no school because the teachers had gone to fight, but he couldn't enjoy the free time, because his mother worried about unexploded bombs and all the drunken people around, so she made him stay in the yard. He was glad when his brother came home. His brother was teaching him how to use a gun so he could defend himself.

Gorazde, 1992–1993

Amela decided that if she had to choose between cows and shelling, she would choose shelling any day: it was much less frightening. After they arrived at her aunt's house Grandma became very organized. She seemed to know what to do. She had keys to a shop owned by a relative and she went there to get some food. Then she found a cow left by one of the departing Serb families, which she caught and brought back. Amela was terrified of all farm animals and could not bear to go near the cow. The family spent most of their time in the basement because of the shelling, but she was scared the cow might come into the hallway and jab her with its horns. This worried her much more than being hit by a shell, and she went on and on at Grandma to kill the cow so they could have some meat. Finally Grandma did kill it, and then they swapped the meat for milk and cheese with another family for a whole month, and felt very well fed.

The front line was very close so they hardly went out at all. There was no possibility of going to school, but she didn't mind. She had all her dolls and had made a small den under the staircase where she could play with them. She and her brother were allowed outside to pee in a basin, then they had to come in. In quieter periods, her mum dressed both of them in white pants and white shirts and let them play close to the wall of the house, which was also white. The idea was that the snipers wouldn't be able to see them.

Amela loved feeling fresh air on her face. At night when it was cold, her grandmother made a wood fire in a pot. It kept them warm, but the smoke was terrible. Her mum was nervous when there was shelling, Amela could tell, but Grandma wasn't frightened at all. *Nothing can hurt me,* she said all the time. Then one day a shell came right through the basement wall. There was an enormous "crack" as something seemed to burst above their heads. Amela bit her tongue and then thought she would choke from all the dust. As it cleared they saw that Grandma had been hit on the head by a brick. It had stunned her but she seemed all right. Amela started giggling. *That's good, now you know things* can *happen to you! Even you!* Mum had been cut too, but not badly. The worst damage was to the wall. It had a large hole in it.

Dad had gone to join the army and was back on the other side of the river. There was no way to cross, so they didn't see him for some months. Amela didn't know if she minded or not. It was nice not having anyone shouting at her, but time seemed to go more slowly when he wasn't there. She could see that her mum was worried about him, and her brother missed him a lot. He would walk up to strange men and say *You're like my dad.* She would rather be beaten than have her brother calling strange men Father.

Up in the hills above town Nina and her mother and sister were thinking about how they could get back to being with her father and brother. Both were based at a local defense unit down in their village. In four months Nina had lived in three different villages, moving to avoid the shelling. She didn't mind. For some weeks they had lived in a village with four other families. She liked the garden and they had enough to eat, but the house was so old that she thought if it got hit by a shell it would just collapse. She could hear shooting in the villages below and she had seen some houses burning. But no one seemed to be shooting at them and she was left to play with the other children. After a few weeks her mother got worried about schooling, so Nina's sister, who was ten years older, gave her and some other children lessons under a peach tree. Then they moved to another house which had a basement, but her mother wanted to get down to their own house. It was concrete and she thought it would be safer, and the family could be together. So they decided to walk down through the woods.

The three of them set off in the morning, heading down through the trees to keep out of sight of snipers. Suddenly Chetniks began shooting at them. Nina could hear the bullets whizzing past everywhere. They got behind a big tree. Mother said *Be glad they aren't shelling or we would all be dead.* Then she said *Run!* They ran so fast through the trees that Nina still felt she was running when they stopped at a small spring. They could still hear shooting but it was above them at the big tree, so the Chetniks thought they were still there. They walked on. Nina was now too excited to be scared. She knew they were getting close to home, and she couldn't wait to see her father. Then she saw their cherry tree, full of bright red fruit, and she rushed to climb it, filling her hands and mouth with cherries. They had never tasted so good.

During the next few weeks there was more shelling. Two airplane bombs fell a hundred meters away, but no one was hurt. Nina had learned to listen for the dull tone that meant a shell was coming in. If she heard that, she knew she had to lie down somewhere at once. The house felt very safe. It was behind a little hill and her father had built a shelter in the underground garage, so that became their home. Their uncles and cousins joined them. She was glad to be with the family, although it was more boring than in the hills. Sometimes, for a change, she would sit in the car beside the house and try to teach herself to knit.

Sometimes she went to a neighbor's house to play with a friend. She was there one day when she heard the sound of a shell flying really close. There was no time to reach the garage so they crouched against the wall of the house. It fell so close she couldn't believe she was all right and was still checking herself all over when her father came, screaming *Where have you been? What have you been doing?*

How could you do such a thing? They ran into the garage. Father was still shouting at them when a strange woman appeared, crying and talking very fast: something about Nina's cousin. Nina had seen her cousin only ten minutes before, smiling and friendly, as he went to put grass in the barn. Her father and sister rushed outside. He was dead; a piece of shrapnel had gone straight into his heart. Nina's sister helped to lay him out in the yard. Then her uncle came back and when he found everyone crying he guessed at once, even though they tried to tell him gently. They took the boy away to be buried. From that moment Nina could not bear to look at the place where he had been lying.

That wasn't the only bad thing that happened. Once when they were all at home they suddenly heard screaming somewhere in the hills. The whole village went outside to listen. It was a little girl screaming, on and on. No one knew what to do. Nina didn't want to hear it. She hugged her mother. Later they found the girl. She had been raped and killed. Nina knew what that meant. She had known the little girl and cried when she thought of her.

A few days later Nina's father saw Chetniks coming toward the house slowly, down the hill, through the fields. He ran into the basement, shouting at them to run and hide. She and her mother hid in the field. Luckily she was wearing an old fur coat which she kept on even though it was summer. It had a hood and she was sure it made her harder to see when she was lying down in the grass, so she felt safer. She thought about what had happened to the little girl, and whether it might happen to her. Then she made herself stop and did what she always did when she was scared: thought about other people who were worse off than she was, and how they were surviving, so she would too. She tried to think of nice times they had had at the seaside before the war and how they would do so again when it stopped. There were some shots. Then her father called them back. The Chetniks had run away. Her father and the other men were laughing. They said the Chetniks probably thought there was a big army unit here, rather than a few men with old hunting rifles, and that was why they left. The village could have been taken in an hour if they had tried.

Nina wondered if they were ever going to stop moving. The family decided to move back to the apartment in Gorazde, because her father's and brother's unit were there. They had a terrifying journey in a truck full of all their food. She and her sister sat on sacks and they drove without lights, but even so the Chetniks saw them and fired at them. She could see the sparks and was really scared, especially when they crossed the bridge. She knew that one grenade would destroy them all.

Everything in Gorazde was different. There were strange people she had never seen before, the air smelled of smoke, and every building in the town seemed to have been hit by shells. There was no water or electricity, and the shelling never stopped. Nina hated being in the basement all the time; she preferred going outside even if it was dangerous. Once she and her sister were almost hit, while they were getting water from the pump at the post office. They only missed it by diving into an apartment building when they heard the whooshing noise. Each time something like that happened she vowed it was her last trip out, but it never was.

She was happier living close to her father and brother. Then her father decided he wanted them to get out of Gorazde, out of Bosnia altogether if possible. He said he couldn't bear being on the front line and worrying about them in the city, it would be easier for him if he knew they were safe. *Besides, the children might learn something good abroad.* So her mother finally agreed.

That was why in the middle of winter and in the middle of the night she was dressed up in five pairs of trousers, five pairs of socks, and three sweaters, carrying a small rucksack and walking with her sister, mother, and uncle in a long line of people through the snow.

They were going over a mountain called Grebak. The lines had been pushed back a few months earlier and people could get in and out of Gorazde this way. They were in two groups, and there were soldiers leading them. It reminded her of the old films about partisans and she felt quite excited.

After some hours, though, she began to feel exhausted. Sometimes the snow came right up above her knees, almost to her waist. The tea in the thermos had frozen, so all they had was some thick plum juice her mother had made. At one point they were going along a stream, but her mother had stopped her from drinking the water. Then right by the stream she saw an old man lying on the ground. He was all blue, and his eyes were open. Nina stared as she walked past; she knew he was one of theirs, and that he was dead. She looked back, keeping her eyes on him as long as possible. No one wanted to stop and close the man's eyes.

Sometimes they took little breaks to do some exercises to keep their circulation going, but no real rest. Then Nina noticed that her family was alone. They had lost the group. They had no idea of the way, but dared not stop with Chetniks all around, so they just kept walking, hoping and praying they were not blundering across enemy lines . . . She had never been so cold. She just wanted to sleep but her mother kept nudging her to keep her eyes open. Then she saw a small house ahead. It was just beginning to get light and there was smoke coming out of the roof. *Mama,* she called, *I'm so cold, let's go inside and get warm, just for five minutes.* But as she got closer the house began to disappear. Instead there was a tree with wide branches. She wanted to weep. Her uncle pulled her along, promising chocolate and saying *Come on you can make it! I am going to tell your cousins in Zagreb how brave you are.* She just had to keep going a little longer. Now the sun was right up and there was another cabin, but perhaps this one would disappear too. It did not, and as they got close they saw the sign for their own police force. They were on their own side.

They walked in and there was a stove and a small bed. Nina went straight over to the bed and fell asleep.

Samir spent two nights sleeping in the hills before they managed to cross no-man's-land to their own side. A group of them were sent in a bus to a town called Visoko. It was better than being trapped in their house in Gorazde, but people were not very friendly. They slept in the school for a month, then were given a room in a house whose Serb owner had left. There were still Serbs and Croats and Muslims living together in the town. Sometimes he thought the Muslims were the worst. He saw some of them selling humanitarian food aid in the shops, when lots of people did not have enough, but one of their Serb neighbors brought them oil and flour and was very nice. Then sometimes when his father was home on leave, local people who didn't know him would send the police around to say he should be on the line. Father had papers now to show what unit he was with, and where he should be, but it felt unfriendly. Other times people would ask *You refugees, when are you going home?*

There was occasional shelling in town—one day Samir counted eight rounds one after the other—so you had to be careful. Once when he was walking home with his friend, a piece of shrapnel hit his friend in the leg right in front of him. But it wasn't as bad as Gorazde or Sarajevo. He could see how things were there on TV, with people dying all the time. Sometimes he and his friends played volleyball in the street. Some of them collected shell casings and bits of shrapnel, but he wasn't interested.

His father was on the line, but he got home every week. He had managed to find some fruit and vegetables to sell to try and get them a little money because they had nothing. Samir started school again, having missed a whole year. The other children were friendlier than the adults and there was a sports hall where they could play games. There was a hodza (a Muslim religious teacher) at the school, so he

was starting to learn a little bit about being a Muslim. He had decided
to start going to mosque.

Narcisa and her mother were bused through three separate towns, including Visoko, before they found one that still had room for refugees. First they were put in a school, then they were offered room in a
house, but then some of the occupants made it clear they were not
wanted, so they went back to the school. They shared a classroom
with five other families. They put mattresses and blankets on the
floor, each family marking its own space. Narcisa didn't think it was
so bad; she could get used to anything, except being without her father. One day she saw her brother Kemal take a picture of Father out
of Mother's purse. He made a kind of frame around the picture and
put it around his neck. When he thought he was alone he would take
it out and look at it. He would talk to it very quietly, but when she
came close he dropped the picture and pretended he wasn't doing
anything. She thought they were all dead. Father, uncle, and grandfather: she would never see any of them again.

At lunchtime one day a girl walked into their room and told
Narcisa's mother there were some men from Gorazde asking for her.
Her mother went out, saying there might be news, and the next
moment everyone was shouting at Narcisa *Your father came!* She
couldn't believe it. She ran down the stairs and there was her mother,
she had not realized how thin she was, but she was laughing and crying, and there was her father! Narcisa ran into his arms, crying and
asking questions all at once: *How are you here? How is my dog? Is she
okay?* Father was laughing and crying too, but he told her he was
sorry, the dog was dead. She had been barking during the shelling
and a man had got scared and shot her.

Where's Kemal? Father asked. Half the people in the room set off to
find him. He came running up the stairs, carrying the tins of hot
food he had collected for lunch, and when he saw Father he just

dropped everything on the floor and they were hugging, and both were crying. Narcisa thought that everyone in the room, everyone in the whole school, seemed to be crying with them. She had never felt so happy in her life.

They spent the next days talking and talking. Father had been in Gorazde. He said it was very hard in the city. There was shelling and there was no food and you had to climb to a place high in the mountains to buy flour or anything. You could get in and get out of the city that way, but it was a very long and dangerous walk, forty kilometers, and you had to walk in silence, at night, without lights.

Narcisa wanted to go home and all the family agreed, home was the best place to be no matter what. So (shortly after Nina and her family walked out over Grebak), Narcisa and her family walked back to Gorazde along the same route. The house was still standing even though it was a mess with all the windows broken. As there was not so much shelling at that time, sometimes she could go outside. All her friends were pleased she had come home.

After what seemed like weeks on the road, sleeping in a bed with five strange children, traveling in a hot, full truck where Nina was scared because she couldn't breathe, her family came to a small town called Kiseljak, near Sarajevo. Nina could not get used to it. The war was going on only a few kilometers away and yet here were Muslims, Croats, and Serbs living together almost as if nothing was happening. The shops were open and you could buy anything—jam, chocolate, meat—just as if you had walked into another world. Nina wondered if people had any idea that other people she knew were fighting and dying and suffering while everyone here was enjoying themselves.

She did not go to school. Her mother said there was no point when their visas for Germany might arrive at any time. They were staying with another uncle, and mostly she played with his two little boys. There was a large sports stadium opposite their house, but they couldn't go there. It seemed to have been turned into a prison. Sometimes Nina watched from her window. She saw that the Croats were in charge there. She wasn't sure if the prisoners were Muslim or Serb, but she saw them being taken from cars and left in the stadium. It was a freezing winter, yet the guards made the prisoners take off all their clothes except their underwear and run around in the snow. Nina couldn't understand it. Why make them run without clothes in the freezing cold? She found it hard to watch. It made her think of her father. Maybe he could be caught, and made to run like that? The thought was unbearable. Even so, she had noticed something about herself. At the beginning of the war, everything had upset her: the little girl, people being hurt. Now after a year she didn't think anything could really shake her up. If she saw burned people, wounded people, dead people, she just felt cold, and she never cried any more.

After three months in Kiseljak, Nina's mother decided they had better move to Zagreb and try from there. So they set out on yet another journey. This one felt like the worst. It took days, because they had to take a bus through Chetnik territory. Twice they got turned back and had to start again with another route. Nina thought she was living on buses. Sometimes Chetniks would get on and search and demand money, then the Croats refused to let her cross their border because they said her mother was planning to put her in school in Zagreb, and they didn't want that. Then they phoned some Croatian friends who came and got them by car and there was no problem. Finally, after a bus journey to Split and another to Zagreb and another to Berlin, they were in Germany, staying in the house of the pastor who had sent their visas. Everything was different. Nina had no idea if she would see her father again, and now she had to learn a whole new way of life.

Foca, 1994

Svetlana was tired of being homeless. She had liked being in Belgrade. They had stayed with relatives and she had gone to school and done well, even though some children had teased her for being a "refugee." But they had used up all their savings, and hadn't wanted to burden their relatives. When they got back to their village it was completely empty, everyone had run away. They didn't dare stay there alone, so they had come to Foca. Svetlana couldn't recognize it, so many houses were destroyed. They managed to find an apartment in town. Then the landlord wanted it for someone else and kicked them out. Then they found another empty apartment. They just moved in without getting permission, and one day when Svetlana was at school the police came and threw all their things out on the street. Only her little brother was there at the time and he was terrified. They called her mother at work and she ran home, but he was hysterical and wouldn't let her touch him. Then Svetlana came and tried to get close to him, but he screamed and yelled and refused to let her—and the same with her father. It took hours to calm him down; she had never seen him like that. Now they were in another apartment. It was very old and the rooms were tiny, and who knew when they would be thrown out of this one. They had heard that their house in the village had been burned down by Muslims, so her father had the right to be given somewhere to live.

That was not the worst thing that had happened. First her grandfather had died. Not because of the war, he was quite old. But she missed him, she remembered him taking her for rides on his horse and how much she had liked that. Then her favorite uncle had died on the front line outside Sarajevo. He was really young and had been so nice to her. She had been so upset. She still couldn't bear to think about him or talk about him. If she did, she cried. If she looked at his picture, she cried. So she tried to avoid doing those things, everyone said that was best.

Both Ivana's grandparents had died. Her mother phoned her in Belgrade to tell her and she cried. At the beginning of the war, Turkish people tried to attack their village, so they came to stay in Foca.

Grandma didn't like it because she wasn't used to sleeping up on the third floor, she was afraid she would fall down. Ivana and her brother thought this was terribly funny. Then the Turks left, and her grandparents wanted to go home, even though the village was empty. They were worried about their cows. So they went back, but the Serb army had put mines around to stop Turks from coming back, and Grandma stepped on one. Then when Grandfather was sick, he couldn't go to the hospital because there were too many wounded people there, and he died too.

Ivana loved being in Belgrade. All her mother's family was there. They were quite well off, had a big house, and lots more relatives came to get away from the war: an aunt and cousins got out of Sarajevo. There was another bad moment for them. Turks made a terrible massacre in a village near Foca called Josanice, and killed some old people and children. They showed it on TV, and her aunt had relatives in that village.

When Ivana's mother came to take her back, she didn't want to go. She had seen what Foca was like on television, with the center of town empty and destroyed. She told her mother she wanted to stay.

Don't be silly, her mother said, *don't you want to see your father? Things aren't so bad now. All the children have gone back to school.*

I don't want to go back.

Well, your brother does. If you don't come with us now, I can't tell you when I will be back to get you, maybe never.

Ivana was not sure she believed this, but her mother looked serious. When they got back to Foca it wasn't quite as bad as she had expected. There was no electricity. A lot of people seemed to be dying. She only saw her father one or two days a week. There were lots of children she didn't know. But they asked her which class she wanted to be in at school and she chose the one with some old friends from her part of town. They could play together, mostly hide-and-seek or ball games. The boys played war, hiding behind trees and killing themselves and one another. They were very aggressive and shouted and pushed, and she thought it was stupid. Asra and her family had gone, she did not know where. When she asked her mother, she didn't know either. Her mother could see she was upset. *They wanted to stay, but they could see people leaving every day,* she explained. *They were scared. It was us or them, my dear. Somebody had to go, or this war will never end.*

After the massacre in Josanice, Dusan's grandfather said *Not a single Muslim ear should remain.* Father and Grandfather never minded when Dusan listened. Father seemed astonished and said *But you were always telling me about "Brotherhood and Unity."*[1] Grandfather had said he was eighty-five years old; he had survived three Balkan wars, the First, the Second, and now this one. In his opinion the Muslims had betrayed the trust of the Serbs too many times in the last two or three hundred years. This was the moment when they should be destroyed.

The best times were when Dusan's brother came back, even though sometimes it was for friends' funerals. He was always filthy and exhausted, and then had to rush off again. He wasn't an ordinary soldier anymore. First they had transferred him to heavy weapons, but he told Dusan the army was a big disappointment: too many people just held the lines and didn't try to advance, they even ran away. There was looting from people's homes, and drunkenness. People took liquor up to the lines with them, or arrived there already drunk, shooting at random from the trucks as they drove up. Then they would fall asleep and get massacred.

Vlado thought there were too many cowards and he despised the corruption. He had got himself transferred to an "intervention unit." Sometimes they were in really close fights; he had to jump into enemy trenches. He brought home some Muslim guns he had taken, but he never talked much about what he did. Dusan knew they moved a lot. The lines extended all the way from Gorazde to Treskavica. His uncles, father, and brother were in completely different places and it was hard to keep track. They had the radio on all the time at home. There was no TV because there was still no electricity. That used to come from Gorazde, so it was cut off. The radio made everyone tense because sometimes the news was awful. Sometimes they sat up all night to hear how many people had died and who they were. He and his mother always wondered: Will it be one of ours?

Nothing worked normally in the town. All the shops were empty, people were hungry. There was humanitarian food aid, but not everyone got it. Father said smugglers and profiteers were taking it. Everyone seemed tense, sometimes people shot guns out the windows just to let off steam. His parents still didn't want him to go out much. Anyway school was not working normally. You would get there and find the classes canceled because there were no teachers. He and his friends played soldiers. Different groups had camps in different parts of the town, so they invaded each other's camps and tried to destroy them. Sometimes they built a fire. It was just like the regular army; girls did the cooking and cleaned the camps. Sometimes the boys collected bullets. When Dusan couldn't play, listening to music on the radio cheered him up. He liked the songs about the war; they made him feel brave and courageous.

Finally his parents decided conditions were so bad that Dusan and his mother should go to Serbia. There would be more food. He could go to school properly. They could live in an old house belonging to a relative. It had no running water or inside toilet, but it would be better than here. Father promised Dusan he could come back to Foca for visits.

Gorazde, 1993–1995

There was a man calling Amela's name as she walked up the street. The shelling had eased off and she was enjoying being outside. She looked around and saw a thin, bearded, very dirty man. He looked just like a Chetnik. She thought of running, but before she could, he caught up with her. He was laughing and put his arms around her. He smelled just like a Chetnik too, disgusting!

Amela, it's your dad, it's me. Don't you recognize me?

She stared at him, pulling back and stepping away. *Okay, so if you're my father tell me something about us that only Dad would know, from when we lived together. Then I'll believe you. But don't come near me until you have!*

All right, how about the time you ran away to the woods when you were a little girl? As he was speaking, there was a sudden crack and a bullet shot over his head, so that he dived toward her, clutching her again. *Do you believe me now?*

She roared with laughter. *Scaredy cat!* It was her dad, and in spite of the beard and the smell, she was really glad he was back; it was more than a year since she had seen him.

Walking home, he told her he hadn't had a razor for a year, let alone a place to shave, so he had chopped at his beard with a knife. He had bad news as well: *Dragan is dead, and his family, I think.*

What happened?

I don't know exactly. I'm told that our lovely neighbors burned down his house with him inside.

Amela couldn't believe it. She remembered Dragan hugging her before she got in the car. She remembered his two little children and presents given every Christmas. *What about Andrija and Diana?*

I think they might be dead too. I'm so sorry, Amela. He didn't want to join in their dirty war, but he couldn't get away. They put gasoline around the house, I think he was tied up inside. Maybe his family tried to help and it was too late.

Amela had a vivid picture of the girls frantically trying to untie their father as flames leapt round the doors and window frames. She started to cry. They were almost the same age she was, one a year older, one a year younger. Her dad told her that their own house had also burned down completely, and all her toys were gone. Of course that was awful, but not as bad as what had happened to Dragan and his family. She had to stop and pull herself together. They were almost home. Her dad seemed to stiffen a little.

They were using the whole house now that there was less shelling. Amela pushed open the front door into the living room. Her dad walked in, and stared at her mum. *So you're not dead then?* Amela wasn't sure she had heard right. Maybe he was joking, but he looked completely cold. Oh poor Mum; to wait a year for this. All the warmth Amela had begun to feel disappeared in a rush of rage. Dad had sat down and was calling Adem, her brother, to sit on his knee, but Adem had shrunk into a corner, scared by this strange, rude man. Grandma was crying, asking him if he had any feelings for his family.

Put a sock in it, you stupid old woman! he shouted. He stretched out on the sofa, his hard military boots still on. Grandma looked at him and retreated into the other room, slamming the door. Mum was crying, and then she bent and kissed Adem on the head. He stayed stuck, frozen in his corner, staring at his dad and refusing to speak. Mum made the coffee and tried to make things normal as she always did. Dad lay with his eyes closed. Amela wondered if he was drunk. He obviously wished they had all died. She wished he had as well. After a couple of hours some of his colleagues came and banged on the door to get him to go back to his unit on the line. She was not sorry.

That was how it continued. Now that he was on their side of the river, he could come home quite often. He came back for meals, demanding the best food in the house. He would question her mother about what food she was using when he wasn't there and shout at her if she didn't keep the best stuff for him. Then he would go out to coffee bars with his friends.

Sometimes he was away for weeks and would say he had been on the line, but Amela knew it was not completely true. She had heard he was spending time with other women in town. She saw her mum slaving away for him, accepting everything, and for what? She knew she should try to help, but how? Amela couldn't understand why her mum put up with him. She could see he didn't love her mum any-more, he just saw her as a housekeeper. He still beat her, and he hit the rest of them, even Grandma, or he kicked them. She didn't think he loved her anymore either.

It was worse than before the war, and she wished she could run away, but there was nowhere to run. Sometimes it was slightly better. When she was alone with him, he sometimes seemed to want to be friends with her, give her advice, just chat. It felt as if he had two faces. Maybe she upset him because she was always on her mum's side. Well, someone had to be, and her brother was always on Dad's side now. Maybe the war had made him sick with his nerves.

One day after a really horrible fight, Amela's mum told him they had to separate and she would take the children. He stormed off. Now he was back on the line again, farther away, so he was not com-ing home much anyway. Their aunt came back from Germany, so they had to move to an abandoned shop near the mosque in the cen-ter of town. The shelling got worse again. The Grebak route closed and you couldn't get food that way anymore, so they began to get re-ally hungry. Still, Amela felt better than she had for a long time. She was getting to be really grown up and could help her mum with everything. Sometimes it felt as if her mum was her sister or her best friend.

Some food came in on the airdrops. You could never be sure where it would land, but sometimes they were lucky. One night Amela and her mum waited in the wrong place for an hour before someone said *No, go there.* They were crossing some woods when they saw the pal-lets dropping from the planes and were terrified they would get hit by one. So they started running. When Amela thought about it, it was pretty funny: running away from "lunch." Then she was crouched under a tree and she had lost her mother. Still she couldn't miss a chance. She grabbed two large cartons. Everyone around her was do-ing the same. She opened one and started to stuff the small packets into her backpack. It was getting lighter and people were hurrying to get away. You weren't actually supposed to get the food yourself. If the police found you, they would take it. Mostly it was supposed to go to the army.

Amela lugged her cartons and her backpack down toward a little stream, filled the rucksack to the top, and hid the cartons out of sight. Then she changed her mind and decided to try to drag them home. The hill was very steep, but somehow she managed to pull them along behind her. When she finally got home, her mother opened the door. She had obviously been crying, thinking Amela was injured or lost. The police had grabbed her stuff and hit her with a gun handle. Then she saw Amela's bags, and then Adem came down all sleepy. When Amela started to pull sweets out of her backpack, Adem was ecstatic; he didn't know what to take first. *When my sister is alive I'm not afraid of anything!* he shouted. He stared at Amela. *I will never forget what you did, sister, until the end of my life.* The next night they went out and loaded up again. Dad came home once and immediately had an argument about it, telling Mum he didn't like her going out, it was not her job. *I have to, because you don't want to,* she replied. *Someone has to feed our children.*

Amela started going to school again. They dug some trenches for protection from snipers, so children who lived farther away could walk in them. There was still some shelling, but she was so used to it that she really didn't mind too much unless she actually heard it overhead. That was scary. And if the Chetniks saw you take cover in a building they might shell it.

Then the shelling got really bad again and they were back in the basement. Sometimes it felt as if they had spent all their lives in the basement. She didn't know what year it was or when her birthday was anymore. It was impossible to sleep for long with the constant noise. Her mother was frightened all the time. Amela tried to play games with her brother to stop herself from thinking. Then Mum would shout at them to be quiet because she was listening to which way the shells were coming, as if that could keep them from falling on the house. Sometimes it was impossible not to listen; you just sat silently wondering if you might get hit. The best thing was when Grandma told stories. She had very funny ones about how when she was young, she was the troublemaker in the house, and how she had started work at fifteen and met their grandfather and built a house with him. Grandma knew this was the best way to stop the fear, just to keep on talking. It was great that she was there.

Narcisa thought the heavy shelling was boring. Her parents had made her and her brother a den in the center of the house. They had everything they needed there: they could play and sleep and it felt very safe. She had her harmonica there. If it was a little quieter they played in the yard and ran in when the shelling began again. In the days when it was really heavy, they just stayed inside. She and her brother had invented a new game around counting the grenades; it made a change from playing cards. Her father was very clever and had found a way to make electricity by putting a wheel in the river. The water turned the wheel and generated electricity, so sometimes they could even watch a video. Neighbors came to watch with them and brought more food and drink.

When the shelling was less intense, she sometimes went to find her father. He managed to come home every three or four days, but in between she missed him. At one point he had a position near the house. She and her brother would put food in a basket and take it up to him. There was a small path up the hill that they could use. If a grenade came over, they just flattened themselves on the ground. But he was only there a short time, and then he moved to another position, then another. Then they would sit listening to the radio waiting for the lists. There was always that moment when they announced that someone was hurt or dead, then the relief when it was not her father's name.

Less shelling also meant that she could go to school. Sometimes it started on the way there or back. One day she was at mekteb, the religious school, where she went to study the Koran. She came out, and as she put on her shoes she noticed two other children and their

mother going past. She and a friend started walking. The familiar
whooshing came, followed by an enormous crash ahead of them.
Narcisa could guess what had happened. She started to pray the
prayers she had learned in mekteb. There were people running by
talking about bodies. Her heart was pounding, but there was no
other way to go to get home. She and her friend turned the corner
and there they were, three mangled bodies lying in the street: the
woman and two children, although you could no longer see their
faces. One body seemed to be hanging over the street, another lay
blocking her way. It was so horrible she thought she would be sick.
The blood was thick and she had to step through it and over the bodies. Later she couldn't get the pictures of cut-up bodies out of her
mind. They kept coming back, especially when she went past that
spot again.

Amela started having bad dreams after her friend was killed. They
were walking near the house, when her friend suddenly fell over, hit
by sniper fire. Amela started yelling but no one came to help and
there was nothing she could do; she couldn't even move her friend's
body. So she ran home to tell her mother. This wasn't the first person
she had lost. The strange thing was that although she sometimes felt
frightened, especially in the dark, and although she had bad dreams
about blood and shootings, she didn't feel so very sorry for anyone's
death. Eight relatives and friends had died. It was hard to have any
feelings such as real sadness when you had no idea if you yourself
would be alive the next day. So she had not cried. Maybe she would
when the war was over.

Foca, 1995

On New Year's Eve in Serbia children played with firecrackers. Dusan
felt that celebrating with things that flashed and banged was rather
strange, and didn't enjoy it very much. His mother had found work

in Serbia, and he was doing all right in school. Finally his father had
let them come back home for the summer holidays. His grandfather
had died a year ago, so he was sleeping in his old room, alone. Then
he woke up, and the oddest thing: there was someone right next to
him, head on his pillow. *Hello, little brother.*

Dusan gave a shout. It was Vlado! He had always liked playing
jokes. He had just arrived from Treskavica and come in especially to
see Dusan. They would talk about everything in the morning. Dusan
went back to sleep happily, but when he woke his brother was not in
the same mood. He had no time to talk. There had been some kind of
emergency and he had to go back to the line right away, but not to
worry, he would be back very soon.

Vlado was killed two days later, while heading home. Dusan was
the first to hear because only he and his aunt were there when the
news came. They had been going off the line and a grenade had fallen
between three of them. Vlado and another man had been killed instantly, the third wounded. Dusan couldn't believe the news; it was
impossible that his brother was dead. Then he wanted to cry and cry;
but as he listened to what people were saying about his brother, all
the stories of how brave he was, some of the pain began to turn into
pride. This was his brother they were talking about: a good soldier,
always first into action, even though he was usually the youngest; always clean; no raping or looting; not corrupt; a great Serb, fighting
for a Serb country.

As the days and weeks passed, though, he couldn't always hold on
to these feelings. His father had come back that evening and was
completely devastated. His mother could not stop crying and he
couldn't bear to see it . . . It felt as if his whole family had died; no one
could talk or think about anything else. Dusan knew he had to be
very strong and keep his feelings inside so he could help with the funeral. That was not always so difficult, because a lot of the time he
just felt empty, he didn't feel like doing anything, so he just did what

had to be done. Other times he felt again that it couldn't be true, there had to be a mistake, Vlado would just walk in with his jokes as he had in the past.

After the funeral, Dusan and his mother went back to Serbia. His father insisted. He didn't want to go. When he got there he felt worse than ever. He couldn't stop thinking about his brother, so it was impossible to concentrate at school. Anyway he had no interest in schoolwork anymore. Sometimes he felt afraid for no reason, because after all nothing bad was happening in Serbia. Dusan knew he wanted to be with his family in his own house. At least he had the video of the funeral. It comforted him to remember how well people thought of his brother. He wanted to be as much like him as he possibly could.

Back in Foca, Ivana was twelve and had settled into a new year at school. The higher up you went the more homework there seemed to be, so she was sitting up in the evening doing biology. There had been some talk of "bombing" and some people at school were nervous, but a neighbor phoned her mother that evening and told them not to worry.

They just want to frighten us, her mother said. *It won't happen.*

Why do they want to bomb us? Ivana asked. She wasn't quite clear who "they" were. *They want our army to move from its positions,* her father explained. *If they don't, then they'll be bombed.* This still didn't make much sense. At nine-thirty she decided to go to bed, leaving her mother standing on the balcony watching the river.

It seemed as if immediately her mother was shaking her to wake up. *Get up, get dressed, they're bombing us; we have to go to the shelter.*

Ivana just wanted to sleep, but she could hear sirens going. She dragged herself out of bed and went down to the cellar with her mother and brother. It was dark, because there was no electricity, and completely full of neighbors. People kept going outside to see what was going on, and coming in again if there was any sound of planes. She wanted to see too. Her brother yelled at her to come and look at the planes. *Crazy guy, those planes drop bombs and they can fall on us!*

But she joined him in the doorway. Suddenly there was an enormous thud and the door fell out of the frame, hitting both of them and knocking them back into the cellar. Ivana got up and checked herself. She was all right. Her mother yelled at them to come in, and they retreated to the lowest level. Ivana was really afraid now and she couldn't stop shivering. The last time she had felt like this was the first day of the war. They had sat in the cellar then, too. She could hear shells falling and got as close to her mother as possible. She felt exhausted. She wished she could sleep, but she was much too tense. What would happen to them all? She couldn't bear it if anyone else was killed; losing Grandma was bad enough. Around two in the morning it seemed to stop, so everyone went back to bed. Next day when she woke up, she didn't feel frightened at all.

NATO bombed off and on for the next few days. Ivana stayed indoors all the time with her mother and brother. The radio was on all the time so they could hear what was happening. All the bridges in town had been destroyed, and when they had TV they could see planes bombing Pale. Ivana heard that the Serbs had shot down a plane and local people had found the pilots and had beaten them up. She wasn't surprised. Everyone was angry. Sometimes at night her fear came back, but it was not so bad. She didn't think they wanted to bomb people. All the same, if the Serb army didn't move, they might bomb more places.

On the other side of town, Svetlana also had trouble waking up. She heard her mother shouting at her to go down to the cellar. So she blundered out in her bare feet, still half asleep, and then a window fell in and she cut her feet. That woke her up. There was blood everywhere. Her mother tore off part of her trousers to bind it and then they sat in the cellar. Her mother was terrified, Svetlana could tell.

She was muttering to herself, saying she wished she had died before the war began. A lot of people were crying and moaning. They all seemed scared. Oddly, Svetlana didn't feel frightened at all. She just wanted to sleep.

Stojan was really scared. He woke up to the sound of a plane going over, and at first he couldn't make sense of the noise. When he went to the window, he could see a fire on one of the bridges, and then he saw a plane flying in that direction and dropping something that looked like a rocket. It felt like a movie, but when he heard the explosion and the sound of glass cracking, he knew it was real. He stood rooted to the spot, shaking with fear. Then his mother came to take him down to the cellar. It was freezing and full of people. All Stojan could think about was: Were they going to bomb people as well as bridges? People were saying it would start with bridges and then go to factories and shops, then houses.

After two or three days the bombing stopped, although planes still flew over the town. This made everyone nervous. Ivana still couldn't go to school. All the school windows had been broken, so they had to wait until they were repaired. Nobody in Foca had been killed by NATO bombs but people were still dying. One day Ivana was sitting alone in the house when she heard the most terrible sound, a little like singing but more like wailing. She went onto the balcony. The woman next door was crying with this high moaning noise. Her son had just died. Ivana phoned her mother to come right away, as the woman was her friend. She felt miserable. The worst thing was that her own brother was supposed to go to join the army in just a few days. What if this happened to him? She just wanted the war to be over, and people to stop bombing and dying.

3

Adjusting to Peace

On December 15, 1995, I was in a convoy of vehicles trying to get into Sarajevo. There was deep snow and the journey up the dirt road from Mostar had taken almost twenty-four hours rather than the expected three. Now we were stuck in our minivan, on the wrong side of Mount Igman, along with French NGO trucks carrying seed and food for Gorazde, and United Nations and NATO personnel in a variety of military vehicles. Supposedly there had been a ceasefire for the previous two months, brought about by the combination of a successful Bosnian and Croat ground offensive and NATO air strikes against the army of Republika Srpska (VRS). Presidents Izetbegovic of Bosnia, Milosevic of the Federal Republic of Yugoslavia, and Tudjman of Croatia, meeting in Dayton, Ohio, had reached an agreement on November 21. It maintained Bosnia Herzegovina as a unitary state and divided that state into two Entities: Republika Srpska and the Federation of Bosnia and Herzegovina. It also stated that all refugees would be allowed to return to their homes, and that those responsible for war crimes would be arrested and tried. It set a series of dates for the transfer of various parts of the country from one Entity to the other, to conform to the agreed-upon boundaries.

The Agreement had been signed on December 14 with great ceremony in Paris, but here on the ground there was no sense that the war was over. Serbs still controlled the suburbs of Sarajevo and were angry that these suburbs would be given back to the Federation over the next few months. Shots had been fired that morning, and no one was sure if it was safe to move. Gorazde was still cut off to all but authorized aid convoys and international forces. It was now an island of Federation territory with all roads to it going through Republika Srpska.

Welcome to Sarajevo, my friends said when I finally reached the foggy, snowbound city that night and we sat huddled over an oil stove. *You see, no gas, no electricity, no water, and the shelling continues. There won't be peace until we can cross Igman, or walk in Ilidza without danger.* The war trickled to an end. There were no victory parades. I saw no dancing in the streets. Gorazde remained isolated and completely dependent on humanitarian aid. Many of the Serbs who did not want to live in Federation territory headed for Foca. Not surprisingly, it was hard, then or later, to get a sense of how or when the war actually ended for the children.

Foca, 1996–1997

Ivana heard that Serb forces had left their positions and an agreement had been signed. She was relieved that her older brother would not have to go to the front line and that the shooting had stopped. Both of her parents had found jobs in the town, although for very little pay. She went to visit her aunt in Serbia for a holiday, glad to be in a city where no one talked or thought about war, and where people had nice things. When she came home, she settled down at school, got good marks, and enjoyed her life.

Stojan did the same. He was glad they could move back to their old apartment. He had a video player and enjoyed watching action movies like James Bond. He had his own room back and stuck posters of his favorite basketball heroes on the walls. He planned to be a sports star himself, and he did well at school. Sometimes he wished they could travel more the way they had before the war, and that the town was a bit more up to date, but he enjoyed life in most situations. There was no reason not to do so now.

It was not so easy for Svetlana. Her family had moved again, to yet another abandoned Muslim apartment. They had no legal standing, so it felt very insecure. The Dayton Agreement meant the owners could come back at any moment, although there seemed little chance of that. Svetlana could think of nothing nicer than for everything to return to the way it was before the war. She longed to see all her old friends again, but knew it was impossible. The war had destroyed everything. There were lots of new people in town, and everyone had changed. There were often fights at school. The atmosphere in town was depressing, and at home her mother was just as nervous as before. Both her parents worked, but neither of them got paid much so they had hardly any money. The war was over but it didn't feel like it. She was fed up with the endless news on TV. She hated it. Everyone always seemed to be arguing, and she worried that the fighting could start all over again.

She was not doing very well at school. Her mother said it was just laziness but she knew it wasn't. She just found it hard to sit still and concentrate. She felt nervous and everything bothered and upset her, even little things. If her mother asked her to wash the dishes when she was trying to draw a picture, she felt like screaming. She thought she might pick up the plates, throw them across the room at someone, and then burst into tears. She had found some ways to escape, listening to music, doing the things she was good at like art or karate training. Talking to her closest friend was the best; they were like sisters and understood each other perfectly.

Dusan came back to Foca with his mother. The town had been renamed Srbinje, but his father said that Vlado had died fighting for Foca, not Srbinje. Dusan saw that his parents were completely exhausted. Luckily people wanted to help. A friend set them up in a small business, so they were very busy and that gave them less time to think. He tried to concentrate on doing well at school to please them. He knew things would never be the same as before.

He hardly ever stopped thinking about Vlado. He visited the grave every week, looked at photos, and thought about all their times together. He liked talking about him with his parents, because it made him feel that in some way he was keeping Vlado alive, at least in his memories. Dusan could think of nothing better than trying to be exactly like his brother. But sometimes it was very painful, and when he was alone he let himself cry. Sometimes he would play with his dog or go for a ride on his bike or play with his friends. That helped him to forget for a while. Sometimes he thought he had no feelings at all.

Physically he was fine, he slept and ate well, but there were still times when he wasn't interested in anything. He felt bored and cut off from everything. Nothing would ever make him happy again. Other times, when he thought about the war, he felt angry. His brother had fought against violence and for Serbia, to save them from living under Muslims, as they had done for five hundred years. He had learned in history class how bad that had been. Now it felt as if his brother had fought for nothing. The family had been pleased about Dayton at first, but nothing was settled. The countries were not separated yet and foreign forces were pushing in the wrong direction. He knew it was foolish to try to put Croats, Muslims, and Serbs in one country. It would humiliate all those who had died in the war, fighting for separate nations. Anyway, if Muslims came back to Foca, what would happen to the Serb people in Muslim houses? Where could they go? It wasn't right.

He thought there would probably be another war in the next ten, fifteen, or twenty years. After all, his grandfather had lived through three. Whether it was Balkan people or outsiders who wanted a war, they always had it here. Ordinary people never had a say; it was always politicians. When there were no proper laws and when people had no money and no food like now, then there were wars.

Gorazde, 1996–1997

Samir worried that there might be another war. Sometimes he talked about it with his mother, and she said she couldn't bear to go through all that again. He and his family had come back to Gorazde in 1997. They could not go back to their house; it was almost completely destroyed. But his father said *You should spend your lives in the place where you were born.* Samir didn't want to live in the old house. If he went inside he remembered the man talking about three knives and felt scared. They had two rooms in a big hut for displaced people. He liked it. They had a TV, he had his own bed. He knew his parents were very worried; they had no money and couldn't get their old jobs back because the factory was closed. Father said the authorities should help them.

The town was getting better. They had rebuilt the school and the sports hall. The trouble was that it didn't feel completely safe. Gorazde had made itself an Open City. This meant Serbs could come back and live there and the police would not search them anymore. Recently there had been two Serb men in their area, and someone said they were armed and had shot a dog. On the radio Samir heard angry Serbs say that if they didn't get a town called Brcko, they might take Gorazde by force. He didn't like or understand politics, but these things made him worry. He felt very confused about Serbs. He thought everyone should be able to go back to their own homes, which meant Serbs should be able to come back too, but not if they cursed or had guns, and not the ones who had wanted to kill them.

His biggest worry was school. In Visoko the teachers had been patient and explained if something was unclear. It wasn't like that here, and he got so nervous when they asked him a question. And there was so much homework to do. He felt a bit lonely. He had always been shy, but since the war and coming back, it felt harder to make friends. He had a couple of good ones, but he would have liked to be part of a crowd.

Another trouble was that he still remembered things from the war, like when he and his family were imprisoned in their house, and then he would just start shaking. Sometimes the memories made him angry, sometimes he just felt really tense and cut off from his friends. It could happen out of the blue: one moment he would be feeling fine and the next he would be afraid. It was getting better, so he didn't tell anyone; he wanted to forget everything to do with the war. Even so, his father knew he was still a little nervous and was going to take him to a local woman who had a special method for taking fear away.

For Amela, the end of the war meant things just got worse. Her father was back, as bad as ever. As usual her mother put up with everything. One night he came home really drunk with a hand grenade and started yelling *Get out of the house, or I'll kill you, it doesn't matter if I die too*. They ran to the police station, but the police wouldn't do anything. Amela knew some of them were friends with her father. She thought he gave them money. They spent the night there anyway and then went back home. Another time he threatened her mother with a knife, and Amela tried to stop him. She was terrified that her mother might die; it would be the end of everything. One night she felt so miserable she decided to take all her grandmother's pills. If she were dead, there would not be all this fear and pain and arguing. She fell asleep, and woke up late the next day feeling sick, drowsy, and amazed and angry to be alive. No one seemed to have noticed, so she decided not to tell anyone. There didn't seem any point in trying again.

Then one day her father hit her mother so hard he broke her jaw and she had to go to the hospital in Sarajevo. The period that followed was one of the worst of Amela's life. They had to stay with her father's mother, who let them go hungry. Meanwhile her father continued to drink and see other women who Amela thought were ugly and stupid. She went to school and tried to work, but it was difficult to concentrate on what the teachers were saying. Often her head would be full of pictures of her father shouting at them. She didn't tell anyone, she was ashamed. She didn't want anyone to know that things were different in their house. Anyway she knew that lots of people had suffered in the war much worse than she had.

When her mother came home from the hospital after four months she went straight to court for a divorce. Amela felt as if they spent the next three months sleeping on the court benches. Father fought to keep Amela and her brother. Amela didn't want to leave the courthouse until she was sure she would be with her mother. Sometimes it was horrible; her father would curse and swear in court. But her mother was really tough. Other times he cried. He said things like *I had everything for thirteen years. I didn't appreciate it, and now I have nothing, and I realize what I have lost.* That was the hardest moment. She thought she might cry too, but she was determined not to.

Finally everything was resolved; Amela and her brother could go home with their mother. They all left the courthouse and walked down the main street. Dad was just ahead. Suddenly he turned to them. *Let's all go and have a drink together! Come on, for old times' sake.*

Amela looked at her mother, who just stared at her father and then burst into tears. *We don't want to drink with you,* Amela said. *When we needed to sit and drink together you weren't there.*

He looked at her. *Don't ever call me Father again.*

Then he turned back to her mother. *And you just remember who I am, I am a man from Montenegro, and you will remember me. Until the day I die, I won't let you forget. I'll find ways to remind you.*

After that things did get better. They moved to a tiny, damp house. Mum said she didn't want his money and could manage by herself. That meant she had to work all hours, so Amela did the housework and took care of her brother after school. She didn't mind. It was better than the fights. Sometimes, to her surprise, she missed her father. She even felt sorry for him. He seemed to be drinking less and was lonely, so she went to visit him and helped with his laundry. Sometimes she wished they could be together, but she knew he didn't want to live with her mother.

As for the war, she tried not to think about it, although every time she turned on the television it made her nervous. There always seemed to be arguments. She was glad about Dayton and about having international troops in the town, but she was still afraid the town could be taken, or swapped for another town, if the troops left. Maybe they would all have to move. That feeling of numbness she had had during the war had gone. She missed the relatives who had died, and thought about them a lot. Sometimes she had nightmares. She had always been afraid of the dark, now it was worse and she couldn't sleep alone. She felt very edgy a lot of the time. She would just yell at her brother for no reason. That wasn't fair, but it was hard to stay calm. Other times even the funniest book was boring. And her memory was still bad. Her mother teased her that sometimes she didn't know what day of the week it was or what she had had for breakfast. At the same time there were things in the past she wanted to forget, but they wouldn't go away.

As soon as Dayton was signed Nina was eager to get back home, she had missed everything so much. She had spent three and a half years in Germany, living in an apartment in the house of the pastor who had invited them. They were the only Bosnian refugees in the small town. Her father and brother tried to join them but couldn't get out of Bosnia. But they called often and she exchanged letters with her friends through the Red Cross, so she knew how things were at home. She liked Germany and settled in well, learning German, going to the local school, and getting top marks in every class. She made friends and loved their host and his family. Her older sister married another Bosnian refugee. Her mother always tried to be happy about their success, but Nina knew she hadn't stopped thinking about Bosnia for one moment. She never had the radio off, even going to sleep with a small transistor beside her. Nina told her that when the war was over and they were back in Bosnia *You will never turn that radio on again.*

When the time came to leave she felt glad and sad all at once. She felt she was leaving her own family. All their friends came over the night before for a party, and when they returned in the morning to say goodbye, she cried and cried. Finally, after a long bus journey, they were in Sarajevo. The bus was hours late, so no one was there to meet them. Her mother called her father, and then they sat on plastic chairs and waited. Nina watched her mother watching every person who came in. Nina had often thought about her father in Germany, wondering if she would ever see him again, and if she did, how she would feel. She had heard stories on the journey home, people saying her father had found another woman. She didn't believe it; she knew there were many false rumors.

There is your father, her mother said. Nina ran toward him and stopped in front of him. She could see he didn't recognize her, and he looked a bit strange too, his teeth were odd.

Nina? Nina? Is it really you? Why you're completely grown up! Then her mother came up and they were all hugging, and everything was all right.

The next day they drove the car over Grebak, a long bumpy potholed dirt road that went back over the mountains, almost the same way that Nina had walked out nearly four years earlier. It took five hours but it meant they could avoid driving through Republika Srpska, and Nina didn't mind. They came to the curve of the road from where you could look down and see the Drina, flat, bright, like metal in the sunlight. Nina loved the water; now she knew she was coming home, she was bursting with excitement, her heart beating really fast. Finally they got to the apartment, and there was an unrecognizable older brother running toward them from a café and hugging them and declaring how grown up she was; and she knew everyone was happy because they were all together again after three and a half years.

That evening she went out to walk around the town with her brother and his wife. Her friends had all changed physically, so none of them could recognize her or she them, but it didn't matter, she was so pleased to be back with them. It was strange how in Germany she had felt like a child and hardly ever gone out at night, but now she suddenly felt very adult. They stayed out late to give their parents time to be alone together and catch up. When they came home, Nina knew right away that something was wrong. It was a two-room apartment; her mother was in one room making up a bed; her father was nowhere to be seen.

What's happened? Where is Papa?

He went for a walk, her mother said in a flat odd voice. This made no sense to Nina—why would he go for a walk alone on their first night back? Why not take her mother with him?

Why did he go for a walk?

He just left. I don't know . . .

Mama, what's wrong? Is something wrong?

Nothing . . . there's something wrong with your father, he is not all right.

Her mother wouldn't talk anymore; she wanted to sleep. Then Nina's brother explained: It was true, her father had had someone else during the war, and he no longer felt the same about her mother.

Nina couldn't believe it. How could this have happened? They were one of the happiest families in Gorazde. Everyone knew that. She remembered leaving Gorazde. Her father had stood by the door and cried. It had been the worst day of her life. She knew his feelings for them, for her, so how could he do this?

The next year was horrible. Her father promised to stop seeing the other woman if her mother moved back to the village to take care of *his* mother, who was blind. She agreed. Because of school, Nina stayed in town with her brother and his wife. Whenever she went home she saw how bad it was: her mother did everything her father wanted, but he was different; it was not a normal marriage. There were always arguments. He was never home on time, and when her mother asked him where he had been, he put on this serious face and said *Who are you to ask me where I was? I can do whatever I want.*

School was not easy at first. Nina had lost a year in Germany because of having to learn the language, so now she was a year behind her contemporaries. But she worked through the holidays and caught up.

After a year, her mother had had enough. She told Nina she was leaving her father if he didn't change. *What kind of a life is that? Why take care of someone or clean up after them, when they don't love you?*

There was no change, and her mother moved into Nina's brother's house and her father decided to have nothing to do with them. He had been seeing the other woman all the time. Nina hated her. The woman looked nothing like her tall and elegant mother. She was small and had children of her own, but she had done something incredible to Nina's father, because he had never been like that before. Nina had heard people say there is some force that can change a man and make him crazy. She knew many men had seen other women during the war. But they had always gone back to their families. Her father had not. What also made her angry was the thought that the money they had kept sending from Germany had gone to that woman. If her mother had known, she wouldn't have sent a penny.

Sometimes Nina felt that losing her father in this way was worse than anything that had happened during the war. It was almost as if he had died. She cried much of the time and became very thin. Sometimes she felt so bad she thought *I'll kill myself, what am I doing here?* She knew that was just something silly in her mind. She would never do such a thing. She wrote everything in her diary, and she talked a lot to her mother and her best friend. She couldn't say everything, but it helped. She also talked to her father. He had started coming around once a month to give her money, and she told him how angry she was. She cried in front of him too, asking him why he had left and why he didn't come back. He still didn't want a divorce, and he sometimes said *Anything is possible.* Then she realized nothing would change and decided she just had to carry on with her life. After all, lots of people were divorced or separated. She was all her mother had left now that her brother and sister were married, and her mother had been so brave.

She finished eighth grade with top marks again and passed the exams for secondary school. She was pleased she had done what she had set out to do. She had many friends and enjoyed her life. Sometimes she thought about her life in Germany, but that whole period had a dreamlike quality. This was her home again now.

Narcisa knew she was lucky. She had not lost any close relatives, her father had come home safely, and their house was still standing. Her mother didn't have a job anymore and her father didn't get paid much, but they were managing. She was beginning to enjoy herself again. She loved school and did well in every subject. She never seemed to have free time because she belonged to a singing group, helped run a school newspaper, played basketball, and went to mekteb. The worst thing the war had done to her was damage her eyesight. She blamed her need to wear glasses on all that reading by candlelight and worried a little that it would mean she wouldn't get boyfriends. That was her biggest concern and she knew it was silly. Sometimes, walking down the street where she had stepped over the dead bodies, she remembered. Sometimes she thought of going another way, but she never had, and now the memory came less often.

In some ways, she didn't want to forget. She thought it was important to remember all the suffering of the last four years. As far as she was concerned, the war had helped them understand what was what. They had seen the real faces of all those people who had seemed to be such good friends. The mass graves had taught them a lesson. When she thought about what she had been like before the war, she couldn't imagine having had such thoughts; she hadn't even understood that there were any differences between people. Even now she knew that not all Serbs were terrible, but the trouble was that the ones who had done the killing gave the impression that all were the same. She knew the Serbs had to be allowed to come back to Gorazde; everyone had to be able to go home. But she would not be friends or mix with them in the same way. She would not forget and she could not forgive.

Most of the time she gave no thought to such things. The war was over and she wanted to get on with her life. She had decided to become a lawyer. The war had made her realize there was a lot of injustice, here in Gorazde and in the world. She wanted to change that.

part two

Understanding
What Happened

4

Why Did We Fight?

Bosnia is a formidable, scary place of high mountains, brutish people and tribal grievances rooted in history and myth born of boozy nights by the fire. It's the place where World War I began and where the Wars of Europe persist, an ember of hate still glowing for reasons that defy reason itself.

—Richard Cohen, *Send in the Troops*, 1995

Did you know what nationality you were before the war?
Tatiana: *No. Actually, one day in the schoolyard, they asked me whether I was Serb, Muslim, or Croat. And I thought it sounded nice to be a Muslim, I liked the sound of the word, so I said I was Muslim.*

—Fifteen-year-old Serb girl, Foca

Milica was fourteen, pretty, dark haired, soft spoken, and shy. She and her family had decided to leave the small town of Ustikolina after the war ended, when the Dayton Peace Agreement allocated the town to the Federation. She sat in the bleak classroom in the primary school in Foca, answering my questions politely, with the slightly bewildered air of one discussing the obvious.

Why wasn't it possible to stay?
How could I stay—there were Turks there.
Did someone say you had to move, or did you want to move?
They told us we had to move, on the news, because the Turks who had lived there were supposed to come back.

Ustikolina was not Milica's original hometown; her family had moved into an empty Muslim-owned house there early in the war, after fleeing from a village near Gorazde. She had happy memories of her old life. Her father had built their house himself, and the family had a smallholding with a cow, pigs, sheep, and chickens. She helped her mother by watching the sheep. Her father worked in a factory in Gorazde. The families in their village were Serb, although there were a few *Turks* living there; and the neighboring village was *Turk.* This was the term she now used for her Muslim neighbors. At school her teacher was *Turk* and her friends were of all nationalities. When the shooting began, all the mothers and children ran away, leaving the fathers to defend their houses. Her father left a few weeks after that. Later they heard that the house had been burned.

After the war, Milica was angry with the returning Turks for making them have to move again, and she missed her old home near Gorazde. Sometimes she thought it would be nice to go back, but she knew it was impossible.

Why? I asked.

Because Gorazde will never be Serb, it will always be theirs.

Gorazde will always be Muslim?

Turk.

Can you imagine ever living with Turks again? I decided to stick with her definitions.

No.

Can you explain to me why not?

She was silent for a while. *Because I don't want to live with them.*

Why is that?

Because I don't like them.

Why don't you like them?

I don't know why . . . Because they're Turks, that's why I don't like them.

But she found it hard to specify the differences between Serbs and Turks. She knew she liked Serbs, and she thought Turks looked different, although some of her girlfriends in the village had been Turks, and they had looked and behaved just like her.

Did you like Turks before the war? She was silent again. This time the silence continued until I broke it. *Did you know who the Turks were before the war?*

No.

So it's only since the war?

Yes.

So what has made Turks since the war so unlikable?

Another silence. *I don't know. Serbs look better to me, umm, and I have more Serb friends now.*

Do you hate the Turkish friends you had before the war?

No! Why? They didn't do anything to me. She looked astonished.

Would you ever like to see those friends again?

No.

Because?

I don't know why.

But later it became clearer. She was convinced that *Turks hate Serbs,* although again she had no idea why.

On another afternoon I visited Milica's parents. The family now lived in another Muslim-owned house, an old two-story building close to the river in Foca. We walked through a door in a high stone wall into a paved yard with fruit trees. Wood was neatly stacked against the wall. I pulled off my shoes, placing them as usual with the other pairs outside the door. Milica's mother ushered me in. She was a sad-looking, pleasant-faced woman with graying hair loosely pulled into a bun, wearing a long skirt of printed material. Her husband joined us in a neat front room that doubled as a kitchen. I was seated on a shiny plastic-covered sofa, while she poured Fanta into glasses, and started grinding coffee with a small hand grinder. When I said that I wanted to understand how things were now and how they had been before, Milica's mother burst into tears. She continued to cry as she talked of her old home, the animals left behind, and her husband's inability to find work in the town. *It was better than now,* her husband said. *It was good until the war.*

Sanela was a Muslim thirteen-year-old who had also lived with her family in a village near Gorazde before the war. They shared a house with her grandparents; each family had a separate floor. They kept cows and horses. She went to school in the suburb of Kopaci, and had no sense of difference between herself and her Serb friends. The only way she could tell was by names. Then the war came and her father was killed in the first year of fighting. Two years later, as Serbian forces attempted to take Gorazde, she fled into town with her mother and her older sister, Jasmina. Now they lived seven floors up in a flat vacated by Serbs and allocated to them by the municipality. She wanted to go home to the village. The whole family felt the same. *I would like to live together, if that's possible,* Jasmina said.

Yet again I was sitting shoeless on the sofa as the mother ground coffee, and we drank Coca-Cola from glasses. *Could you live with the people who killed your husband?* I asked Sanela's mother.

Well, it wouldn't be the way it was before but we have to try . . .

Many families I talk to in Foca say "If we live together again we'll all kill each other. So we have to live separately."

Jasmina roared with laughter. *They know we wouldn't kill them. They pass through this town safely, nobody stops them. But when we go through Rogatica, they stop you all the time.*

Sanela thought it would be much safer if everyone went home: *If they don't come back there's a possibility of war.* I asked her to explain. *If they were together with us, they wouldn't start a war.* She couldn't say why she thought that, it was just how she felt.

I would like it to be so that everyone could forget everything that happened, said her mother. *Friends. I mean before the war Serbs and Muslims worked in the same factories together, they were sitting in the same cafés, they were using the same buses, I mean my husband was a driver, he was driving Serbs—*

Jasmina interrupted: *Why couldn't we try to do that even now?*

I don't know, her mother replied. *With some nice things everything could be forgotten, you have to go on living.*

There is a story told about the war in Bosnia. It has variations, but the central theme is constant: Balkan peoples have always been fighting; they are tribal, primitive, and barbaric; and the animosity between them stretches back not just centuries, but millennia. The hatreds were temporarily frozen in the ice chest of communism, but after Tito's death the age-old animosities emerged intact. The story was useful to the domestic elite in Serbia to support its claim that it had no part in the fighting in Bosnia and that this was a civil war arising out of unresolved long-term grievances. The story also had a powerful hold on the public imagination in the West. It was used to justify Western neutrality and the policy of non-intervention championed by the British government.[1]

Yet the story bears no resemblance to the lived experience of any families I got to know in either city. On the contrary, the descriptions of prewar life were not of unspoken tensions and repressed hostility, but of what now seemed like a halcyon period: when hard-working young families had just begun to feel prosperous, when almost everyone earned good wages and few gave much thought to the nationality of their neighbors. As winter turned to spring, I drove up and down the river valley, past the burned-out houses to which no one had returned and the convoluted piping of the chemical factory which no longer functioned, listening to words and phrases that became very familiar. The recollections took on an elegiac quality: mourning for a period of lost grace.

Everything was good then. When you could earn enough to build a house in two years that was good.

It was wonderful, we were free, the children were healthy. We could live like normal people. We could go to the coast, to the mountains. I don't think it will ever come back.

They brought us eggs at Easter; we all ate cake at Bajram.

We used to go to work together. And at every holiday I used to get a big piece of roast meat like a Christmas present.

We were so close to each other.

I had more Serb friends than Muslims and I never thought that my colleagues would shoot me.

My best friend was my Muslim neighbor and we were in the same class.

I didn't know then who was Muslim, who was Serb. All my friends were the same for me.

They were always helping us whenever we asked.

I did not feel that I was in danger.

His first teacher was Muslim and he was great in the school.

It was much better while we were together.

We were all together somehow before the war. There was much more company then than there is now. And I think we were all honest, and everything we did, we did it together.

It would be wrong to dismiss this as retrospective nostalgia. In any careful reading of history, Bosnia is notable for the half-millennium in which four different faiths (Orthodox, Catholic, Muslim, and Jew) lived together remarkably free from violence. The conflicts that had occurred prior to the most recent war were no more frequent than those between other European nations, and were largely instigated by outsiders. Intermarriage, though still rare in rural areas, was accepted and increasingly common in cities.[2] According to a survey on national tolerance carried out by a consortium of Yugoslav sociology institutes, in 1990 Bosnia had the highest index of tolerance, 3.88 on a scale from 1 to 5. This was well above average.[3]

This war, far from arising out of ancient animosities, actually created them. Families who formerly shared many aspects of a way of life and celebrated their differences now felt that they had been dispossessed. Children who previously had no strong sense of ethnic identity and no feelings of enmity toward their neighbors now knew who they were, and many perceived the other ethnicity as a threat to their safety.

So what happened? I wanted to discover how the families had made sense of the events that led to the shift in neighbor's perceptions of neighbor. Most of the children had not been aware of anything different until actual fighting began in their community. Their parents thought the changes had begun a little earlier. It was the parents' understandings, whether spoken or not, that helped to shape their children's worlds.

Foca

National parties, Nikola's parents told me. A university-educated professional couple, they had their own book-filled apartment in a highrise by the river in Foca. *Everyone started to separate. Nobody asked you to join. Everybody joined his own people. The Muslim National party was created first, then the Croat National party, and then the Serb National party was formed.*

Simo Mojevic, headmaster of one of the primary schools in Foca, had previously been head of the primary school in Ustikolina. He had gone to the founding meeting of the Stranka Demokratske Akcije or Party for Democratic Action (SDA), the party predominantly supported by Muslims, held in Ustikolina's youth club. He was the only Serb present, invited as a guest. *I suddenly realized that Muslim people were not satisfied with Yugoslavia,* he told me. *They all talked as if Muslims were in danger! Some uneducated people started to shout things about not sleeping together, about separating the children, making separate kitchens. Someone even said that Serbs who didn't want to be killed should go to Montenegro. I think I understood then that Yugoslavia would be divided. Serbs started doing the same, but a month later.*

Anyone who gave it any thought knew that the evil was coming, said Nikola's father. *Television had an enormous influence.*

Everyone I met in both cities had TV sets, no matter how impoverished they were or whether or not they still lived in their own homes. The set occupied a prominent position in the living room or kitchen and was invariably switched on. Before 1992 families in Foca could watch television stations from Sarajevo and from Belgrade. They could also buy the main Serbian daily newspaper, *Polityka,* and a number of magazines. For the three years before the war, Serbian TV and newspapers had told them the same disturbing story: Serbs were in danger and under attack all over Yugoslavia. They had seen "Albanian separatists" beating Serbs who were protesting for their rights in Kosovo, and they had watched Serbian President Milosevic promise *No one will beat you again.* They had heard horrifying accounts of the rape of elderly Serb women in Kosovo, and of attacks on Serbs by Croatian militias using the same flag as the Ustashe, the Second World War Croat fascist regime. Finally, many thought, the truth about Serbia was emerging: the historical facts that had never been properly discussed, such as how many Serbs had been killed by Ustashe in concentration camps or massacred by Muslim SS collaborators during the Second World War. It seemed that Serbs had sacrificed a great deal, and for what? Milosevic reminded them that Serbs had never been conquered or exploited by others; they had always liberated themselves and tried to help others do the same.

Serbs were always for Yugoslavia, and maybe the biggest Serb tragedy was in 1918 when they let Yugoslavia be created instead of a Greater Serbia, Dusan's father told me. He had been a Communist Party member for seventeen years, even though it was the party that had put his own father in jail. No one wanted communism anymore. He thought Tito had been part of the problem. He had made a constitution in 1974 which benefited every nation except the Serbs, at Serb expense. Muslims, for example, had been given National status, and yet everyone knew they were Serbs who had converted to Islam when the Turks came.

It was a euphoric time, there were so many people on the streets, Ivana's mother recalled about the period before the war. *Now we know that those people in power were just communist Serbs, and now they are Radical Serbs, the same people, just changing places. Muslims and Serbs simply thought that those who got the most votes would be in control. It was just the same between Croats and Serbs in other places.* She and her husband did not vote. They hoped it would all die down.

Svetlana's mother was not so hopeful. *That was the end of everything, I was terrified. My neighbor said how good it was to have National parties and asked why I was frightened. How could not I be afraid when two people start a fight? I couldn't see how so many people could make peace between themselves. Maybe they knew something I didn't, they were all going to meetings, I didn't know anything.*

Her husband was more confident that there would be no war. *Because we lived together so nicely, we had good relations. I had worked twenty years with Muslims, I couldn't imagine us fighting. My Muslim friends felt the same.*

By the summer of 1991 everyone felt uneasy. The three National parties had all won proportions of the votes that reflected their constituencies and formed a coalition government with a rotating presidency. Dusan's father hoped this was a continuation of "Brotherhood and Unity" without communism, but most Serbs in Foca did not trust it. They watched as Slovenia and Croatia went to war against Serbs and Yugoslavia. Serbs in Croatia defended themselves by forming their own autonomous regions. Radovan Karadzic, president of the Srpska Demokratska Stranka or Serb Democratic Party (SDS), said that Serbs in Bosnia should do the same, and called for a united Serb state that would bring Serbs from Croatia, Bosnia, and Serbia together. That sounded sensible to some. Dusan's parents saw that

"Brotherhood and Unity" was over. Alija Izetbegovic had told parliament he would sacrifice peace for the sake of an independent Bosnia, and what kind of Bosnia would that be? They knew that Izetbegovic had dedicated his entire life to creating an Islamic country with only Muslims, no Serbs or Croats. That was why he asked for Bosnia-Herzegovina to join the "Organization of Islamic Countries." He had gone to prison years ago for writing a statement that said as much. Dusan's father wished they had never let him out.

There was a strike at the bus company, Foca Trans. Stojan's father explained it to me. The Muslim director had been accused of corruption. For Stojan's father the issues were clear. The director had been smuggling wood to Italy, and all the workers went on strike against him, but then Muslim politicians came down from Sarajevo and took the director's side, the Muslim workers went back to work, and the abandoned Serb strikers were fired. So they had no choice but to set up their own bus company. A few years earlier, when a close friend had married a Muslim, Stojan's father had been best man at the wedding, but now he realized that he and his Muslim friends interpreted every event differently, so it was hard to be together anymore. The whole town seemed to be going the same way. He knew it was ridiculous, this was the late twentieth century and yet Serbs and Muslims took separate buses and drank in separate cafés.

Things that had not seemed significant a few years ago suddenly seemed to matter: that wedding, for instance. Both sets of parents were religious and were against it, particularly the Muslim parents of the bride, although they had always been very friendly to Stojan's father. There was a big fight about what to call the first child: the girl's parents wanted a Muslim name, and the boy's parents wanted a Serbian name. After all, it was normal for a child to be named after the father's family. The couple decided on something completely neutral, and asked him to help them make peace between the grandparents, but it was not a friendly occasion. The girl's father kept saying that he

couldn't forget that Chetniks had killed his brother in the last war—
even though it was fifty years before.

*What's that have to do with your son-in-law when he was not born
then?* Stojan's father asked. *He lives with your daughter. They have a
son. Why should it spoil their life?*

No, the girl's father said, *I cannot forget.*

*After we left my Serb friend's father said "Did you see that Balija?"
That's a bad name for Muslims. You use it if you want to insult them.
Because there were some Muslim units in the Second World War, called
Ballist Units, which collaborated [with the Nazis]. My friend's father
went on, "I was sitting in the corner." Then I realized he had spent the
whole time sitting in a corner so that no one could sit beside him. He
was just waiting to be attacked. He had a gun with him! And he told me,
"If that Balija had come toward me to attack me, I would have killed
him."* Stojan's father laughed as he told me this story, but it was clear
he thought it significant. None of his generation had been interested
in all the stories their parents had tried to tell them about the past,
but now the memories seemed more important. Those experiences
had become relevant.

Then there were the rallies. The SDA held a large one. Muslims
came from all over Yugoslavia: Kosovo, the Sandzak (the area of Serbia with a predominantly Muslim population), waving green flags
and talking of building an enormous mosque, as if the town didn't
have enough mosques already. *It's not just a coincidence that that big
SDA rally was here,* Stojan's father told me. Foca was a key point on
the "Green Road." If that road was cut, Muslims from Bosnia would
be separated from those from the Sandzak and Kosovo, so of course
Muslims paid special attention to Foca. The Serbs believed it was the
bridgehead for any putative Islamic front driving up from the south-
east. *When someone comes from another republic with a Turkish flag
and walks around town provoking people . . . if it was just a Muslim
town okay, but it was half and half. Every country has its own flags, so if*

someone comes with other flags . . . It's a wonder someone didn't throw a bomb.

In August 1991, Mojevic arrived at work one morning to find the monument in the schoolyard destroyed. It commemorated a partisan killed by Chetniks and Italians in the Second World War, and it had stood in front of his office, surrounded by roses. A note on the shattered stump was addressed to him. It said *You will finish in the same way.* Mojevic decided to join the SDS. *I said to myself that I have to join with my people. I was afraid for my physical safety, I had no other choice.*

The coalition government, with its joint parliament, was not working. Serbs resented SDA support for Slovene and Croat attacks on Yugoslavia, at a time when they believed Serbs risked extermination in those countries. Karadzic had suggested peaceful ethnic separation. Dusan's father hoped it would work, but the Muslims had rejected the idea. Serbs knew Muslims wanted their own country, which they could dominate. So in November, when the SDS held a plebiscite, for Serb voters only, on whether or not to "remain in Yugoslavia together with the Serbs of Serbia, Montenegro, Krajina, Vojvodina, and Kosovo," most voted yes.[4] If Muslims wanted to leave Yugoslavia, let them, they had that right. Serbs also had the right to refuse to go with them.

None of the Serb families I knew voted in the referendum on Bosnian independence the following February. Stojan's father hoped it was a joke. By now Ivana's mother had begun to feel out of place when she went to Gorazde. She had a close Muslim friend, but couldn't seem to talk to her anymore, and she knew she was not a nationalist, not like some of her Serb colleagues. After that "Muslim" referendum, she noticed a real change. She could see that it was a *great moment* for the Muslims. They seemed proud, as if they finally had their own country. An experience at the bus station told her which way things were going. She met an elderly Muslim gentleman and said "Dobar dan" (good day) as she always had, and a young Muslim man turned around and said in a very threatening way *After today you cannot say Dobro Dan, you have to say Merhaba.*[5] She had never given any thought to how she greeted another person before. Suddenly she was afraid, it felt as if there was no more tolerance or life together.

In the few weeks before the fighting began, all the Serb families could see that both sides were arming. The National parties were giving out guns. One day Headmaster Mojevic saw a Muslim colleague wearing two pistols and a rifle. The colleague told him he was a hunter and liked collecting weapons. Mojevic knew the hunters' club was legal, but he was sure it was a cover for gathering weapons, just the same as the Serbs were doing. He was worried, because in his area there were 70 percent Muslims and only 30 percent Serbs. The good thing was that the Serbs did have better weapons, real ones, not just hunting rifles, although they had had to buy them. Nothing came free, but he was determined to defend his homeland and his people.

He hoped they could avoid a fight. He continued to behave perfectly correctly in school. However, he remembered what had happened to some local Serbs in the Second World War. The Muslims had tricked them, disarmed them, and said they were sending them to work in Germany. But they had hanged them on trees by the river. The widows and orphans survived to this day in his village. The day before the war started he warned a Muslim colleague at a funeral: *This time you won't cheat Serbs. You won't stand on Serb land. And you won't have the chance to put any Serbs in prison.* He was not planning to fight a war, just to defend his home and his family if they were attacked.

Dusan's mother respected and admired her son's Catholic teacher, but she was disappointed that now she seemed to award marks on the basis of nationality rather than merit. And there had been an incident with a little Muslim girl who had worn a crescent moon around her neck. One day she had made nasty remarks about Serbs to

Dusan, and he had got in a fight with her, and the teacher had slapped him, quite unjustly. They had always been a religious family, but they believed religion was a private matter. There was no need for anyone to wear symbols and no need to show off who you were by singing national songs. That was what they had always taught Dusan.

Some families still did not believe there could be a fight. In Svetlana's village Muslims and Serbs kept watch together. Mirko lived high in the hills above the town, on a small farm. In his village, the SDS came around and offered all the men guns, for "defense." Mirko's father thought it was completely unnecessary; he couldn't imagine his Muslim neighbors attacking him or he them. But the SDS insisted it might be necessary, just in case the neighbors did attack. So he accepted the weapons. Some families were warned. Bojan's uncle told his family to go to their grandmother's house because there would soon be fighting. Then a man came to give out guns and told Bojan's father to start keeping watch. A courier came and ordered Jovan's parents *When the war starts, take whatever you can and leave.*

Sometimes as I listened to these accounts I could see how things appeared to the speakers. I could look down from the school psychologist's apartment to the garage where she said she had seen her Muslim neighbor handing out rifles, and imagine how disturbing that might be. I could sit in a midtown café and picture the streets full of people shouting and waving alien flags. I had been similarly discomfited, walking through Belgrade in the summer of 1990, when suddenly surrounded by a running, angry, flag-waving crowd yelling *Kill Albanians! Give us guns! Kill Albanians! Give us guns!* I was pushed into the street, and people swirled past, unseeing and uncaring. It was my first direct experience of the frightening indifference and power of a mobilized crowd.

I would drive back to Gorazde, swinging around the curve of the river where the name TITO was still marked out in stone, prominently visible on the hillside, even though sheep grazed on the uncut grass and no flags flew from the poles. I thought of Nina telling me how excited she had been to be made one of Tito's "pioneers" in first grade. That was in 1990, and she was the last of her kind. She had a white shirt, a blue beret with the red star, and a blue scarf. There was a procession from school and a ceremony and they all sat in chairs and listened to speeches, and then repeated, after *some old man,* an oath to respect professors and parents and protect the country. Then there was a party at school and *everyone was happy.*

Gorazde

Families in Gorazde did not talk so much about the distant past, although they lamented the loss of the more immediate one. Narcisa's parents, like Nina, had been Tito's pioneers at school. They had believed in the oath. Milosevic's meetings in Kosovo had disturbed them. They had heard him in 1989, at a rally of nearly a million Serbs, threatening that Serbs might have to fight to protect themselves—even though no one was attacking them! *The non-National parties weren't strong enough. We all thought if we chose something else we would lose protection, security. And we believed that nothing would happen to us.*

Fikreta's father was a cook. He had worked away from home most of his life, in Germany, Libya, Sarajevo. They had an old house in town, with a garden. His wife looked after their children well, but it was tough. He thought that after forty years there was no point in voting for the communists, who just offered old ideas with new names. The new parties might give them a better life, but having been born a Muslim, he did not see how he could vote for the Serbs or Croats, they wouldn't want him. Samir's father had thought the SDA was for everyone, Serbs and Croats as well as Muslims. When he realized it was just a National party like all the rest, he knew things were going wrong.

If anyone had a reason to join nationalist parties, it was Bosnian

Muslims, said Elvira's father. He ran a business in Gorazde and we were sitting in his office. *We didn't have the same rights as others in Yugoslavia; we weren't even able to declare ourselves as Muslims or Bosnians for a long time . . . Seventy-eight percent of the officers in the JNA were Serb. And look at things here in town. Serbs were 27 percent of the population but they had more than 90 percent of the administrative jobs and occupied more than 70 percent of the state-owned apartments besides. When the National parties formed . . . Serbs felt they were losing some of that power . . . they felt jeopardized, so of course we were in conflict immediately.*

Personally he had hoped war could be avoided. He and some other professional people, Serbs and Muslims, had set up a citizens' group, an association of people with good intentions who wanted to be between the National parties. But it was difficult, they were only a small group and there was pressure. Serbs in the SDS criticized the Serbs; the SDA bullied the Muslims. He thought the National parties appealed more to people from the villages than to those from the city.

In her village, Sanela's mother felt bewildered. She was a Muslim, her husband's parents prayed regularly, but her generation hadn't bothered so much, just observed the customs. Her Serb neighbor always came to her house for coffee at Bajram and her family returned the visit at Christmas. Sanela went to mekteb, the religious school, and she learned that there were just different ways of worshiping God. No one had made problems. Sanela's mother had traveled all over Yugoslavia and loved each part equally. Everyone was always welcoming, and even in Belgrade she could drink that special kind of Bosnian coffee. She was proud of their army, the JNA, their flag, and their generals. When it came to voting she circled all the parties, Serb and Muslim.

Families in Gorazde had anxiously watched what was happening in Slovenia and Croatia. If those republics left Yugoslavia they couldn't imagine how Bosnia could stay. Milosevic had made it clear he wanted Yugoslavia to be Greater Serbia. They had watched him send tanks into Kosovo, declare martial law, close the Albanians' parliament and university, stop them from using their language, and sack them from their jobs. If Muslims stayed in Milosevic's Yugoslavia they would be treated like Albanians, they would be second-class citizens without any rights.

There were some big rallies in Foca, both Serbs and Muslims. Not many people from Gorazde had gone to the SDA rally. It was people from the Sandzak, all protesting about how badly they were being treated in Serbia. That showed how things might go for Muslims. You just had to listen to the president of the Serb party, Karadzic: he had already called for the creation of a unified Serb state. The Serbs did not want the government to work. They kept walking out of parliament. They wanted to control their own areas of the country, but that was ridiculous, because everyone lived completely mixed up together. There was no way to separate nationalities without forcing people to leave their homes. Then Karadzic had made a horrifying speech saying that if Bosnia did not stay in Yugoslavia, all the Muslims would be killed and disappear. And then in January 1992 he had actually declared a separate Serbian state in Bosnia. It looked as if he and some Serb extremists were determined to divide up the country.

People in Gorazde knew there were tensions in Foca. There had been that affair of Foca Trans, when some experts from Sarajevo tried to calm things but the Serbs started their own bus company. Yet even with all this madness and stupidity, Muslim families in Gorazde could not imagine that a war could happen in their town. Everyone got along too well. Neighbors were all talking to each other, the children were happy in school. People were sure that if the worst were to happen, the army would protect them. The JNA would never allow Bosnian people to be killed.

The Bosnian government held a referendum on independence, on February 29, 1992, open to all citizens of the republic. It asked: "Are you in favor of a sovereign and independent Bosnia-Herzegovina, a state of equal citizens, constituted by the peoples of Bosnia-Herzegovina: the Muslims, Serbs, Croatians, and members of the other peoples who live there?" Gorazde's Muslims all voted for independence. *In Foca,* I said to Fikreta's mother, *they can't understand why you didn't want to stay with them in Yugoslavia. They see that referendum as a declaration of war.*

Never mind what they say, she responded briskly. *If they wanted to live with us, if we lived together as well as they said, why didn't they vote to stay with us in an independent Bosnia? We didn't want a Muslim Republic of Bosnia. Anyway Milosevic would have tried to create a Greater Serbia whether or not we were independent.*

Samir's father had thought he was voting for all the nationalities to live together equally in Bosnia, as the referendum stated. He thought it was the best solution because Yugoslavia was broken. Muslims could never have any say if they stayed in Milosevic's Yugoslavia, or any important positions. He wanted one country that would be equal with all the others, and where everyone in it would be equal, so anyone could be president: Serb, Muslim, or Croat, he didn't care.

After the referendum the Gorazde police split into Serb and Muslim forces. Hasan's father was in the police reserve and it made no sense to him, but the Serbs insisted. This was happening all over Bosnia and there was no way to stop it. President Izetbegovic had been determined to show that there was no threat from the Muslim side. He had told the Territorial Defense forces to give all their weapons back to the JNA, so they had tried to cooperate. In the police they had divided up the automatic rifles between them. Now Serbs were checking everyone all the time, and they seemed to have heavy weapons as well. Hasan's father assumed they had got those from the JNA. He had seen loaded trucks arrive at the Ministry of Internal Affairs one day and then drive off around the town.

His family had just finished building their house. He had been in the Communist Party all his life and thought it had been a good system. He hoped that with time all the crazy people who had appeared in the National parties would just disappear. Meanwhile he went on going to work in Kopaci. Most of his colleagues were Serb. When he asked his workmates what was going on, they said they had no idea, but not to worry, nothing would happen here.

None of the other families in Gorazde recalled being given weapons before the war, although they thought some party activists might have had some. *The Serbs had a plan*, Elvira's father told me. *It was to make a Greater Serbia. They had had it for seventy years. I wish we had had a plan, then we would have been ready for this war and fewer people would have died. Our National party did nothing for their own people. They got us into the war but they didn't prepare us. So we defended ourselves with our bare hands and made our own weapons.*

Nor had any couriers brought them warnings. Even so, when I arrived six years later with the hindsight of the nightmare that followed, I found it almost impossible to comprehend why, in April 1992, with non-Serbs being killed and driven out of cities all over northern and eastern Bosnia and refugees arriving with harrowing tales from Foca and Visegrad, Muslim families in Gorazde had still believed their own city could avoid war.

Some families noticed a change in their friends and neighbors. Armin's father saw that the Serb staff members at his factory were having a lot of meetings. He got fed up with all the partying, the shooting of guns in the air, and the singing of Serb national songs near his house, so he thought they should move to his parents' village for a while. His wife's Serb best friend, who was also their next-door neighbor, had not called round, or come to work for two months. Yet no one believed there would be a war. *Every day you said No, it won't happen, it won't happen,* Elvira's father told me. They looked at all the Muslims who had come to Gorazde from nearby towns, and thought there were far too many people in town for a war to start. And if the worst happened, Samir's father said, *We thought that the world would stop it.*

5

What Became of Our Neighbors?

We put to fire the Turkish houses,
That there might be nor stick nor trace
Of these true servants of the devil!
From Cetinje to Tcheklichte we hied
There in full flight the Turks espied;
A certain number were by us mown down,
And all their houses did we set ablaze;
Of all their mosques both great and small
We left but one accursed heap,
For passing folk to glance their scorn.

—Petar Njegos, *The Mountain Wreath,* 1847

I'd never been aware how beautiful my house is
until I saw it burning.

—Goran Simic, "A Scene, after the War," 2003

Foca must once have been a beautiful town. There was a city here in pre-Ottoman times, lying on the trading route between the Mediterranean port of Dubrovnik and Constantinople. The Ottomans took a liking to the place, endowing it with mosques and other public buildings. The oldest part clustered on a hill in the V where the Cehotina joined the Drina. Here was the Orthodox church, with its cobbled yard and its white-plastered monastery; a marketplace and a mosque; an Ottoman clock tower; and a cluster of small shops with wooden shutters and tiled roofs. Steep flights of steps led down to the newer city with its public buildings and apartment blocks. They were of no particular charm but were set in tree-lined streets and parks beside the river, alongside the graceful sixteenth-century Aladza mosque. More villas were spread out downstream along the Drina toward the prison and the hospital, and upstream toward the timber factory. These were three-storied affairs with gardens and balconies to catch the sun and the view of wooded hills: houses built, or bought with hard-earned wages, by both Serbs and Muslims, to hold whole families. Before the war just over forty thousand people lived in the municipality, 52 percent of them Muslim, 45 percent Serb.

When I arrived in the autumn of 1997, it was a dispiriting place. Coming upriver from Gorazde I would pass the Serbian police checkpoint and cross the Bailey bridge constructed by the UN Stabilization Force (SFOR) to find myself in Donje Polje. This had once been the predominantly Muslim part of town. The villas were still there. Arson does not have the same impact on a house as shelling. When a shell hits, the walls are destroyed or collapse inward from external impact. Brick buckles and crumbles into rubble. The steel of reinforced concrete protrudes. Kerosene and matches have a different effect. The outer walls usually remain standing: an empty, windowless, and roofless box. Each villa now had its own small wilderness, roses blooming in tall grass, lavender struggling with nettles. Here and there were signs of new occupancy, plastic over windows, a freshly dug vegetable patch, hens in a coop. Mostly there was silence.

In the center of town, things were slightly livelier. People were sitting on the terrace of the Hotel Zelengora, an ugly 1960s high-rise, whose residential portion had the heavy lines of laundry indicating refugee occupancy. In the marketplace, traders sold synthetic clothing, portable radios, bright plastic satchels, and the cheaper brands of athletic shoes, along with local chocolate, cigarettes, and peppers. There were few customers, and half the stone trestles were empty, as were most of the small shops that lined the street curving up to the top of the town.

The whole town had a neglected, deserted, and disjointed air. There were too few people on the streets, and too many oddly placed spaces like the one beneath the old watchtower: a large sunlit area of rubble, lined with the shells of burned-out or blown-up shops. The Aladza mosque, with its slender fourteen-sided minaret, its motifs of roses, carnations, and pomegranate flowers, and its colored wall paintings, had gone without a trace. The site it had occupied was indistinguishable from the surrounding park, with only a few turbaned Muslim tombstones leaning askew amidst the litter. The fourteen other mosques that had graced the city had also disappeared, although one shattered dome still stood near the watchtower.

In another unkempt public garden farther along the road, in front of another shattered building, there was a monument, a plain white piece of marble that read: "This is to thank Marshall Tito and the people of Foca for liberating the town and helping to found the Socialist Republic of Yugoslavia." Something metal that had stood in front of the plinth had been ripped away. The marble was scratched and damaged, the listed names almost obliterated by graffiti. *How sad,* I remarked to Biljana, my translator. *If they died fighting for something, they still deserve remembering.*

I agree, she said. *And the same with this war.*

Biljana's parents had moved here from Sarajevo after the Dayton Agreement. They had felt unable to stay in what they perceived as a Muslim-controlled city. Danica herself did not know Foca well, and like most of its newer occupants called it by its new name, Srbinje. She was not sure what the destroyed building with the monument had been, though later I learned it was a school, named after a Croatian partisan hero, Ivan Goran Kovacic. It was his statue that had been ripped away. The school had been knocked down to make room for a yet-to-be-built Orthodox church. The town was full of spaces about which people were either not quite sure or altogether silent.

At the beginning of my study I had asked children aged thirteen to fifteen to write stories about "What war means to me and how it has

affected my life." They had done this at school, during class tii
pervised by Biljana and me. The exercise was voluntary, no o.. ..au
to do it—but 127 young teenagers did. We collected the stories, un-
signed, with their authors identified only by age and gender. When
we read them, the texts seemed full of odd spaces and silences, like
the town itself.

The children had plenty to say. Some were unsatisfied with a mere
forty minutes of class time and took the stories home to finish. Understandably, for the most part they focused on their own worst
experiences. A quarter of the young authors wrote movingly of losing
a close friend or relative in the war, and a similar number wrote of
the pain and anxiety of separation from people they loved. A few had
experienced atrocities at first hand and wrote vividly of them. (I will
return to these in Chapter 9.)

For the majority, the worst experience had been the NATO bombing of Foca's bridges in 1995. Accounts of this event often revealed
anger at NATO (in phrases like *American killers*); pride in Serb courage and sacrifice (*since they existed, Serb people have fought for their
survival;* they *fight to defend the dignity of the Serb people*); and the belief that *Muslim terrorists, Ustashe,* and *powerful foreign people* were
to blame for starting the war. In some the bitterness toward the other
side was palpable. One fourteen-year-old boy wrote: *I had to run to
cellars or shelters to hide from those threatening, hostile warriors who
killed and slaughtered without mercy. They raped innocent girls. They
did not care if it was a boy or a girl, baby or child; they enjoyed [killing],
as if it was their hobby. They did different genocides and sometimes
even drove trucks over innocent souls and killed them.*

A number referred to the *defense, stabilization,* or *liberation* of
the town, or more vaguely to their current *freedom* and the *situation
being calmed down.* One boy wrote: *Our town was full of grief, but
it departed with our enemies. When the town was liberated everything
was easier and more cheerful. Although we grieved for the towns
that were still occupied, since their liberation, only scars remain from
those difficult times.* All this was to be expected. Yet the stories were

almost completely silent about what achieving this "liberation" and "freedom" had entailed: the total disappearance of half the town's population, some twenty thousand people, their neighbors and schoolmates.

There were plenty of unspecific references to the destruction of the town, and to burned houses: *I cried when houses were burning*, wrote a fifteen-year-old girl. *I do not know why. I just found it difficult to watch a house burning, when people had put so much effort and hard work into it. Well, it was someone's house.*

But most stories gave no clue as to whose houses were burned. A few stated that most of the burned houses belonged to Serbs, although only three Foca children mentioned their own houses being burned (a loss of such significance one would expect it to be mentioned if it had occurred). In contrast, many lamented the destruction of the bridges by NATO. A thirteen-year-old girl wrote: *The black birds were making circles in the sky like hawks searching for prey. Why do they do that? Don't they ever think about their children? But it seems that children are the greatest victims of this war [. . .] blood and sweat with which our fathers built the bridges, they were no more, and all my memories were destroyed with them.* And an older girl: *I was waiting for the day when Father would take us back to Foca. I considered it the most beautiful town in the world. Then the bombing came. The awful roaring of planes and the destruction of bridges. I cried, not from fear, but because I felt sorry for the bridges on the Drina.*

Children referred to the bridges with poetic eloquence as *the spine of my town*, and as being in need of protection because they *connect people*. In contrast, only one story mentioned the destruction of a mosque. Many of the young writers described having had friends of all nationalities before the war, and missing friends in general. Only one hinted at what had occurred in the town and specifically mentioned Muslims being driven out. *But some didn't have anywhere to go, and they had to watch and listen to all those massacres, blood, shooting. It was awful. After a while Muslims were expelled from Srbinje. Serbs came back to Srbinje.*

Although all of these young writers had been in school for at least six months when the war began, and a third of them had had two and a half years in ethnically mixed classes, the majority did not mention missing Muslim schoolmates. The handful of exceptions were striking. A thirteen-year-old girl wrote:

Daddy explained to me what war really means. I asked him when we could go back home. He said we could not come back immediately because the town was destroyed and some houses burned down. We came back to the town and I thought all my friends would be there. My father and mother told me that I had lost my best friend, Lejla. I started to cry. I was sad because she would not be with me in school. I remembered Lejla and I still do. War took my best friend. It took my joy and happiness. Today I am happy, but I will never be like before the war, awful war. It destroyed all my nice dreams and everything I hoped for. I thought I would never lose Lejla, but it is all for nothing. Lejla is gone. I can still remember her face. She is still in my heart.

But for the most part it was as if, like the mosques, the Muslim population of the town had never existed.

By 1997 the International Criminal Tribunal for the Former Yugoslavia had indicted nine individuals for their involvement in the ethnic cleansing of Foca. The charges included crimes against humanity, grave breaches of the Geneva Conventions, and violations of the laws or customs of war. The indictments and a Human Rights Watch report, all publicly available at that time, gave a different picture of what had happened in the town. I sat in my room beside the Drina, trying to tie together the dry language of the reports with the children's stories.[1]

Before the outbreak of war, the community had begun to split along ethnic lines. Bosnian Serbs formed a crisis committee, similar to those formed in other Serb autonomous regions in Bosnia, to plan and carry out the takeover of Foca. They inherited heavy weaponry from the JNA, which had withdrawn from Bosnia, and they organized assistance from paramilitary troops and reservists from neighboring Serbia and Montenegro. Many of these troops were thought to be under the control of Zeljko Raznatovic, also known as Arkan, and the Serbian radical politician Vojislav Seselj, both notorious for other brutal mass murders and ethnic cleansing campaigns. Muslims also formed a crisis committee and armed themselves with light weapons. Between April 7 and April 17, 1992, Serb military forces occupied and took over Foca town and rapidly defeated the lightly equipped Muslim forces. Surrounding villages remained under siege by Serb troops until mid-July 1992.

The occupation was immediately followed by the destruction of Muslim shops, homes, and mosques, the forced expulsion of thousands of non-Serb inhabitants, and the detention of thousands of others. Most detainees were Muslim civilians, who had not been charged with any crime. Muslim men, including the ill and the handicapped, were kept in Foca prison, commonly known as the KP Dom, one of the largest prisons in the former Yugoslavia. Women, children, and the elderly were held in houses, apartments, and motels in Foca or in surrounding villages. Many of those detained were kept in inhumane conditions and terrorized, tortured, beaten. Many died, or were summarily executed by Serb forces. Women and girls as young as twelve were systematically sexually assaulted.

The majority of detainees were exchanged or released during 1992 and 1993, but the KP Dom remained a detention facility until October 1994. Between six hundred and a thousand men had been detained there, and 354 of them are still missing. Former prisoners told harrowing stories: "There was one guy hanging a meter off the floor at the wall. Ropes held him up there and on one side there was hot water falling on one of his shoulders and on the other side there was cold water and he was crying . . . It was really hot water and he was really suffering and he was screaming."[2]

Other prisoners had watched guards carrying what seemed to be human bodies in blankets and dumping them in the Drina. A woman reported seeing, on repeated occasions, a yellow minivan driven out to the TITO sign above the river. Serbs then led out small groups of men, forced them to strip and hand over money and identification, and then murdered them with knives and threw their bodies into the Drina. Many Muslim residents of Foca fled to the hospital, thinking it would be safe. However, it had been taken over by Serb irregular forces, and the staff had to work in harsh conditions with little food or supplies. Muslim patients and staff were in effect imprisoned there, and many of the male patients were transferred to the KP Dom, from which some disappeared.[3] The Partizan Sports Hall near the police station in the center of town, and the high school where I now worked, had both been used as "rape camps":

Many of the female detainees were subjected to sexual abuse during their detention at Foca High School. From the second day of their detention, every evening, groups of Serb soldiers sexually assaulted, including gang rape, some of the younger women and girls in classrooms or apartments in neighboring buildings . . . The soldiers threatened to kill the women or the women's children if they refused to submit to sexual assaults. Women who dared to resist the sexual assaults were beaten . . . The detainees lived in constant fear. Some of the sexually abused women became suicidal.[4]

Serb soldiers came every night. They told the women, aged between twelve and sixty, to strip and chose the ones they wanted. They often chose a mother and daughter together. One woman had watched five soldiers rape an eighteen-year-old and had been selected twice herself. While she was being raped by two men, one said, "You should have already left this town. We will make you have Serbian babies who will be Christians." Another had been gang-raped in an out-

door stadium by soldiers: "I counted 29 of them. Then I lost con-
sciousness." Sometimes the girls were not brought back: "When they
take you away they may kill you. So if you are raped, you feel lucky. At
least you're alive."[5]

The stories seemed endless. Human Rights Watch reporters found
Nihada in a refugee camp, lying sick on a cot, with bandages on her
arms and inner thighs. She was a widow with three daughters between eleven and eighteen. They had lived near Foca. They had hidden in the forest for four months, but they had gone back to their
house to get food when a soldier arrived with a piece of paper and
said he had been ordered to kill her and her children. He had put a
grenade on the table and started loading his gun. "He then said 'Listen closely to what I am going to tell you. I am going to cut a Serbian
Cross into your face and throw salt in your face.' I told him that he
couldn't do that, and then he said he would tattoo me 'with sixty-
four letters.' I told him he was crazy. He then got angry and said he
was going to kill my children, that he was going to cut the fingers
from my children's hands and make a necklace out of them. I got
scared and I let him tattoo my body." Nihada had removed the tape
and shown the interviewers the hastily made tattoos saying "Rade—
husband" and "Rade—don't forget me." After tattooing her he had
tried to shave a Serbian Cross on her eleven-year-old daughter's
head.[6]

In September 1997 there were posters of Radovan Karadzic plastered
all around the town. The poster said "Don't touch him," a warning
from the current inhabitants of Foca to the international community
not to arrest their wartime political leader, who was wanted by the
International Criminal Tribunal for the Former Yugoslavia for genocide and crimes against humanity. Not that any arrests seemed likely
at that time. At that point the French SFOR troops who patrolled the
town had not arrested even one war criminal, although several lived

and moved freely in the community. Dragan Gagovic, one of the first to be indicted for rape as a war crime, owned and ran the Krsma bar, where "Tuta," also known as Janko Janjic, one of the most notorious leaders of a paramilitary gang, regularly drank coffee. Tuta had also been filmed on the Hotel Zelengora terrace next door to the International Police Task Force headquarters, bragging of his crimes and showing off the hand grenades on his belt while French NATO officers drank coffee nearby.

Others who had played leading roles in creating an "ethnically pure" municipality also retained their influence. Petko Cancar, who had arrived in Foca in early April 1992 and had led the crisis committee to, in his own words, *stop the threat of Islam* on the Drina, had been mayor during the war and had continued in that position until April 1997. Velibor Ostojic had been Karadzic's minister of information. Three days before the takeover he had demanded, at a public meeting, that all the Muslims give up their weapons and concede that Foca was Serb territory. He had told them to leave for a concentration camp at nearby Jabuka mountain "or else the last Muslim seed will be destroyed in Foca." In September 1997 he had just been made head of the commission for human rights in the Bosnian parliament. (Dusan's family had told me this; they found it uproariously funny.) The literature professor Vojislav Maksimovic had apparently told local Bosnian Serbs that if they would not take up arms and start shooting Muslims he would call for reinforcements from Serbia. He had been responsible for supplying weapons, training SDS (Serb Democratic Party) members, and coordinating the irregulars. Now he was rector of the University of Republika Srpska. He kept a house in the Foca woods, an apartment in the town, and his influence in the local SDS.[7]

Neither Karadzic nor the SDS was particularly in favor at that moment. Unemployment in the town was running at 99 percent and local people were fed up with the increasingly visible corruption.

They had turned in large numbers to the Serb Radical Party (SRS), a branch of the party led by Vojislav Seselj, another Tribunal indictee.

In the first months I spent in the town, I too was silent about these matters. There were many reasons for this. I wanted to hear about the children's own war experiences, their suffering, their losses, and the disruption of their lives, without putting them on the defensive. Their initial hostility toward me as a citizen of a NATO country had been made clear by the messages a few had attached to their stories: one child had drawn a hideous picture of a figure of indeterminate sex saying *I am a war criminal, the more Muslims the better.*

Somebody survived war and then you bombed us. Why? Dusan wrote. *You think that we suffered so little fear and grief, that you should give us more. Muslims, Croats, and Serbs took part in the war. Why did you bomb only us? Could you answer our questions?* Then at the base he printed in capitals SERB PEOPLE FROM REPUBLIKA SRPSKA ARE AGAINST WAR BUT ALSO AGAINST PEACE WITH SFOR. WE ARE FOR PEACE WITHOUT SFOR, WITHOUT PEACE STRANGERS, and finished it off with a diagram of the Serb symbol of the four Cs and *God protect the Serbs.* Interestingly, Dusan had been keen to be interviewed. I knew that if I wanted to learn how these young people felt about ethnic cleansing, I had to let them take the lead.

Some of them did. They spontaneously mentioned the *liberation* or the *stabilization* of the town, and I asked them to explain what this was. With others I asked open questions such as *What happened here?* Or the topic came up indirectly through discussion around related themes, such as whom they held responsible for the war or what they thought the war had achieved.

I began to notice that there were two quite distinct groups of children. Those in one group were curious. They took an active interest in these sorts of questions. They wanted to discuss why the conflict had taken place and what it had been about. Svetlana *just wonder[ed] why this happened. I ask myself, but I don't know the answers.* When

Dragoljub Kunarac, one of those indicted for rape, handed himself over to The Hague that spring, she talked about it with her friends and asked her father what Kunarac had done. *He said he didn't know, because he wasn't with them.* Mirko knew that all the Serbs were *fighting to kick out the Turks* from the town. His brother-in-law had told him the Turks wanted to kick out the Serbs but the Serbs were stronger. He had seen *special units* come and burn down houses in the Turk village opposite his. He asked his father why the shooting and shelling had started in the first place. His father didn't know either and just told him *It was stupid, it was a war.*

The children in the other, larger group had distanced themselves from these events. They often discussed their personal wartime experiences in moving detail, but through verbal and nonverbal language they made clear that questions about what had happened in the town and why were boring and unimportant. The distancing took different forms. Some were completely uninterested. Milica had no idea why the war had started, or for what her father had been fighting. She never discussed it with her parents and had no interest in doing so. She liked living in Foca, liked her new friends, and hoped things would get better. Ivana, in spite of having witnessed what happened to her friend Asra, told me she never spent time wondering why it had happened. Nor did she appear very curious about Asra's fate.

Some, when asked, were able to give quite well worked out answers as to how they made sense of things, but were untroubled by gaps or inconsistencies in their knowledge and made clear that they had other things to think about. Stojan said he didn't know much, because he hadn't been in Foca during the war and didn't understand, but he thought the town had been *liberated very fast.* When I asked him what *liberation* meant he explained that the Muslim people had been transported wherever they wanted to go by bus. He thought that was best for them because once they had been defeated, they had had nowhere in the town to which they could retreat. He had no idea what might have happened to them if they had stayed. *Maybe they signed this kind of a peace; they saw that a lot of people left, so that's why they left too.* All the same, he thought the town had been *better before.*

Marko had been evacuated to a village. He had been in third grade then and was in high school now, a pleasant, diffident boy who wanted to become an engineer. He had returned to Foca six months after it *was already liberated.* I asked what he meant by liberated. *Everything was burned down. Everything was destroyed.* He felt *awful,* although his own house and his predominantly Serb neighborhood were undamaged. He noticed that it was mainly Muslim houses that were burned, including those of all his Muslim friends. They had already left.

How did you feel about that? I asked.

I don't know . . . I felt safer because there wasn't a threat anymore that somebody could meet you on the street or something . . .

What did you feel threatened by?

Well . . . He was silent.

Did you feel threatened before you left for the village?

No . . .

But when you came back you felt safer?

Yes.

Seeing that I was confused, he explained that he had not known he was in danger until he came back to Foca and saw what had happened. When he saw all the destruction, he realized that Muslims could have done the same to them, and then all of the Serbs would have been without their houses.

So were you pleased the Muslims had gone?

Well, I don't know.

Did you miss any of your friends?

Well . . . partly. Later it passed.

Fifteen-year-old Susana lived near the center of town. Her parents were professionals and she was doing well in high school. She liked

listening to music and told me her favorite film star was Richard
Gere. She wrote in moving detail of the death of her cousin:

> *I can still remember some moments I experienced in that awful
> war. It is as if I am watching now: my mother crying when she
> heard the words "Your cousin Mihajlo has been killed and his re-
> mains could not be removed from that furious battle." I felt grief in
> my heart. To know that he would not come again, with wet shoes,
> which my mother would have dried carefully, made some special
> food, and taken care of him like a sister for her brother. It was both
> difficult and painful.*

Susana made a clear distinction between these kinds of details
from the war, in which she took an interest, and those in which she
had none. She watched war stories on television, particularly when
they were about people who lost close relatives. But she had no explanations for and no interest in what had happened to Muslims in
Foca. *I don't know. They didn't like being together, they wanted something,* she responded vaguely when I asked how she made sense of the
war. *It's all finished. They wanted to separate.*
Everybody wanted to separate? I asked her.
I guess so. I didn't follow that.
She had never discussed such questions with her parents or her
teachers or followed the topic on TV. The news bored her. She preferred movies and soap operas like the one about an Australian high
school. There had been no tensions or troubles in school before the
war. She had had friends of both nationalities, *as was normal.*
Did you have a best friend? I asked
I had Vasvija. She's Muslim; she's not here anymore.
At the beginning of the war there had been a panic and everyone
had left. Her family had taken her to the village for ten days and then
they had come back.
When was the last time you saw your best friend? I asked a bit later.
It was in the school. She wasn't my best friend. I also had the other

friends . . . all those who were Muslims left, but it didn't stress me or shock me.

Do you know why they left? I could see from her expression that Susana was already a little bored with the conversation.

I didn't.

So can you explain it?

Susana looked incredulous. It was as if I had asked "What color is butter?" I apologized. I was an outsider, I said, perhaps these things were obvious to her, but I didn't want to rely on what I read in newspapers and reports. She gave a little laugh. *Because they were other nationalities. We just split up, separated.*

How was it when you came back to Foca?

Two houses next to mine, Muslim houses, burned down. Actually one, and then when I came back, the other one. She had watched the second one burn. *I could see other places, houses, burning. Every night some house was burning.*

She did not know who had set her neighbor's house alight—probably outsiders who had come from somewhere else. She had heard about the house burning when she was in the village, so she had expected to see it when she returned. *I wasn't very upset.*

Did you know the neighbors who owned that house? Did it matter?

Yes, I knew them. They were our next-door neighbors. But they had left at the beginning. So I knew they wouldn't come back. She had particularly liked the small girl, who had visited her often. But before the war the girl's parents and grandparents had stopped her from coming around so often, and when she had come, she had talked about the SDA. Nothing unpleasant, just stuff about political parties that Susana thought the family must have told her to say.

So it didn't matter that the house was burned down?

No.

You didn't care?

She gave another small laugh. *No.*

How would you have felt if it had been your house that had been burned down?

I would have felt sorry. Everybody is sorry when their house is burning.

Not all the Muslims had left by the time Susana returned to Foca. *Those who stayed longer, they were forced to leave.* She did not know how. She had not seen.

Susana said she hadn't been very scared by the NATO bombing because she knew they were aiming at military targets. She had been far enough away, and felt secure enough, to watch from her windows. She thought the destruction of the bridges made the town *awful.* I asked if it was just the bridges, or if the earlier destruction had upset her as well.

It was mostly Muslim houses that were burning.
And mosques presumably?
Yes.
Was that a problem? Did you mind?
No.

When it came to discussing the question of responsibility for the war, a pattern began to emerge. The teenagers who had shown the most curiosity about events were also the most evenhanded, tending to hold both sides, or no one at all, responsible for the conflict. Svetlana did not blame anybody and was not angry with anyone. Some of the disengaged teenagers, in contrast, tended to see Muslims as more to blame. Milica was sure that Turks had started the war, although she had no idea why. Stojan believed *Muslims wanted to have the power, to have the president of Bosnia.* Others blamed outsiders, such as the West, who they believed wanted to weaken Yugoslavia or destroy it.

Almost all told me they had worked these things out for themselves by *watching television* or *listening to adults talking.* When the more curious children had tried discussing the war directly, they had received unsatisfactory answers and given up. Some sensed that it was not something to be discussed. Divac, a high school boy who had moved from Sarajevo in the first year of the war after his father had been injured on the line, said he *listened and overheard things; I thought things out for myself. I didn't consult anybody or ask anybody. My parents didn't want to worry me with that and I didn't ask them.* Others wanted to protect their parents. The war had taken Jovan by surprise. His parents had a shop in town, and they had sent him to the village when the courier came to warn them. He had asked questions at first, *then I didn't want to ask anymore. I knew this was hard for them . . . They have their own problems.* He hadn't wanted to upset them. Similarly, Stojan said *They don't want to talk about that.* Dusan was an exception in that he and his parents had often had lengthy discussions, but as time passed he too was concerned with protecting his parents and himself from distress: *I don't want to remind my parents and I don't want to remember what happened.*

Their parents agreed. They wanted to protect their children, or thought the children were not interested and had other worries. *We don't wish the children to see what we saw,* one father told me. *She isn't interested, she is interested in books.* Another, contradictory explanation was that *the children know everything,* because *they saw for themselves.*

This mutual silence covered an unspoken, shared understanding of events. Svetlana's mother sounded as bewildered as her daughter: *It's hard to explain. I don't even know myself how I explained things to her.* Ivana echoed her mother's experience at the bus station with the elderly Muslim man when she said the problems had begun *with people not respecting each other, they were not saying good afternoon to each other.* She shared her parents' view that it was *us or them.* Her father had fought to prevent Foca being *their territory, to stop them occupying it so we would have to move from here.* None of the families denied that some terrible things had happened to Muslims in Foca, although many felt that the Muslims and the Western media had exaggerated events, or had not understood the danger faced by Serbs that had precipitated the conflict. All were convinced that *kicking Muslims out,* as Jovan's mother put it, had made them safer. *If we stayed together, no matter whether it was Serbs or Muslims, it would be more dead people,* Ivana's father said. *That's how it is: Muslims are running away from here, somewhere else it's Serbs, somewhere else, Croats.*

The parents, like most of the children, distanced themselves from these events in a number of ways. Many told me simply that they had not been present when the worst excesses occurred. Women were with children out of town, men were on the line in another area. They thought the real crimes had been committed by *outsiders, criminals,* and *psychopaths.* Many described personal assistance they had given to help friends escape, and the danger involved in doing so. Many Muslims had left of their own accord right at the beginning, Nikola's parents assured me, and it was only those with nowhere to go who had stayed. They themselves had helped a family get to Montenegro and intervened to get the husband of one of the daughters out of prison.

Why were most of the men put in prison? I asked.

I don't know how it was regulated, men were in prison. The same as Serbs were in prison in Gorazde and they don't know why they were in prison.

So were any Muslims actually forced to leave?

They knew how they would live if they stayed here, Nikola's father replied.

Nobody trusted anyone, his wife added.

I asked how those who did stay had been treated, but they said they only knew about the ones they had protected, who had therefore been all right. It had been very dangerous to protect people, so no one knew about it.

Nikola's mother had worked in the hospital. She told me that things had carried on there *just like before the war. We worked together. My boss stayed there. Every night we had dinner together, we were drinking coffee, laughing together. When he left, he was crying.*

Why did he leave?

Because he was Muslim. But nobody touched him in the hospital.

He had to go, Nikola's father explained. *It was safer for him.*

But the staff treated him fairly, Nikola's mother said. *Everyone got along well, he didn't have to go because of the staff. He had absolutely no fear of me.* They were anxious that I should understand and continued to speak in turn:

It was not an organized army.

Nobody knew what night could bring.

Or who could come into an apartment with a knife. We criticized the Serbs who stayed with the Muslims, and they criticized Muslims who stayed with us. Asking them why they were staying, why don't you come to us? Muslims, Serbs, Croats. It was like a nightmare.

Dusan's father felt aggrieved that the West had not recognized the Serbs' restraint. *Serbs could have liquidated all the Muslims on that road if it had been to their advantage. You drive from Ustikolina to Foca all the time. It's ideal for destroying people on foot. Two guns and nobody would have got to Gorazde alive. But the Serbs had nothing to gain . . . To be honest it's a pity they didn't do it, because they shouldn't have let them reach Gorazde. To be honest I think it's a great mistake that we didn't exterminate them. We had the possibility, but the commanders and the people in power, parliament didn't let us. And now they are called war criminals!*

All the families set the ethnic cleansing of Foca in the context of what they perceived as a completely symmetrical war. *It was us or them,* I was told repeatedly. If Serbs had not acted preemptively, Muslims would have attacked with equal brutality. As evidence of this they mentioned the occasions when Muslims were known to have attacked and committed atrocities, such as the concentration camp of Celebici near the town of Konjic, which was run by Bosnian government forces and held Serb prisoners, and where, according to Human Rights Watch, "prisoners were bestially beaten in the Celebici barracks and many died as a result." There was the execution of around sixty civilians in the village of Bratunac near Srebrenica. And after

Bosnian government forces had partly lifted the siege of Gorazde in 1992 they had attacked several hundred Serb civilians who had left the town by bus. Three hundred were alleged to have been killed by Muslim machine-gun fire.[8]

Many families had had experiences which confirmed their view of an entirely equal conflict. Stojan's relatives in Sarajevo had been unable to get out of the city, and had been forced to do manual work on the front lines. His father did not believe many Serbs had stayed willingly in that city. Dusan's uncle had been imprisoned by Muslims and had seen his house burned down in Foca at the beginning of the war. If the Muslims had not been pushed out of the town he would surely have been killed. Four of the children said their own homes had been burned. The most horrifying event was the massacre of at least sixty-five Serb civilians, mostly elderly people and children, in the neighboring village of Josanice. Some had been relatives or friends of the families I interviewed.

In early 1998, while I was still in Bosnia, the Bosnian press accused Foca's primary school headmaster Simo Mojevic, in his role as a member of the Ustikolina crisis committee, of having supervised the ethnic cleansing of Ustikolina and been involved in the disappearance of fifty Muslim men. There were two witnesses, and the charges were repeated in the Human Rights Watch report.[9] Throughout my stay in Foca, Mojevic had done everything possible to help my work. No international agencies were working in the town at that time except the bureaucracies of the Organization for Security and Cooperation in Europe (OSCE) and the United Nations. A youth club run by foreign aid workers had been closed down by the local authorities. However the headmaster had told me that he ran an *open school*, even if Foca was not an *open town*. He had provided space for me to work, encouraged parents to meet with me, and given class time to parts of the project. He confirmed the heterodoxy of his views by boldly displaying a calendar with a photo of Biljana Plavsic, a hard-line nationalist and a former close colleague of Karadzic who had just been elected president of Republika Srpska. She was being courted and supported by the West for her apparent support of the Dayton Peace Agreement and for her criticism of her former colleagues. Many in Foca despised her for yet again bringing disunity to the Serbs.

The headmaster invited me to his house for the evening. He asked if I believed the accusations against him. I said I felt quite unable to judge, and that it was not my job to do so. He wanted me to hear his story of what had happened in the war, and he poured it out over rakia. It was a long and complicated tale of killings by Muslims, betrayal of Serbs in the Second World War, and massacres by Serbs in response; of deals done and broken between local units on opposing sides and corruption and self-interest by all parties during the recent war; and of criminal profiteering and self-interest since. He was convinced that outsiders—Americans, the CIA, the Vatican—had started the war for their own interests. Perhaps Milosevic was even an American agent? Why would local people want to break up the land of his grandfathers? He wanted to make clear that his only concern had been to defend his homeland: Yugoslavia.

Mojevic distanced himself from the ethnic cleansing of the region in the ways that I had begun to find familiar. I had made a list:

> *minimizing:* it was not as bad as people said
> *scapegoating:* others were responsible
> *absenteeism:* I was not there at the time
> *equalizing:* they were just as bad, guilty, and criminal as we were

He did not deny that atrocities had occurred. Over a few days he had watched old people and children fleeing Foca: *Everyone who could move was going in carts or walking to Gorazde.* He had seen Serb soldiers join in the looting of Muslim houses in Foca: *It was a rich part. Because Muslims didn't take everything.* He thought the accounts were exaggerated: *They said people were killed, butchered . . . Something happened, but not even 10 percent of what people said in fear. Probably frightened people made things up, because it's difficult to leave your house, especially for older people.* He blamed Muslim journalists for exaggerating the threat, for saying things like *A thousand Chetniks are coming.*

When the main atrocities had been perpetrated in Ustikolina, he said, he had not been present. *It was paramilitaries and irregulars from Serbia or Montenegro. People released from prison or from hospitals for the insane. They killed the best people who wanted to live with us.* He thought it was *the greatest tragedy. They also killed Serbs who wanted to protect those people.* He had sent a group of women, including his oldest sister and a few cousins, to protect his neighbors, but they had been threatened as well, so he had not been able to do anything. There was no command or organization so everyone did what they wanted without telling anyone else. *They burned all the houses . . . They killed innocent people inside the houses, and they took truckloads from the houses they robbed. Mosques fell down. The extremists came out on both sides.*

He told me he had ensured that no atrocities occurred under his command. On the section of the road where he was in control, he had forbidden his men to shoot any fleeing civilians. On one occasion he had helped a group of elderly Muslim people trapped in a village to escape. On another he had saved two Muslim boys. Like all those I interviewed, he set these events in the context of all the equally terrible things that had happened to Serbs in the war, such as at Josanice, and the brutality and treachery of some Muslims.

Instead of just listening as usual, perhaps from weariness or too much rakia, I challenged him, pointing out that while no one denied the atrocities committed by Muslims, this insistence on the symmetry of the war was hard to accept, given that Serbs had taken control of 70 percent of the territory in the first two months. During that time approximately a million people had been displaced from their homes, and several tens of thousands of people, mostly Bosnian Muslims, had been killed. The headmaster replied that this was simply because Muslims had not had enough guns, because of President Izetbegovic's foolishness in removing Muslims from the JNA. This rather undermined his earlier insistence on symmetry, but he did not appear to notice.

I told him there was no equivalent on the Bosnian side of what had happened during the fall of Srebrenica. The headmaster's wife, who had been listening to our conversation in between serving enormous quantities of food, interrupted, asking me exactly what had happened in Srebrenica. So I told her of the organized murder of at least seven thousand men, by soldiers under the command of General Mladic, and the forced expulsion of the rest of the population, some twenty-five thousand people, from the town. She and her husband both listened quietly, and when I had finished she looked deeply upset. *If it is true, it is terrible,* she said, and I had the sense that she was hearing this story for the first time. *We lived very near to the Partizan Sports Hall,* said the headmaster. *Believe me, we knew nothing of what happened in there.* Then we had to stop talking because Red Star was playing a football match on TV.

The more time I spent in Foca, the more I became aware that the war had reduced each family's world to their immediate neighborhood: relatives, friends, how to survive, with no attention to anything else, not even what is going on in the house next door. The media continued to play a key role. In England, I had been able to watch or listen to reports on the entire war from almost every part of the country. After the takeover of the local transmitter at the beginning of the war, families in Foca could only get Serbian Radio (and Serbian Television when there was electricity). This always showed Serb forces as fighting for freedom and to protect themselves from Muslim forces. Muslims were fighting a religious war and were intent on forcing Serbs to belong to an Islamic state. The Serb side never attacked: *The Muslim authorities are holding Sarajevo under siege from within* was typical. A single broadcast from Foca in August 1992 mentioned *Alija's wanton hordes, Ustashe chauvinists, Islamic chauvinists,* and *Islamic fundamentalists.* There was no discussion of the strategic goals of the war, no maps to show who controlled what, no pictures of the destruction inflicted by Serb forces, and the only victims ever shown were Serb.[10]

So it was not surprising that many Serb children believed the Serbs had suffered the most violence in the war, in places such as Josanice or Celebici. The majority had no idea what had happened in Gorazde, just up the road. *How could I know?* one asked me in some irritation. When a child had first-hand knowledge and did not depend on adults or the media, this made a significant difference: Jovan told me *I was only watching one side,* but went on to say that he thought Gorazde had suffered more. A gun emplacement near his house had been used to shell Gorazde, so he knew that *there was the shelling of the town,* and that *in the Muslim part I know they had very bad living conditions, they didn't have food for some time.* He did not know why they were shelling.

The war was not symmetrical. There was no organized ethnic cleansing of Gorazde. The prewar population of the municipality was approximately 57,000, of whom 70.2 percent were Muslim and 26.2 percent Serb. In the city there were about 9,600 Muslims and 5,600 Serbs. Gorazde was of crucial strategic importance in any attempt to create an ethnically homogeneous Serb area in eastern Bosnia. It lay on the main road between the cities of Foca and Visegrad, both of which were rapidly and effectively "cleansed" of their non-Serb populations in the first months of the war. Gorazde also possessed a large armaments factory, located in the western half of the city. The majority of Bosnian Serb residents left Gorazde in the weeks and days before the outbreak of fighting. They believed the local Serb leaders' assertion that they faced an Islamic takeover and would be killed if they stayed. As in Foca, most families sent women and children out of the town immediately prior to the fighting. At the beginning of May 1992 Serb men withdrew to prearranged positions and began shelling the city. Bosnian Serb forces hoped to take the city as rapidly as they had taken neighboring Foca and Visegrad. Then Serb families would be able to return.

They had miscalculated. First, unlike the situation in Foca and Visegrad, there was no place to which Gorazde's non-Serb population could retreat. Second, although poorly armed, the Muslim population included a larger number of men of fighting age because of the influx of refugees from the neighboring areas. And third, in the previous weeks the less trusting local authorities had refused the offer of JNA "protection." Thus indigenous Bosnian Serb forces at this point lacked JNA support. The "siege" continued for three and a half years. For the first four months the bombardment was intense, then in September 1992 the Bosnian Serb forces were pushed back and a narrow corridor was created over the mountains (the Grebak route) allowing communication between Gorazde and Sarajevo. Further offensives occurred intermittently, and shelling and sniping continued, throughout the four years, most notably in the spring of 1993 when the Grebak route was lost and in 1994 when General Mladic attempted to storm the town. Bosnian Muslim fighters also launched offensives out of the enclave and were on occasion responsible for serious abuses of human rights, such as the destruction of villages and the massacre of civilians. Human Rights Watch states that these actions appear to have been perpetrated by individuals rather than as part of a premeditated plan.[11]

After the closing of the route over Grebak in 1993 the town of

Gorazde became completely dependent upon its own resources and what could be obtained from airdrops. Convoys carrying humanitarian aid over land were repeatedly blocked by the Serbs. Electricity, which had come from Foca, was stopped, and the fresh water supply was disrupted by shelling. Around seventy thousand people were trapped in the city, all subject to the same harsh living conditions.

The Serbs who remained were those who did not wish to join the Bosnian Serb nationalist enterprise, those with nowhere to go, and those who had not managed to get themselves exchanged. Veljko, who had worked as a factory manager, was one of the first group. He voted in the Bosnian government referendum in February 1992, because he wanted a unified Bosnia. He was convinced that from the outset Milosevic had been bent on the division of Bosnia, and for him the choice was simple: a divided Bosnia or a unified, independent one. Some fellow Serbs called him and said that if he voted he would be killed. He thought it was intimidation like this that had stopped most of his fellow Bosnian Serbs from voting. *They went into Serb homes and said if you vote you will get shot. The only people who mistreated me were Serbs.* He showed me two repaired walls that had been destroyed by shells, and the holes of more than 250 sniper bullets. In the 1994 offensive, Serbs called him by name from across the Drina, saying they were coming to get him.

Sladjana and her mother stayed because they could not make up their minds about going, and because they had no money and no offers from anyone to take them to safety, whereas it seemed that many of their neighbors had both. Sladjana's mother found it difficult. She felt attacked by both sides. When the shelling was particularly intense one neighbor said she was going to kill them. Another threatened her in the shelter, saying *If there are any Serbs in this building we should kill them.* She had no desire to quarrel. *None of our neighbors helped.*

How can you say that, Mum, when neighbors came with food and coffee? Sladjana said.

That was not help! That was not saving my life!

Sladjana turned to me. *We never had any complications, and they never mistreated us. They just didn't like making conversation because of what was happening.*

That is mistreatment, her mother interrupted.

But some Serbs were kicked out of their homes and put in some kind of prison, weren't they? I asked. This was what I had heard.

Refugees came, Sladjana replied, *people who had suffered and been kicked out themselves and seen death. Some of them wanted to take Serb flats by force. I found some people I knew and we took them in, but I could see by the way they looked at us that they wanted us to get out and give the flat to them. There were around twelve people here for two years. Then they found another place.*

She explained that the authorities had warned the Serbs in 1992 and 1993 that it was not safe to stay in their homes and had moved them into collective centers in town. Their own neighbors, though, had insisted they stay in their flat. Others had moved, leaving their property vulnerable to takeover, looting, and burning. Furthermore, many Serb houses had been in the area that Serb forces recaptured in 1994. These soldiers were not local and in ignorance had burned Serbs' houses.[12] I knew the area, a pretty rural suburb on a small road on the eastern side of the Drina, winding up to Cajnice, with the same overgrown unkempt gardens and the same deserted silence as in Donje Polje. Some two to three hundred Serbs had been murdered, Veljko estimated. The worst violence had occurred during offensives against the city.

The children I interviewed in Gorazde were not silent about their Serb friends' leaving. For many of them the mysterious disappearance of children from school in the month before the war had been what first made them aware that something was not right in their town. *One day two Serb children would be missing, the next day another one, until all of them escaped,* Suada recalled. She had been in third grade. Nedjad, another third grader, had had a Serb best friend: *He said he was going to visit his grandparents and he would be back in a* month. *I didn't see any change on their faces. All of them left just before the war.* Jasmin had also had Serb friends in that class. He had noticed no tension, but *they left. They ran away [. . .] before the war started. They didn't say anything.* Ten-year-old Iris, like Amela, had been jealous: *They said they were going on vacation, and I said "Oh, why couldn't I do the same thing?" I didn't understand why they were leaving.* Iris was in her second year of primary school. *My teacher was a Serb but I really loved him very much, regardless of his nationality. He stayed until the day before the war and then suddenly he just seemed to disappear.*

Iris's parents were professional people living in the center of town. Serb neighbors had warned them: *It was strange because almost all our Serb friends said to my father, you should leave, but they didn't explain anything. Why should we go? Actually we were supposed to leave, but then my father decided not to go, and I didn't want to leave either. I couldn't imagine living somewhere else. Mother's family came to stay with us and they were refugees from Foca, so we couldn't just go and leave them.* The relatives had brought tales of their experiences. *In the area where they lived in Foca, they used to come to their house every night to look for weapons. And they threatened them, if you don't leave, something like that, we will kill you, and then the shooting started there, and so they left. When it started in Foca, I knew the same thing was going to happen here, and sometimes I thought maybe it would be better if we went somewhere else, but anyway it is best to be at home.* Senad's aunt had a Serb friend who warned her that there would be a war. His parents sent him out of the country to Spain with the aunt and her children. They thought of going too, but they had good jobs in the factory and delayed until it was too late.

Many of the Serb adults had simply departed like the children. Jasmin's neighbors suddenly got in their cars and disappeared. Then he noticed Serbs building barricades behind his house. *Then I heard that some young Serbs left Gorazde and went to the hills; only old Serbs stayed in my neighborhood. Then the war started. They started shoot-*

ing. We started to take shelter. They started to shell. It was like that all through the war. The shelling had been so intense in the first months that *we couldn't move, we couldn't go on the streets, and that's why, to protect the center of the town, the Muslims drove them far away from the town.* The siege of the city had been lifted on September 18—*the date of the liberation of Gorazde,* Jasmin called it—the same day his father had been killed in the fighting.

In contrast to the situation in Foca, where Serb children had returned to a relatively calm city, *free* of Muslims, for Muslim children in Gorazde the departure of their Serb neighbors from town did not signify the disappearance of Serbs from their lives or the end of fighting in the city. On the contrary, they now discovered that the parents of their former school friends were the ones shelling them from the hills.

As in Foca, I had asked a large sample of children aged thirteen to fifteen to write anonymous stories for me; in Gorazde 155 children did so. The vast majority gave graphic and powerful descriptions of being shelled or shot at. Most of these described witnessing death or injury, often of more than one person, often of family or friends. Almost a third of the children told of losing a close relative or friend. More than a quarter wrote of being displaced. Many wrote of the harsh living conditions. Ten recounted having been wounded themselves. A few, like this thirteen-year-old boy, wrote of their personal experiences of imprisonment or ethnic cleansing:

In 1992 I was a prisoner in Rogatica. I was imprisoned with my mama, sister, grandma, and grandpa, who were killed near the house. My father ran away so they could not catch him. He fled to the forest with his friends who had no guns. The Serbs drove us down the street, which was full of people from that street. They took all of us to the priest's house. We did not eat for three days. On the fourth day they brought us beans that were not cooked very well, just water and beans. We were there for ten days. Then the Serbs came and told us we were going to a school where there were lots of people from Rogatica. In that place they raped girls and women, separated children from mothers, brothers from sisters . . . We got in a bus and were driving along. As we were driving we went past the street that would have taken us to that school. Then the driver told us we were going to be exchanged in Zepa. That was easier.

There was an interesting silence in many of these stories as well. Foca children, although mostly absent during the initial fighting, had mostly been present when NATO bombed the town, and usually identified the perpetrator by name, accompanied by understandable anger. However although the majority of Gorazde children were in town throughout the bombardment, only a third of them mentioned an aggressor, often in the matter-of-fact manner illustrated above, and half of these simply used the term "aggressor" without identifying this as Chetnik or Serb: *The war started in 1992. My family and I went into the basement. We only came out during the night. The aggressor from the hills was shooting a lot of projectiles around the town and people.*

Most of the stories were dominated by concrete descriptions of horrifying events that seemed to come out of nowhere: inexplicable and bewildering catastrophes. They started abruptly: *One morning grenades woke me up . . .*

They often mentioned injuries and multiple losses, as this thirteen-year-old girl did:

The shell fell suddenly when I was in front of my building with my friends. One of my friends was killed and the other and I were wounded. We were in the hospital a long time. When I came out of the hospital I visited my friend Mirela. I saw she was without her leg. I was so sad. I heard some shelling on my way back. My father told me some time later that one shell hit Mirela's flat and she was killed. I was so upset because she was my best friend. We had been together in school, at the same desk. I was sad for a long time. I wish she were alive and we could be together now. But that is Destiny. I will never forget that day. It is always on my mind.

Or, like this thirteen-year-old boy, they mentioned witnessing terrible events:

One day the war started in my town. There were a lot of shells falling down. There were many dead people who were killed on the street next to me. I was on the street one day when the shooting stopped a little bit, with my best friend [. . .] We were playing the game Ganje. My best friend was killed by a sniper on the way back. I and the other friend were next to him. We took him in our arms and we put him behind the house trying to hide ourselves. We were very sorry for our friend. Then we went home [. . .] I was wounded at the same place a few days later. I was wounded in my leg. It was very painful for me and I thought about my friend who was killed next to me. The war impressed my life with many sad things.

In at least two-thirds of the written stories the children made no mention of the perpetrators of these actions. I would suggest three reasons for this silence. First, the events themselves are so numerous and overwhelming that describing them filled the allocated time and was given more importance than explanations of responsibility. Second, one child mentions Destiny. Such mentions were not frequent in either the written narratives or the interviews, but stoical acceptance of death is part of Muslim culture and faith, and was mentioned quite often by parents. Third, this silence makes sense in the context of the Muslim families' complete lack of preparedness for the war. In their anxiety to prove that they had no aggressive intent, the Muslim officials in the tripartite government had constantly reassured their own people that there was no danger and would be no war.

Even after Karadzic famously threatened the Muslim population with annihilation, on the night of October 14, 1991, Izetbegovic said, "I want to tell the people of Bosnia-Herzegovina not to be afraid, because there will be no war . . . Therefore sleep peacefully." Many Gorazde families, when I talked to them six years later, saw this as a great failing on his part. It was the main reason why they held their own politicians equally responsible with the Serbs and Croats for the conflict.[13]

The writer Mark Thompson suggests that the Bosnian state media, particularly RTVBiH (Bosnian state radio and television), strongly influenced by its hard-line communist past, was determined to play an "impartial" role in covering both the wars in Slovenia and Croatia and the events leading up to the Bosnian war. Being impartial meant presenting all parties as equally responsible for the descent into violence without analyzing the context or the details of their positions. The journalist Zlatko Dizdarevic noted in his Sarajevo diary for June 1992: "Journalists from the International Press Center want to know 'when will Bosnia-Herzegovina's television start to use a terminology about this war that describes what is actually taking place?' (In the interests of moderation Bosnian TV journalists have avoided naming the aggressor or any of the parties involved in the conflict.)" Thus in contrast to the Serbian media, which had for the previous three years been warning Serbs of an Islamic threat and reminding them of their unresolved historic grievances, the Bosnian state media had left Muslims psychologically unarmed.[14] This explains Narcisa's family's readiness to trust the JNA guarantees about security in Visegrad, in spite of refugees' experience to the contrary, and the disbelief that anything could happen in Gorazde. It also explains the perception, revealed in many of the children's narratives, of an anonymous "war" that erupted out of nowhere. This perception altered with time and hindsight, as my interviews with the children made clear.

When I discussed responsibility and explanations for the war with the Gorazde children, I could distinguish two groups, as I had in Foca. Those in one group were curious and wanted to understand more about the conflict, and those in the other group were less interested in these questions and distanced themselves. Here, in contrast to what I found in Foca, the distinction between engagement and distancing seemed to be related to the amount of violence the children had suffered during the war. The children who had not been present during the worst of the siege, because they had been refugees abroad or living in a safer area, had more distance. The children who had experienced the most violence were the most engaged in trying to make sense of what had happened to them. Moreover, also in contrast to Foca, the children in the distanced group were much more evenhanded about assigning responsibility for the war, while those engaged in looking for meaning ascribed greater responsibility to the Serbs.

Suada, for example, had left for Germany with her family a few days after her Serb neighbors disappeared, and had returned a year after the war was over. In Germany she had watched television news and worried about her grandparents and friends. Now back in Gorazde, she had little interest in discussing the war at all. She was friendly and happy to talk to me, especially about her current life. I tried all sorts of approaches:

When you try to make sense of what has happened, what explanations do you come up with?

I don't know really.

So how will you explain it to your children when you're grown up?

I don't know.

Nor was she very interested in other people's explanations: *Nobody*

really says anything about that, but the Muslims say the Serbs are guilty and Serbs say the Muslims are guilty.
And do you have an opinion on that?
No.
Do your parents?
I don't talk to my parents about it.
Because? You're not interested?
I'm not interested in that.

In contrast, the children with the worst experiences were the most interested in making sense of them. Amela, who had managed to escape from her house thanks to the decency of her Serb neighbors, had spent most of the war being shelled, and had lost close friends and relatives, thought it would be best if people forgot the war, but she herself wanted to understand why it had happened. Her explanation was that *Serbs wanted to live by themselves [. . .] because they don't like living together. I don't know why. But I also blame both sides because our people killed their people also, as well as them killing us.* However she thought the Serbs had begun it: *Well at least they started the shooting, I don't know about politics.*

Sanela, who had had to flee her home and whose father had been killed, had thought a great deal about why the war had happened. *It's interesting because if you look at the purpose of the war, I mean you wouldn't like to have it again.* She thought that *Serbs wanted us to be under their religion, and they wanted us all to be only one nation, they didn't want to have Muslims and Croats and other nationalities who live in Bosnia [. . .] Those who would accept their religion, they would keep them, and those who wouldn't accept being Serbs, they would kill them.*

Why would they want to do that? I asked. But as with most Gorazde children, the logic underlying this plan escaped her.

I don't know, she replied.

As for Muslims, according to Sanela, *Muslims wanted peace and freedom [. . .] They wanted to be free and not to have war; they wanted the situation to be as it was before the war.*

Did they want Serbs to become Muslims?

No.

Sanela had worked things out for herself. Gorazde children did not discuss the war very much with their parents. *Nobody wants to talk about that subject,* Amela told me. Those who wanted to know more listened in on adult conversations and the news, but avoided asking direct questions, for the same sorts of reasons as had children in Foca. They did not want to bother their parents or remind them of unpleasant times. Nedjad said *Maybe they wouldn't know how to answer me exactly, because I think the war came like a surprise for them too.*

Parents agreed that they did not know what to say. Samir, his parents told me, sometimes asked about his Serb friends, but they didn't know how to answer. *I mean I really don't know where his old friends are and what happened to them,* his mother said. Like quite a few other families in both cities, they underrated their son's curiosity: *I never explain to him, and I believe he doesn't know,* said his father, who thought it *better not to talk about that, so that he doesn't hate all the Serbs or all the Croats. Because I admit that there were some good Serbs and Croats in the war. I mean I don't want to create any hatred toward these people.*

Many parents felt that their children already knew as much as they needed to know. *They were old enough to see everything that happened, and they know who was attacking, so we don't need to explain anything to them,* Armin's father told me. There were more important things to do than discuss the past. Now it was time to move on.

6

What Country Is This?

We urged . . . that the country be called, simply, "Bosnia and Herzegovina"
. . . "Giving up the word Republic is giving up nothing" . . . Owen told
Izetbegovic. The second point was more difficult. "That name [Republika
Srpska] is like the Nazi name" Izetbegovic said. We replied that the name
meant nothing, and that the governing—the overriding—sentence was
the preceding one that recognized Bosnia-Herzegovina as a country "with
its present borders"—that is a single country of which R.S. was a part . . .
But I regret that we did not a make stronger effort to drop the name
Republika Srpska. We underestimated the value to Pale of retaining their
blood-soaked name.

—Richard Holbrooke, *To End a War,* 1998

When people say "What country are you from?" what do you say?
Susana: *Republika Srpska.*
Is that part of any other country?
Susana: *I think it's independent.*
So what is Bosnia-Herzegovina? Does it exist?
Susana: *I think not.*

—Fifteen-year-old Serb girl, Foca, 1998

What's the name of this country?
Narcisa: *Bosnia-Herzegovina.*
And what does it consist of?
Narcisa: *It's broken, [only] some towns.*
Have you heard of something called Republika Srpska?
Narcisa: *I think that is Serbia.*

—Fourteen-year-old Muslim girl, Gorazde, 1998

Stojan and I sat in his room in Foca. It was a comfortable teenage boy's room, computer in the corner, posters of basketball stars on the wall. He told me that he wanted to go to America to play basketball professionally because they had the best leagues. Then he remarked that if he was in a competition he would say he was from Yugoslavia, because nobody had heard of Republika Srpska. *Why not Bosnia-Herzegovina?* I asked. Because he didn't think Republika Srpska was part of Bosnia-Herzegovina. He knew it was not really part of Yugoslavia. Apparently Republika Srpska was in a strange no-man's-land called "the former Bosnia-Herzegovina." *The Federation calls the part that it got Bosnia-Herzegovina,* he explained. He knew that people in the Federation included Republika Srpska in the country of Bosnia-Herzegovina, but he did not agree with that. *Serbs don't include themselves in Bosnia-Herzegovina.* Seeing my puzzlement, he said he would prefer to be called Yugoslav because only Serbs lived in Yugoslavia and *in Bosnia-Herzegovina they are mixed.* Coming from Yugoslavia would give him a clear ethnic identity. Living conditions were better there as well, he added as an afterthought.[1]

As I talked to Stojan I realized that the quickest way to get a grasp of these young people's sense of identity was to ask them where they thought they lived and how they felt about sharing their part of the country with others of a different ethnicity. Their answers were revealing, but understanding those answers requires a brief diversion to explain the Dayton Peace Agreement.

The Dayton Peace Agreement that ended the war was formally signed in December 1995 by the presidents of Yugoslavia, Croatia, and Bosnia-Herzegovina (a lineup that clearly demonstrated the importance of outside players in Bosnia's war). The Agreement appeared to be the win-win solution of which conflict resolvers dream: taking something from everyone, and providing something for everyone. The Muslims got the multi-ethnic, independent country for which they had fought. This would be a sovereign, internationally recognized, unitary state, in which a central tripartite government would have control of foreign policy, a central bank, a single currency, and a constitutional court. They had to give up part of the country's name. It would no longer be the Republic of Bosnia-Herzegovina, just Bosnia-Herzegovina. The Serbs gained political control of a large proportion of the territory from which they had expelled the non-Serb population. This was achieved by dividing the country into two Entities, each with its own parliament and its own security forces. The Bosnians and Croats would share 51 percent of the territory as one Entity called the Federation. The Serbs would get the other 49 percent of the territory as an Entity whose name included the crucial republican prefix that Bosnia-Herzegovina itself had lost: Republika Srpska.

The Western sponsors of the Agreement insisted that this was not de facto partition, and thus a reward to the Bosnian Serbs for their brutal campaign of ethnic cleansing and terror, because Dayton also ensured the right of all residents to return to their homes, freedom of movement, and the possibility of voting in democratic elections in one's own hometown even when not physically present. These provisions would restore the status quo ante, an integrated Bosnia with an integrated population. How this was to be achieved given the continuing presence of the political and security forces who had conducted the campaigns of terror in the first place remained unclear. The newly created International Police Task Force (IPTF) was only there to monitor and train local police and had no mandate to act in the face of any abuses of human rights. The international military presence, the Implementation Force (IFOR), later to become the Stabilization Force (SFOR), was there to enforce the military aspects of the Agreement, with no obligation to enforce civilian aspects such as freedom of movement or right of return. They had the authority to arrest war criminals, but again, they were not obligated to do so.

Some aspects of the Agreement were achieved rapidly. International troops poured into Bosnia, local forces pulled back from the front lines, and after almost four bitter years, the fighting stopped. The agreed reallocation of territory between Entities proceeded on the agreed dates. Yet even in those early months the contradictions and weaknesses in the Agreement were apparent.

In March 1996 I went to Banja Luka, the new capital of the new Serb Entity, to discuss my proposed research with Dr. Kuzmanovic, the deputy minister of health. He believed the Serbs had won the war. He was delighted that the world had finally recognized that *Serbs want to live alone* and had given them Republika Srpska. He explained to me at length that the world had tried to use the Serbs to destroy Bosnian Muslims in order to stop the spread of Islam, but that all the Bosnian Serbs wanted was to live alone in their own land. He was very pleased with their success in achieving this, and assured me they would be good neighbors. The West would also appreciate that they would be *a dam against Islam.* We had blundered in making an *Istanbul of Sarajevo. It is going to be a bomb from which every evil will spread to Western countries.*

It felt as if little had changed. Dr. Kuzmanovic was sure the Federation would fall apart: *Islamic extremists cannot live with Croatian fascists, but everyone enjoys living with Serbs.* The remark contrasted oddly with the views he had just expressed about Muslims, and with local events. Only a few days previously a thousand Serbs had demonstrated violently at a nearby village to stop three Muslim families from returning to their homes, a harbinger of things to come. Moreover, he saw little chance that the twenty thousand Muslims forced out of Foca could return home, as Foca was full of Serbs who had just left Sarajevo.

In the first months of 1996 there was a massive exodus of the Serb population from the suburbs of Sarajevo when these areas were handed to the Federation under the terms of the Agreement. Yet again the Bosnian Serb leaders had convinced Serbs that it would not be safe to live with Muslims, and that they would be traitors if they did so. They had been helped in this endeavor by the actions of some Muslims, harassing and intimidating Serbs who had thought to stay in Ilidza, the first suburb to change hands.

That March I witnessed the effect of those actions and the propaganda during the handover of Grbavica, another Serb-controlled
part of Sarajevo, to the Federation. This area above and around the
Jewish cemetery had been controlled by Bosnian Serb forces from
the beginning of the war. The steepness of this hill in the center of the
city had given the Serb gunners, camped out in the ruined fortress
that was the Partisan memorial from the Second World War, a full
view of much of the riverside and the center of town. They had tuned
these areas into a shooting gallery. The Brotherhood and Unity
Bridge had been a front line marked by barbed wire, tank traps, and
sheets of metal and old buses that gave some cover from snipers.

By March 1996 this detritus of a divided city had been pushed
aside and you could walk across the bridge. Most of the buildings not
damaged by shelling had had doors, windows, and roof sections carefully removed. I watched as residents loaded them into cars and vans
already stuffed with furniture and miscellaneous household goods: a
bathtub sticking out of a car's trunk, a child's blue mattress strapped
with dining chairs to the top of a small Yugo. Some people had only
what they could carry. I met an elderly woman struggling up the hill
weeping, weighed down by four large carrier bags, one on each
shoulder and one in each hand. They contained what looked like
clothing, shoes, and light fixtures. The woman was a primary school
teacher who had taught Muslims, Serbs, and Croats all her life and
had never known the differences. She had escaped to Belgrade and
hated it, had come back home, and now was walking four kilometers
to Lubavica, the first village in Republika Srpska. She could not stay
in Grbavica, she said, she was terrified. She had heard it was not safe.
On another street tired-looking elderly people, waiting for a bus to
take them they knew not where, told me it was impossible to live with
Muslims: *I would rather live under a tree than in Sarajevo with Siladzic
[Bosnia's wartime prime minister] and Izetbegovic,* an old man told
me. *If it was possible to live with Muslims we would not have had
this war.*

At the police station the Serbian police sang their national anthem, then ceremoniously lowered the Serbian flag and rolled it up. Dignitaries lined up to kiss it and the deputy minister of the interior made a speech about how special units had raised the flag in 1992, but unfortunately according to Dayton a region which had been Serb for centuries now had to be given to the other side. (In fact the ethnic composition of the prewar population of Grbavica had been mixed.) The ceremony was accompanied by explosions. Fifty meters away a house burst into flames, and smoke rose in plumes from the remains of others similarly gutted. What the Serb community could not keep, they were reluctant to leave for others. Italian troops arrested three Serb teenage boys with grenades in their pockets, pushing them, hands splayed, against the wall and searching them. It looked tough, but IFOR could only detain them for seventy-two hours, then they would be handed over to their own police. They knew they would be released in a couple of days.

Not all the Serbs left. Eleven thousand stayed in Grbavica. The relatives of friends of mine had lived through the war in a mixed apartment block where all had acted collectively to protect their Muslim neighbors. They were determined to stay. In the days leading up to the handover the Serbian police visited them regularly to ensure that they were leaving. The family had devised a strategy to avoid harassment. They pointed out two packed suitcases placed near the door as a symbol of imminent departure. Dr. Kuzmanovic felt sorry for such people. They and any other Serbs who remained in Federation territory, he said, were likely to be *hunted down and killed like animals* by *Islamic fundamentalists,* and no one would be able to help them.

In failing to prevent this exodus, the international community and the Bosnian government had contributed to the ethnic separation and consolidation of both Entities. The exodus also highlighted the inherent weaknesses of a peace agreement that did nothing to challenge the mind-set of the domestic elites who had gone to war for ethnic separation in the first place.

Over the following years these weaknesses became ever more

apparent. Instead of something for everyone, Dayton had become nothing for most people. Far from reversing ethnic cleansing and creating an integral, functioning democratic state, Dayton had given legitimacy to leaders who still trumpeted the benefits of an ethnic separatist project built on paranoia, murder, and forced expulsion. The lines of ethnic partition were frozen solid. Indicted war criminals retained their prestige and influence, and corruption was rampant. Biljana Plavsic described Republika Srpska, of which she was then president, as "a State in which the budget does not actually exist, where Police are involved in smuggling and stealing from their own state, and where a majority of the population live in abject poverty."[2]

These contradictions were particularly apparent in the Drina valley. Gorazde was the only enclave in eastern Bosnia to hold out against the Bosnian Serb assault. Dayton had designated the municipality as Federation territory except for one suburb of the town, which had previously had a Muslim majority but went to Republika Srpska. The Serbs called this suburb Serb Gorazde; the Muslims called it by its old name, Kopaci. Gorazde was supposed to be connected to the bulk of the Federation by a new highway, constructed on a corridor of Federation land over the mountains between Sarajevo and Ustikolina. Three years on, the promised highway was still lines on a map, and a potholed dirt track still switchbacked over the mountains, four hours of choking dust in summer, impassable in winter. Those who took the main road, which went through Republika Srpska, risked assault and kidnap.

When I first arrived in Gorazde, one year after Dayton, it still wore the war like an old winter coat. The footbridge to protect pedestrians from snipers still ran under the central bridge. Homemade waterwheel generators still floated in the Drina, and almost every house was pitted and cratered by shrapnel and blast damage. Many were shattered and roofless. The roads were treacherous with potholes. Every untended garden, every field in the surrounding countryside, carried the risk of mines and unexploded bombs. There was no power, no running water, and no phone connection. Women still did their laundry in the Drina.

Over the following two years I watched the town come to life. Electricity and clean water were reconnected, buildings roofed and repainted. The schools were reequipped and a new sports hall built. There was a cultural center running local TV and radio shows. On summer evenings the streets and cafés were full. The energy in the town was in marked contrast to the gloom and quietness of Foca. Even so, Gorazde still felt as if it was economically and politically under siege. Local businesses struggled to pay the exorbitant costs of transporting goods through risky territory. Local professionals felt isolated. In spite of projects to restart local factories, there were few real jobs and young people just wanted to get out. They recognized that Gorazde was an island. In a divided Bosnia of mono-ethnic communities, the town made no sense. *An appendix,* one friend quipped. It was an appropriate metaphor: easy to inflame and not difficult to cut out.

The international community pushed through the first municipal elections in 1997. More interested in finding an exit strategy from the region than in building a democratic state, they ignored the fact that the conditions for holding elections were neither free nor fair. Large numbers of displaced citizens, the majority of them Muslim, still lived in squalor and uncertainty far from their original homes, and freedom of movement was still a myth. These elections did nothing to contribute to democratic change. Not surprisingly, given the continuing insecurity, most people voted for the National parties that had fought the war on their behalf. In Kopaci, the local Serb authorities, recognizing that a vote reflecting the composition of the prewar population would throw them out, discouraged and intimidated displaced Muslims who wished to vote, and registered large numbers of nonresident Serbs to ensure their own victory and consolidate their hold on the area. (About 3,500 people registered to vote although the maximum prewar population was estimated to be 2,000.)[3] I sat in a shrub-fringed lay-by, one warm September afternoon in 1997, counting the many buses and cars with Serbian number plates, as they brought in the suddenly enlarged population of this rural suburb to cast its votes.

In Foca the votes of displaced Muslims had succeeded in returning some of their own politicians. They had to be given protection to travel there, and council meetings were usually deadlocked by disagreement between the ethnically based parties. Three years after Dayton not a single non-Serb had been able to return to live in the town. Visits by former Muslim residents to relatives' graves had to be organized and protected by international police and still met with hostility from local Serbs. The community oriented itself politically and culturally eastward, toward Yugoslavia. Many local people preferred to travel the single-track dirt road to Montenegro, then drive for four hours to Podgorica, to go shopping, rather than travel for an hour on a reasonable highway to Sarajevo. Local businesses used Yugoslav dinars. Television in Republika Srpska still referred to Bosnia-Herzegovina as "the former Bosnia-Herzegovina" and put all news from the Federation in the "foreign" news (this ended when SFOR took over one of the television transmitters in November 1997). The local Serb authorities still appeared to be closely associated with those who had organized the terror and ethnic cleansing of the town.

Because of this noncompliance with Dayton, the international organizations continued to refuse to release aid to the town. This left local Serbs confused and impoverished. I spent part of Easter in 1998 visiting a teacher and friend living in the hotel cum collective center in the middle of town. She had fled from the fighting at the beginning of the war and now lived in a small room containing one cheap dresser and a bed, with all her possessions piled in boxes around her.

She had no hot water and cooked on one electric ring. She had invited me to learn how to decorate Orthodox Easter eggs, so the ring now warmed a saucepan of melting wax. We sat on the bed and the one chair while she deftly painted the red wax onto the eggs and talked.

She hated Foca. *They are horrible to refugees in this town. There is no collective spirit. No one cares. People know my situation but no one asks me to eat, or even for coffee. They know I don't have hot water. Do they ever offer me a bath?* The tirade went on and on. Given her unhappiness and obvious discomfort, I asked if she would consider returning to her hometown in the Federation. Under Dayton she had a right to reclaim her house there, and even to receive some assistance to get it rebuilt if it was damaged. She had told me how much she loved it before the war. *Absolutely not!* She looked at me in bewilderment. *Why did the West give us our republic if they want to make everything the way it was before?* In a few words she had identified the contradiction at the heart of Dayton.

The teenagers I interviewed in Foca may not have known the political and physical geography of the new country, but they grasped the psychological reality of Dayton completely. Although the Inter-Entity Boundary Line (IEBL) was only fifteen minutes up the valley from the center of town, more than half of the children thought Republika Srpska was not part of Bosnia-Herzegovina. They avoided the word Bosnia and were uncomfortable if pushed to use it. When I asked Ivana where Republika Srpska was, she replied *On this territory where this country is, where war was.*

Okay, I said, *I'm not being clear in my questions. Is Republika Srpska inside any other country?*

I don't know, she responded, then definitively: *No.*

Is it inside Yugoslavia?

She hesitated. *Maybe.*

Well, where is Bosnia-Herzegovina? I asked, finally giving up the hope that she might mention it herself.

She paused, then laughed. *I guess on Turks' territory.*
And is Republika Srpska inside Bosnia-Herzegovina?
No.

Many of the children thought that Bosnia-Herzegovina had ceased to exist. Dusan thought that Republika Srpska was independent. He was uncertain where Gorazde was, but thought it might be in the Federation: *That's the name of the country of the Croats and Muslims.* Svetlana was sure that Republika Srpska was inside Yugoslavia, and that there was no more Bosnia.

Half of the Muslim teenagers in Gorazde also believed that the Federation and Republika Srpska were not in the same country, and had a similar vagueness as to where Foca was located. Their descriptions of the country were both more confused and more complicated than those I heard in Foca. They believed Bosnia-Herzegovina existed, but many did not think Republika Srpska was part of it. Some thought that Serbs still had parts of Bosnia, such as Serb Sarajevo and Serb Gorazde, and consequently these were no longer in Bosnia. *There were a lot of towns that were in Bosnia before and now they are not in Bosnia, because they were taken by them [. . .] they're in their territory [. . .] That territory is in Yugoslavia now, and before they were in Bosnia,* one boy explained, firmly and nonsensically placing a suburb of his own town in a completely different country. Narcisa thought Republika Srpska was in Serbia. Foca was in Bosnia, she said, but it was *occupied by Serbs from Serbia, not Bosnian Serbs.* Samir thought Republika Srpska was *down in Belgrade* and not part of Bosnia-Herzegovina at all.

The children's ideas about where they lived connected to their ideas about with whom it was possible to live. Sara thought her town, Foca, was now in Serbia and Yugoslavia. Sara's family had just finished building their house in the town before the war. Her best friend had been the daughter of her Muslim next-door neighbors, who was in her class at school. When the friend fled three days before the war,

Sara had already left for a village. Her father had been badly injured driving over a mine but had recovered. She missed her friend and wanted to see her again, but still thought it was better to live separately. She had heard adults talking about Muslims hating Serbs and Serbs hating Muslims: *If they hate each other they can't live in the same town.* She worried that if Muslims returned there would be another war *because we were together before and war happened then.*

Almost all the Serb children were opposed to non-Serbs returning to Foca, and those who had been displaced from cities within the Federation had no wish to return home. It was not because they felt personally antagonistic toward Muslims; many liked the idea of seeing their old friends and did not hold them responsible. But living together would be dangerous. Their logic was simple: they had lived together before, and there had been a war, so if they lived together again, there would be another. *They're starting to come again today,* Susana told me in her usual slightly offhand manner, shortly after former Muslim citizens of Foca made an arranged visit to the graveyard. *I think everything will be the same as it was before.* She didn't mind, she didn't hate them; but she thought there would *probably be a war, because we are together again.*

Another concern was that people living in the Entity belonging to another ethnicity would be treated as second-class citizens. Helena had come to Foca from Sarajevo at the beginning of the war. She had loved Sarajevo. They had an apartment in a predominantly Muslim area; her mother worked in a public company, and had deliberately not had Helena baptized in case she chose to marry someone of another religion. When the war began, Helena's father did not want to join the Muslim militia in their street. He had hoped to avoid the fighting by moving to a village, but he had been called up by the VRS, and had been killed on the front line in the first month of fighting. In spite of this terrible experience, Helena was not angry with Muslims. *Only one man killed him. Not all of them. They are not all guilty.* She thought she would like things to be as before, because they had been so good, but she also worried that living together would lead to war, because there was likely to be discrimination and jealousy. *For example, if in some factory the director is a Serb, maybe the Muslims will only get bad positions.* Jovan had seen on local television that Serbs who had tried to return to the Federation had not been able to work on their own land and had been treated badly.

Many felt that even if ordinary people could get along the extremists would cause trouble. Divac had shared a shelter with Muslim neighbors in his street in Sarajevo at the beginning of the war, and when Serb forces had taken control his father had acted to protect those neighbors. Divac said he would go back to Sarajevo the next day if only others felt like him. But bad people on both sides would destroy the situation, the same if Muslims returned to Foca, and there would be war again. Nothing could be done about such people. Everyone should get new houses and live separately. Helena's mother had very similar attitudes to her daughter. She was still grieving for her husband and spent much of our time together in tears, but kept insisting *I don't hate anybody.* All the same she wanted to live separately from Muslims because she was afraid *they will have some laws which will make us lower-class people.* She had friends who had returned to Sarajevo and could not get jobs. *At this moment I don't think it is possible to live together. We can't find a common language.* The problem was not with people like her but with extremists.

Can't you do something about extremists?

It's impossible, only the law could do something, and who believes in the law [. . .] We ordinary civilians can't do anything. Even a lot of us together can't do anything [. . .] I don't believe democracy can live here. We are the kind of people who need to be told what to do. She had been watching the RS assembly on television and found it ridiculous. *I think the intelligent people left and only the uneducated ones are still here. How can people who only went to high school be in parlia-*

ment? She had had a passport in 1992 and now wished she had had the courage to emigrate so her children could have seen *somewhere civilized.*

Not everyone felt like Helena's family. One thirteen-year-old boy in Foca wrote: *The war caused me great pain because my family was killed. That's why I hate Islamic criminals. Because of that I would never live with those cretins, jerks, Ustashe, and merciless people. The news about what those heartless people did in Josanice upset me the most.*

Many felt that no matter how good relations had been before, the war had generated so much hatred that living together now would be impossible. Dusan could not imagine how he could live next door to the Muslim neighbor they had seen with a gun. *His son died, too,* Dusan's father said, *so how do you think we can live together? We will see who can throw the other in the Drina first. I'm younger, so probably I will manage. I won't let him do it.*

Even children who had not suffered personal losses told me it was impossible to go back. Radmila had lived in a mixed village where her mother worked the land and her father had a factory job. It was not an easy life, but relations with her Muslim neighbors had been good. She told me that after the Serbs had *kicked out* the Muslims from Foca, her family had feared reprisals and had moved in with Serb neighbors on the other side of the river. Her Muslim neighbors had done nothing to threaten or harm them; they were afraid and had fled as well. After fleeing the fighting a number of times and being bombed by NATO in Ustikolina, Radmila had ended up on a farm formerly owned by Muslims. Her family had managed to keep their own animals and take them along. Their relatives were in neighboring houses so it felt like home. Radmila liked it much better because it was easier to get into town and see friends. She did not want to see her prewar Muslim friends, because the war had changed everything.

I think they hate us.

Do you hate them?

I do.

Why?

Because they are a different nationality.

She said she did not hate other nationalities on principle. Normally she thought all kinds of people could live together. But Muslims were different from Serbs in ways that she could not define. She was worried that they might attack. This was the same discussion I had had with Milica. Both girls now had a hatred of Muslims based on a new perception of difference and a belief in the others' hostility. Their hatred had arisen because they had had a war. Radmila was clear that it was the war itself that had made her feel like this.

The most significant argument against living together had nothing to do with the children's feelings of safety. The war had been fought so that Serbs could live alone. If Muslims came back to live in Foca and other parts of Republika Srpska, it would make the effort meaningless. A fifteen-year-old boy in Foca wrote: *Some people dear to us gave their lives for our liberation [. . .] When everything was liberated my town got a new name: Srbinje, that name presents the face of our town and the determination of its people to fight for Serbs and unity [. . .] Now they are trying to take from us that for which we gave our young lives, our sacred country, Republika Srpska, but they will not succeed however hard they try. While there is one Serb in this area they will stay forever.*

Like my friend in the hotel, this boy had touched the heart of the contradiction within the Peace Agreement. When the international community stated that it wanted to return refugees to their homes, it was in effect saying that the creation of Republika Srpska through territorial aggression and ethnic cleansing was an unjust and criminal project that should be undone. Yet by creating an Entity called Republika Srpska, albeit reduced, and at present within the confines of Bosnia-Herzegovina, it appeared to be telling the Serb community that this had been a goal worth fighting for.

Some children wrestled with the complexity of this issue. Vesna had been driven barefoot from her village near Sarajevo by Croat and Muslim forces. Her family had moved to a relative's home in the Sarajevo suburb of Ilidza. They had not wished to leave after the Agreement handed it back to the Federation. However, when Muslims took over the police and local authority, they had done nothing to make them feel welcome. Every day more neighbors departed, more Muslims moved back, and they heard stories of other Serbs being attacked, so they felt *there was no place for Serbs. I don't know who set the terms. We just had to move out. Everybody was saying it is much easier with your own people.*

Vesna had cried when they left and did not particularly like their new home in a village near Foca. She had a loving, close-knit family and was one of the brightest children in her class at high school. She planned to be an engineer. I asked her how she thought things could be healed after the war.

We have to help each other, she immediately replied. *People have to help each other. Nobody can live alone.*

Do you mean people should go back to their homes?

I don't know, it would mean that the war was for nothing. Why did we fight if they come back?

She was clearly uncomfortable with her own conclusions. She was not sure that separation achieved by war was a good thing: *I don't believe things can be separated like that.* But letting Muslims return to Foca would mean the war *was for nothing, because after the war some people left their homes. Probably they were forced, and now if they came back . . . Why were those people fighting if they are . . . Why did they separate it at the beginning if they are coming back? Why did so many people die just to be together again? Because it can happen again. I never thought about things like this.*

When telling me about leaving her original village, Vesna wept. It was the first time she had talked about it in detail for six years. She was surprised at her own reaction and insisted on continuing. Later in our conversation, again on the edge of tears, she assured me that she did not want to return to her old home, nor did anyone she knew, because nothing would be the same. I wondered how much her own certainty on this point, combined with her obvious distress, had to do with feeling a need to give meaning to the sacrifices her own people had made, even as she sensed the moral ambiguity of the separation project as a whole.

Dusan felt his brother had fought and died *for nothing* because the countries were still not properly separated. The international community was wrong to force Croats, Muslims, and Serbs into one country. *It is humiliating for so many people who died during the war.* They had fought for separate nations. *I think Muslims should live in a Muslim country, Croats should live in a Croat one, and Serbs should live in Republika Srpska or a Serb country. Later if people want to, they can mix. I think it's awful that Serb people who moved into Muslim houses should have to leave because of Muslims who want to come back.* Anyway he did not think many Muslims genuinely wanted to return; they were being pushed by their politicians.

Many children expressed the feeling that the return of Muslim neighbors would make a mockery of the sacrifices of the war, and would mean that Serbs had fought for nothing. Perhaps another, unvoiced reason was that such a return would also require meeting former friends and hearing firsthand the means by which separation had been achieved. A painful essay written by a fifteen-year-old boy hints at this:

> *I imagine how things would look if this war had not occurred. I imagine people who are not here anymore. I tell myself that it would not be better, I am deceiving myself, but it doesn't matter because it helps me look at the present in a different way. The present is here and it cannot be changed, and that is why we have to accept it. The Muslims want to live with us again, they ask "Who did this to all of us?" We have to accept the present time, but not with them. I don't want it. It is true that we talk the same lan-*

guage, listen to the same music, write the same way, but they are completely different and I do not want to erase that difference. There is no more peace and no BIH. We can look at each other only through gun sights and be together only in the Olympic Games. I was educated to love and not to differentiate people on the basis of religion. But I cannot love someone who does not love me. Many of my friends were Muslims before the war, we never had a fight, and I remember them, but the question is what our meeting would look like now. I don't have the courage to think about that meeting and also I don't want to, because who knows what it might bring.

Not all the children in Foca were totally opposed to return. Svetlana said that she would *love* to have her Muslim friends and neighbors come back and saw no danger from that. *They are people; they are human beings just like us.* Ivana thought the best way to make peace was for everyone to go home. *Everybody should live their own life and not interfere with other people.* Some children were ambivalent. Helena did not care which Entity she lived in or what it was called. She wanted to go back to Sarajevo and live with her Muslim friends again. She also felt Muslims had the right to come back to Foca. Her conversation slid from saying that living together would be dangerous, to wanting to do so *but without war,* to deciding it *would be the best to stay like this, Serbs on one side and Muslims on the other.* I could sense the difficulty the issue caused her from her sighs while answering.

These three girls had had very close contacts and friendships with non-Serbs in their own childhoods. As with other aspects of their understanding of the conflict, there appeared to be a pattern. For the most part, it was the children like Svetlana and Helena, who were trying to understand what had happened in Foca, who were more enthusiastic about living with Muslims again. Children like Milica, Radmila, and Susana, who distanced themselves from what had happened in the town, were also more forthright in their opposition to

Muslims' return. Disengagement and distancing allowed for certainties; curiosity could lead to openness, but sometimes to confusion and distress.

The families in Foca assured me that Muslims in Gorazde were equally opposed to living together. If I was told differently it would be because they were lying or manipulated by their politicians. A few of the Gorazde children's written stories did make such feelings clear, such as this one by a fifteen-year-old girl:

> I've lost my father, my life changed a lot with his death. I was very happy when he was alive [. . .] four years have passed but every day it's just worse and worse [. . .] I wonder very often why he had to die. Why? But I know I will never get an answer to this question. I just know one thing, he is not here anymore. I will never be able to live with the people who gave me all this pain. I cannot stand the fact that they will return to Gorazde and live as before the war. I am not scared of them but I just hate them from the bottom of my soul.

Gorazde had changed by the summer of 1998. Many of those who had been refugees abroad had come back. The international community had finally clamped down on illegal checkpoints and imposed a unified number plate policy. This meant that it was no longer possible to identify the Entity from which a car originated, so it was safer and easier to travel through Republika Srpska to Sarajevo and the rest of the Federation. Visiting sports teams came for matches. More small shops and cafés had opened. Young people commuted home at weekends from Sarajevo University. Most significantly, in November 1997 the local authorities had decided to make Gorazde an Open City, committing the municipality to facilitating the return of non-Muslim refugees and protecting them from any abuses. This was pragmatic. Local officials knew they would be rewarded with more international aid. They also knew that someone had to break up the peculiar game of musical chairs in which the different ethnic communities appeared to be engaged. If Serb returnees were offered their homes back in Gorazde, the mayor of Serb Gorazde could no longer argue that the Serbs in his town needed the houses that belonged to their Muslim neighbors. There had been a steady trickle of visitors and former inhabitants ever since, as well as cars driving through from Visegrad to Foca. It was not surprising, therefore, that the majority of children and their families to whom I spoke in Gorazde were in favor of living together again, although some were ambivalent.

The ambivalence was most evident in the children who had been in Gorazde through most of the siege and who had had some of the worst experiences. Their uncertainty focused on two issues. One was the same question raised by Foca children: If one had suffered directly, how could one live with the people who had inflicted the suffering? Iris thought living separately was better. *Most of my friends have lost fathers, sisters, they can't imagine living with someone whose parents were killing their families.* Later she said that if things went back to the way they were before, without misunderstanding, *I don't know, in a way they should return, in a way they shouldn't, I don't know. And probably all the people who did the killing during the war wouldn't return.* But as it might not be possible to distinguish the innocent from the guilty, how could one live with any of them? Armin thought families who had lost someone might want revenge and then take it out on the wrong people.

A second issue was a feeling of personal insecurity. This was not the Foca children's fear that another war might arise automatically if the two communities mixed. In Gorazde all these children repeated, almost as a mantra, *Everyone has a right to their home.* They knew this meant allowing Serbs back into Gorazde. In contrast to Foca, they almost all felt that living separately would result in another war, while living together would foster long-term security. However, direct encounters with particular Serbs had created anxiety for some.

Amela demonstrated all these contradictory feelings. She told me about an incident that had scared her. A Mercedes with Serbian plates had parked in front of her house, a short distance out of town, and a somewhat aggressive man had asked the way to Gorazde. She had helped him and he had driven off leaving her feeling *unsafe*. She had been afraid the man would hit her. She could not say why, simply that he was an impolite stranger and she wondered why he had picked her. Even so, she said, she would help the next Serb who asked, and she did think they should come back, as long as things went back to the way they had been before the war, when the only distinction was religious belief. She was not afraid of life together. *It will be easier if we are all together, sharing the life we had before [. . .] If we go on living separately I think it will be a disaster . . . Because there are a lot of Bosnian areas in their hands, so if they came back, Bosnians could go back to their towns.* She thought Gorazde would look better if Serbs repaired their houses. She had also noticed that many of the factory managers were Serbs, and she was worried that the Bosnian Muslims lacked the education and skills to restart the economy by themselves.

In a later meeting Amela repeated her wish *to continue the life we had before the war*. She thought the solution to any difficulties was for no one to talk about the war. *Even if we can't forget it, I don't want to mention it.* She still felt that living together was the only way to avoid another war. But she had been watching television and listening to adults talk and had heard that Serbs still wanted a town in northern Bosnia (Brcko), and that they still wanted Muslims to leave Gorazde and wanted to take it for themselves.[4] This horrified her. She thought the Serbs were making impossible demands.

I told her that Serb children in Foca believed living together was not safe. *Then maybe it will be better . . . It would be better if they don't want that, then it would be better . . .* She looked very sad and sighed. *They don't want to live together with us. And we want that. Just to avoid the war. If our people try to do something by force, to live together again, then it is war again. Well maybe that is impossible. But maybe the way is to forget everything that happened. Let's all forget everything that happened.* Then she came full circle again: *But I think it can't work because everybody talks about the war. So I think we can't live together.*

All the children in Gorazde distinguished between war criminals and others. No one wanted the criminals to come back. There were also stories of Serbs who had actively assisted them, while other Serbs were seen as ordinary soldiers because they had no choice. Samir said *My father has . . . had, a good friend, Serb. He didn't fight in the war. He had a house at the seaside and he went there. If some Serbs didn't have enough money to pay to go, they had to go and fight, even if they didn't want to, they forced them to. They were saying "We'll kill all your family if you don't go."* The solution arrived at by most ambivalent children was usually that Serbs should come back and live in their own homes, but that they personally would have nothing to do with them. *Gorazde is an open town,* Nina said. *And by law everyone can live in it. And I don't care, I don't really mind. I have my own friends to socialize with, so it doesn't matter if they come back.* She wanted a normal country like Germany or America where people lived together.

The children who unequivocally favored the return of their Serb neighbors were those who had been some distance from the worst of the siege. They did not think things would be the same as before; they wrestled with the dilemmas of whether they could or should forgive and forget what had happened, but they felt that normal life and security meant living together. Fikreta put it in bald pragmatic terms: *Everyone should go back to their own homes, because if they don't return the Muslims won't return to Foca and to Visegrad.* She did not think she would have any problems living with Serbs again. On the contrary, she found it hard to imagine life without them. *I learned that in school, and my parents taught me: because we have to be with others and we can't live alone because, for example, if now our neighbors are Serbs or Croats, we have to be with them, because how can we*

*be alone in the house and not be with anybody else? How can we not
talk to them and not spend time with them?*

Fikreta felt as many did that a mixed life was the best one. As in
Foca I found that children's views were similar to those of their parents. Fikreta's mother told me that if Serbs and Muslims did not return to the towns from which they had fled during the war, *we will
never have peace, it will never be good, nobody is for that.* She believed
that living in a mono-ethnic state carried its own risks. Although
religious herself, she had no desire to live in a *Muslim Republic of
Bosnia. I don't want to go covered; I don't want to live in Iran. I will go
and live in Republika Srpska,* she said, laughing, *but I will not have
a cloth on my face. I don't have to be dressed completely to be Muslim.*
Living together with other groups was a protection against the
extremism of one's own.

Other parents thought a multi-ethnic society was a better guaran-
tee of democracy. Armin's father was helping an aid agency rebuild
Serb-owned houses. *Just Muslims* was not a good way to live: *They
will rob their people and ours will rob our people [. . .] There are a lot of
poor people here and there are also a lot of poor people there.* Of course
there might be *some fear, some period of silence maybe.* But with time
everything would be okay. *Because before, Serbs and Muslims were always helping each other,* Samir's father told me. *If only Muslims ruled
there wouldn't be any democracy because only their families would be
on the top.* He believed that in a mono-ethnic society some families
would be privileged at the expense of others, whereas in a mixed
one Serbs and Muslims would protect each other's rights. If Serbs
and Muslims had real equality there would not be another war.
*The Bosnia I fought for was multi-ethnic, not dependent on Croatia or
Yugoslavia or Serbia.*

Gorazde and Foca felt much more than thirty minutes apart. Foca's
Serbs had fought for ethnic separation. A generation of young Serbs
was now growing up convinced that ethnic cleansing had been a de-

fensive necessity, and that the only way to avoid future war was to live alone, in squalid poverty if necessary. The return of Muslims would mean the Serbs had lost the war and their parents' struggle and sacrifices had been for nothing. Down the road in Gorazde, Muslims had fought for life in a mixed society, so whatever their anxieties about meeting their former neighbors, for them only a unified and mixed Bosnia could signify victory. Young Gorazde Muslims were growing up in a town whose isolated population had no viable existence outside a multi-ethnic state. But the different perspectives were not just the result of a flawed peace agreement. Serb and Muslim children's different aspirations regarding future living arrangements also related to the very different ways in which they thought about themselves.

7

Where Do They Come From?

Although the existing name [Foca] is pretty old and etymologically contains our roots, in its adapted pronunciation it has acquired the form of a Turkish name, and that with an overtone that was bound to irritate us Serbs, since it continuously reminded us of the centuries of slavery under the foreign Islamic oppressors. [The name Srbinje] contains at its root the word which distinguishes our national name and essence. In this war the fighters from Foca and from the [surrounding] region were worthy defenders of Serbianness and Orthodoxy. Therefore they have merited that their regional capital and the entire region carry a name with an emphatically national hallmark.

—Vojislav Maksimovic, former mayor of Foca, 1994

It is a tragic illusion that war, ethnic ideologies and the fixing of boundaries are necessary for the realization of the self, through the production of a pure culture and a return to roots . . . This approach leads only to the use of force and a falsification of history, past and present. Its advocates and propagandists do not realize how dangerous it is to their own pure culture and much loved nation, for it is a process that leads nowhere except to a ghetto mentality, to cultural stagnation and eventually death.

—Ivan Lovrenovic, *Bosnia: A Cultural History,* 2002

There is a saying, "If you respect yours, you respect others," and it says in many books, and my father told me as well: If you respect your own nation and your own religion, then you respect other religions and other nations.

—Muslim mother, Gorazde

I had never been aware I was a nation
until they said they'd kill me.

—Goran Simic, "A Scene, after the War," 2003

History Lessons

Ask the Muslim people, "Where do Muslims come from?" Igor said to me.

I will if you like, but my question to you is "Why does it matter?"

It doesn't matter to me, said Adriana, Igor's wife.

It matters because it's a source of tension, it was a problem in the past as well, Igor replied.

Igor and Adriana had invited me to their tiny apartment because they wanted me to understand Foca better. Neither was happy with the city at that time, the winter of 1997. Adriana, who had loved her university life in Sarajevo, missed the past. Igor was bitterly disappointed in the present and the hopes of the promised future. They thought of emigrating. As usual the television played in the corner much of the time. The evening news appeared to consist mainly of Republika Srpska politicians attacking each other in the run-up to the Entity elections. We could watch either Biljana Plavsic in Banja Luka castigating the corruption of her former friends Karadzic and Krajisnik in the Serb Democratic Party (SDS), or the leader of the Serb Radical Party (SRS), banned in Banja Luka at that time, on Srbinje TV.

Biljana, my translator, despised and distrusted Plavsic for being a turncoat, interested only in power for herself, and for dividing Serbs yet again. Adriana despaired of them all. She saw the SDS as a party that had forced impoverished and uneducated people to fight while the leaders' own children were out of the country. The SRS were the same as the SDS: *Serbs, Serbs, and again Serbs.* All the parties were the same as in communist times; only the names had changed. *They pay more attention to religion and ethnic identity but we can't live on these things.* She wanted *a party that would open us up and take us to the West.*

Igor had just come home from an SRS political meeting. He liked the SRS because its program offered *discipline, work, and order.* He could see I looked a little startled at this phrase and, perhaps recognizing the resonance, immediately added, *not work as in Arbeit Macht Frei, as in Auschwitz. Our program is based on tradition, history, culture, and environment.* I asked why he admired the radical Serb politician Vojislav Seselj. *Because he wants to build our country without criminality and corruption, to bring us back to Serb traditions and the history of the Serb people, which we all shared. He would never let Albanians in Kosovo use a different language. They would all learn Serbian.*

My friends in Foca would like you to tell me where you think Muslims come from, I said to the school psychologist in Gorazde a few days later. *I have no idea. Does it matter?* he replied. *I can answer that question,* said Hasan's father. *I was born in Foca but I came here forty years ago, so originally I am from Foca.* I often encountered this problem in these indirect exchanges. Both communities used me as a kind of carrier pigeon, winging messages and questions to their former neighbors on the other side. However, the conversations frequently became derailed, because the starting points and basic understandings were not the same, particularly when it came to questions of ethnic identity, origins, and history.

Origins and history mattered to the Serbs in Foca, both adults and children. They were clear about their own identity and its roots, and the town echoed with historical references. Some of these were newer than others: The name of the primary school had been changed from Ivan Goran Kovacic, a Second World War antifascist hero, to Sveti Sava. Saint Sava was a member of the Nemanja dynasty that had created the short-lived medieval Serbian empire, which at its zenith in the mid-fourteenth century had stretched from the Danube to the Peloponnese. Sava founded and headed an autonomous Serbian Orthodox church, had his own royal family sanctified, and was canonized himself after his death. We celebrated his saint's day with a special service in church, a holiday from school (although as the teachers were on strike for lack of pay this did not count for much), a visit and blessing from the priest, and a lavish breakfast of roast meats and plenty of rakia in the staff room.

Children learned in third grade about Prince Lazar, whose portrait watched over their classroom. Lazar had lost that same medieval kingdom at the battle of Kosovo. Sara, a seventh grader, told me that Prince Lazar and Milos Obilic, who had reputedly assassinated Sultan Murat during the battle and lost his own life doing so, were the kind of Serbs *who fight for everybody*. They should be distinguished from those *who only want power for themselves*, like the Serbian traitor Vuk Brankovic, whose betrayal of Prince Lazar had allowed the Ottomans to begin their occupation of the Balkans.

They also learned about the origins of Muslims. In their seventh-grade history textbook they discovered that under Ottoman rule some Christians converted to Islam for a variety of reasons, but mostly to retain their property. The majority of Islamicized Christians were in Bosnia-Herzegovina. During the Ottoman years most Christian Serbs, they read, were "feudal tenants," while most Muslims were landowners or privileged because of their religion. "Christian feudal tenants had bigger obligations than Muslim feudal tenants . . . Christian citizens and clergy could never have the top positions in a Muslim state."[1]

We learn that they took children, Sara told me, referring to the Janissary system in which, according to her textbook, the sultan had Christian boys kidnapped and sent to Turkey to be Islamicized and trained in the military. *Children became Turks so they could have more soldiers, and all Serbs who became Turks were made into leaders.* This was bad because *those Serbs who became Turks were against Serb people. They were raised to be warriors. Then they took other children, and killed some of them.* Sara had read Ivo Andric's famous *Bridge over the Drina.* It had bored her but she remembered the part where *some Serb who became a Turk built a bridge and he put two children into the bridge.*[2]

Helena knew that Turks had *enslaved Serbs and plundered and looted* from them. Jovan similarly had absorbed the message that *Turks were bad.* When I asked if Turks and Muslims were connected, he said he thought they were. *They are the same religion, and they are similar. They spoke the same language. Turkish warriors killed people.*

I asked Ivana why she mostly used the term "Turk" for Muslims, as many of the children did.

Well, if we are Serbs, they are Turks, Croats, and so on.

So, what is the connection between Muslims and Turks?

They are the same I guess.

I asked if everyone in her family used the term and she seemed embarrassed, mumbling quietly that she didn't know. She had never used the term about her best friend, Asra, nor had she heard Muslims use it about themselves. She knew they would not like that, she told me with a disarming smile. But history lessons about *the fights for Kosovo* had taught her that Turks and Muslims were connected.

Adriana and Igor talked about this connection. *People always learned that Turks lie,* said Igor. *They say one thing and do another. And now we feel the same about Muslims.*

You do, not me, Adriana corrected him.

I do, he agreed.

Eighth graders learned from their textbooks that "besides the aboriginal Serb population, this territory [Bosnia] was settled by Albanians and Turks. The Serb population was oppressed by Muslims who had come as settlers from the countries which Turkey lost in 1878, as well as organized Albanian groups influenced by the Turkish government." Muslims were either Serbs who had given up their real identity for material gain and benefited at the expense of their poorer Christian neighbors, or incoming colonizers. In the Second World War, as on previous occasions, they behaved perfidiously, siding with the Germans and the Croatian Ustashe, forming their own SS unit, and killing hundreds of thousands of Serbs. Jovan's teacher told students that the Croats created concentration camps in the Second World War, and that *the same thing happened in this war.*

Yet Serbs, Dusan's father told me, had continued to act with extraordinary generosity and forgiveness. They had agreed to give up their own national interests and to form a common state with Croats and Muslims, who as Islamicized Serbs were not a people. *First of all they don't have their own land, they don't have their own alphabet, and they don't have history.* They had their own religion, but no unique culture or customs. The heart of the problem, for him, appeared to be the Muslims' failure to understand and recognize their Serb roots, their treachery in turning on their own ancestors through the centuries, and Serb generosity in ignoring this for so long. *We were good to them, they used it.*[3]

Children now learned in school that Muslims had supported a system that had oppressed Serbs for half a millennium. It was to prevent a reversion to such a system that Serbs had had to go to war when Bosnia became independent. Dusan told me his brother had *fought for Serbs against violence,* because of the danger of being *like it was before, to be under Muslims. Because Muslims wanted to make their country in these areas [. . .] I know that from a story my grandfather told me, and now I know from history that we were under the Turks.*

In Gorazde neither parents nor children were particularly interested in disputing the historical points. Fikreta's mother laughed and said she did not care where she came from. She had been very impressed when a prominent Bosnian Muslim politician recently said on television that he had Croat ancestors. Fikreta's father echoed his wife: *I don't ask where do Serbs come from [. . .] they are people like us, Serbs, Croats, different religions, but I don't see any difference. I've never wanted a Muslim republic here in Bosnia.*

Most of the Gorazde children saw their differences with their neighbors as religious and cultural and had not thought about ethnic origins. Samir agreed that Muslims might have been Turks originally. Narcisa pulled a terrible face when I made the suggestion, but then thought about it and said *maybe before the Turkish empire.* It wasn't a problem for her. The relative indifference was perhaps not surprising given that Samir's and Narcisa's parents had been taught in the Tito period, from textbooks similar to those Serb children still used in Foca in 1997–98. *It's very confusing,* one teacher told me. *I learned that Princip was a hero, and the Austro-Hungarian empire bad. Now children [in the Federation] are taught that Princip was a terrorist and the Austro-Hungarians good.*[4]

Postwar Federation textbooks certainly attempted to create a new awareness of Bosnian national identity and its roots. A far larger proportion of the new history text was devoted to "Bosnian History" than to South Slav or Yugoslav history. I had a sense that the primary school textbooks had been written rather fast, patched together from previous materials with new sections pasted in and old ones rewritten. While the narrative message that came across in the Serbian books was a long struggle for Serbian self-determination against the odds, with outside powers that acted to further their own ends, the Federation narrative message focused on the attempt to define a specifically Bosnian state, first within the Ottoman, and then within the Austro-Hungarian empire. While Serbian texts stressed the "anarchy, corruption," and "economic, political, and cultural backwardness of the Ottoman empire and the Turks," Federation texts emphasized the political and religious tolerance of the Ottomans and failed attempts at reform.

The Federation texts included the nineteenth-century attempt to define "Bosniak" as a multi-confessional national identity linked specifically to the region, and the growing importance of a secular Muslim identity. They presented Serb rebellions as having failed because of internal quarrels or despotic leadership, or as having succeeded because they had co-opted other "Bosnian Christian" reform movements.

Serb successes were linked with plans for expansion and domination by Serbia, as in the first half of the nineteenth century: "Serbian attempts to exert influence on the situation in BIH were evident. In these plans the proposed union of Bosnia with Serbia was dominant." Or as in the proposed Serbian National program of the late nineteenth century, in which "Serbia would include the greater part of Slav countries in the Balkan Peninsula (BIH, Montenegro, North Albania, Macedonia and Bulgaria)."

The most significant difference was that Federation textbooks included attempts to destroy or exterminate the Muslim population. Seventh graders in Foca learned that the Balkan wars liberated Serbs from Turkey and the feudal system, "increased Serb confidence," and left Muslims "confused and surprised." Seventh graders in Gorazde learned that during the Balkan wars Muslims "were executed, exiled, and converted to Christianity by force. The aim of Serbian and Montenegrin policy was the extermination of everything non-Orthodox by terror."

It was these attempts at extermination, rather than stories of historical origins, that stuck in the Muslim children's minds. A number of them told me of *six genocides* against the Muslim people. *The first one was in 1610,* Narcisa said. *The organizer of everything was the Orthodox church and Serbia and Montenegro.* She felt that her own experiences helped her to understand how it was for people in the past. *Not everything is the same, but in some lessons there is some connection with this war [. . .] Because it already happened, so we can have some picture in mind of how it was before.*

If claims to territory are based on a blood-and-soil discourse of what group was there first and what was their racial ancestry, then identifying origins, proving one's own historical continuity and the discontinuity or false claims of others, becomes important. The Serbian textbooks gave a clear picture of a people with a long historical pedigree struggling against colonizers and traitors for a unified state in which all Serbs could live together. There was another message as well: that attempts to create a Bosnian state, whether by imperial (Austro-Hungarian) or communist design, had been futile. Muslim children, in contrast, learned about the continuity of the Bosnian state rather than of a particular people, and about themselves as members of a collective that included multiple ethnic identities: Muslim, Croat, and Serb. Yet here too one could trace a contradictory message of ethnic exclusivity in the references to the victimization and oppression of Muslims and to the longstanding expansionist and genocidal tendencies of the Serbs.

I saw both these strands of thinking in a seventh-grade history class in Gorazde. They were discussing the Congress of Berlin in 1878, when, according to their teacher, a weakened Ottoman empire allowed Austro-Hungary to *occupy* Bosnia-Herzegovina, while Serbia and Montenegro gained their independence. The favored method of teaching in both cities was by rote learning and recitation. Grades were awarded for the capacity to memorize and recite the selected text. As I watched children stand up, either confident and word-perfect or nervous and tongue-tied, in scenes reminiscent of Dickens's *Hard Times,* it often struck me that the most useful reform would be to teach and reward them for questioning, arguing, and seeking answers for themselves. Then the content of their textbooks would matter less.

The teacher of this class had told me he favored a more Socratic approach, but I sensed that the child pulled to the front of the class to join in "the dialogue" knew what answers the teacher expected.

What does occupation mean? the teacher asked.

To take over someone's country by armed force.

So we, Bosnia, were some object, given to anyone, first to the Ottomans then to Austro-Hungary, it was unfair and imperialistic. But who benefited?

Serbia and Montenegro.

And who was helping Serbia the most?

Russia.

And who is helping Serbia now?

Russia.

So all the changes in the world are made by the Great Powers.

The primary school where this class took place, a large, graceful, and solid building built by those same Austro-Hungarian occupiers, had largely withstood the shelling. It had been beautifully refurbished by a Swedish relief agency. It too had changed its name, from Nikola Tesla, the Serbian inventor, to a local religious intellectual, Husein Efendija Djozo. In Foca, meanwhile, as the primary school switched Croatian partisan for Serbian saint, the high school retained Nikola Tesla. The ghosts of the past were also moving to their "ethnic homelands."

The modern scholarly consensus is that Bosnian Muslims and Bosnian Serbs are both of somewhat mixed origins, like most of the peoples of Europe today. Prior to the Ottoman period, indigenous Bosnians were Slavs, and the region was dominated by the Catholic church. However, the remote mountainous landscape, the distance from Rome, and competition with the Orthodox church all allowed for the development of an independent church and various forms of folk religion. In the two centuries after the arrival of the Turks, many Bosnians converted to Islam. The conversions don't appear to have been forced, they included large numbers from all classes of society, and Christians who did not convert could keep their land. The Muslim population was also boosted by slaves captured in various Ottoman wars, as conversion meant freedom, and by Islamicized Muslims who had retreated with the withdrawal of the Ottoman empire from areas such as Hungary and present-day Croatia.

Bosnian Serbs, particularly in the Drina valley that borders on Serbia, are part of the indigenous Serbian Orthodox community. This group also includes those who assimilated and converted over the centuries, such as the non-Slav nomadic Vlachs, Catholics, and colonizing Greeks and Albanians. Paradoxically, the arrival of the Ottomans in the fifteenth century seems to have assisted the expansion of the Orthodox church in Bosnia, through both conversion and colonization. During much of the Ottoman period the Turks maintained a strong alliance with the Orthodox church, to the benefit of both in their fights with other Christian powers.[5]

The Ottoman era, for all its contested symbolism, was outside the living memory of the families in both cities. The Second World War was not. Every child had grandparents (living or dead) whose memories and personal stories of that time had acquired significance since the most recent war. The power of the period to produce strong feelings was brought home to me by the incensed commentary on a Federation textbook from one of my Serbian translators. She was most upset by "the game with numbers"—by what she saw as Muslim attempts to reduce the size of the crimes against Serbs and to exaggerate the harm done by them.

There is no doubt that the Second World War was a horrifying and desperate period in Balkan history. There were at least four wars going on in the region. There was an initial war between Germany and Italy and the Yugoslav state, and a second war between the Axis occupiers and the various Yugoslav resistance movements. There were also two civil wars: one between the Croatian fascist regime, established by the Nazis, and the Serb population of Bosnia and Serbia; and another between the two main resistance movements, the royalist Chetniks led by Draza Mihajlovic and the communist partisans led by Tito. Almost a million Yugoslavs died, most of them killed by other Yugoslavs. The Serbs lost the largest number (209,000 in Bosnia alone) and the Bosnian Muslims the greatest proportion (8.1 percent) of their respective populations.[6]

People of all ethnicities fought on all sides, and some changed allegiances during the course of the war. This was especially true in the Drina valley, which at different periods was the headquarters of Tito's partisans or under Chetnik control. There was a Bosnian SS division. There were Muslims who either acquiesced or actively collaborated with the Ustashe. Muslims also protested against Ustashe atrocities against Serbs and Jews. There were leading Chetniks who advocated the creation of a homogeneous Serbia from which all non-Serbs should be removed. There were Chetnik massacres of Muslims, for their collaboration with both Ustashe and partisans, and Muslim massacres of Chetniks in retaliation. Muslims and Serbs fought together as partisans, and even Muslims and Chetniks cooperated on occasion. From this dismal period, one could find evidence to support every perspective and to justify every new outrage of the recent war.[7]

In schools in both towns children were learning to play the history game, with the selective use of facts. *In the Second World War,* Marko in Foca told me, *Germany wanted to put everything under their control, and now maybe Muslims want it. They [Germans and Muslims] were together in the same army fighting against the Serbs.* In Gorazde, Jasmin learned that Muslims had protested on behalf of Serbs against the Nazi policies of extermination, and that the Chetnik leader, Mihajlovic, had wanted to annihilate Muslims. *They were on the same side but Serbs wanted to destroy Muslims [. . .] because they always wanted to govern all of Bosnia, and they couldn't stand Muslims living in Bosnia, and they are still bothered by Muslims.*

Many of the Muslim children used the term "Chetnik" as a disparaging way to refer to Serbs. Unlike the term "Turk" when used to describe Muslims, this is not always a term of abuse. Some Serbs use it with pride because of its historical associations: its original use was to describe heroic Serb bandit fighters who struggled against the Turks in earlier times.[8] Iris said she usually called *those Serbs who were in the war Chetniks, but I can't call a Serb child a Chetnik.* Nor could she use the term for Serbs who had stayed in Gorazde during the war. She reserved it for those who had been *involved in this aggression against us.* Samir told me it was the term for those Serbs who

called Muslims Balija, and for criminals. He would not use it for a
Serb friend, because a friend would not call him Balija either.

Identity and Belief

It was Ramadan, the month during which Muslims fasted during the
day. Narcisa, who had always been the most devout member of her
family after her grandmother, was fasting, as she had done since she
was quite small. Her father and brother were abstaining from alcohol
out of respect and support for her. I asked them *What does it mean to
be a Muslim?*

Believe me, I don't know, her father replied. *I was brought up a
Communist; Tito was Allah for all of us . . . especially Muslims. He gave
us a nation in 1971, so of course we are glad about that.*

How do you define a Muslim?

People who believe in Allah.

So can you be a Muslim?

He grinned at me, seeing the contradiction. *Yes.*

Although you don't believe?

I am almost an atheist.

And still a Muslim?

Well, I can't be an Eskimo.

War had made him more aware of his specific identity as something different from other national groups. *You know what—if you
were in Foca, Visegrad, Zvornik . . . The Muslims there were slaughtered
because of the hatred [. . .] All the Serbs in Gorazde ran away from here,
they wanted to get out of this hell.* But even before the war he had been
quite clear that being a Muslim was his heritage and tradition because that was how his parents and grandparents had defined themselves. *My parents were religious. It was my choice [not to be].*

If both parents are Muslims then it is natural to be a Muslim,
Narcisa's mother explained. *I respect my mother because she respects*

*Islam. I'm not religious myself. During that period [after 1970 in com-
munist Yugoslavia], I had no need to go to mosque and my parents
never made me. It was qualifications that mattered. We celebrated
Bajram in both families.*[9]

Why not? her husband interjected. *Lots of baklava and cakes!*

I didn't have time to learn about religion, Narcisa's mother continued. *I just celebrated because I belong to my people.*

They said their daughter's more serious approach to religion had
always been her free choice. *We aren't worried about it. We see that besides school she has lots of other activities. She's not especially religious,
it doesn't preoccupy her.*

The conversation, typical of many that I had in Gorazde, brought
home to me how soft-edged and fluid Bosnian Muslim identity was.
There were no references to the distant past, to land, or to historic origins. People were Muslims because their parents and grandparents
had been, because it made them part of a community and represented what they saw as a good way of living, with particular moral
and cultural practices they valued. It did not necessarily entail religious belief, and for many of the parents born in the 1950s and 1960s
it had not done so because religious belief was not compatible with
Party membership. The sense of community arose from established
traditions, such as Ramadan and Bajram, that distinguished them
from their neighbors.

They enjoyed their neighbors' different traditions as well. Elvira's
father, a Muslim married to a Croat, said *The customs we have as
Muslims are very good and very practical.* He took pleasure in wearing
new clothes and visiting for Bajram as well as for Catholic and Orthodox Christmas. It was this sense of belonging to a shared country—Yugoslavia, then Bosnia—and at the same time enjoying differences, that was the striking feature of the Bosnian Muslims' identity.
Their sense of themselves was inclusive, and it depended in part on
living with others who were not the same.[10]

Tito seems to have recognized both the inclusive and the soft-edged aspects of Muslim identity. He clearly hoped to make use of this identity in his construction of a second Yugoslavia out of the ashes of the Second World War. At the outset, although the Final Resolution of the Antifascist Council for the National Liberation of Bosnia-Herzegovina (1943) recognized the "equality of Serbs, Muslims, and Croats" in their "common and indivisible homeland," Tito denied Bosnian Muslims the possibility of identifying themselves as a people *(Narod)* in the same terms that were available to both Croats and Serbs.[11] His plan was a centralized state with a new Yugoslav identity into which he hoped Muslims would be the first to assimilate. By the late 1960s he recognized that while a centralized policy benefited the more geographically dispersed and numerous Serbs, it caused tensions with all the other ethnicities. He moved instead to promoting diversity, in a more decentralized federal state, as a way of balancing national interests and retaining control. This culminated in the famous 1974 constitution, now despised by the Serbs for undermining their interests, but welcomed by the other nationalities for increasing their power and standing within the Federation. Over this period Bosnian Muslims rose higher on the complex ladder of categories of national identification within Socialist Yugoslavia, and from 1971 they could define themselves as a "people." This was one reason Narcisa's parents and many other Gorazde families saw Tito as their champion.

The sense of inclusiveness and multiplicity appeared to have survived the war and been passed to the younger generation in Gorazde. When I asked the children how they identified themselves, most used multiple categories. Alma had been a refugee abroad during the war and had told her schoolmates she was *Bosnian, and then they asked me my nationality and I would say Muslim.* All agreed that being Bosnian meant being a citizen of a multinational state which included three nations: Muslim, Serb, and Croat. They regarded the distinctions between these as religious, and for some like Senad and Samir it was being Bosnian that mattered most. Senad wanted Serbs and Croats in Bosnia to use the terms "Orthodox" and "Catholic."[12] The state had also tried to grasp this nettle of the double meaning of the word "Muslim" and had recently introduced the term "Bosniak" so that Muslims had a nonreligious way of defining their national identity. In Gorazde, when I was there, the term had not caught on and seemed to be a source of confusion. It had produced fury in some families in Foca, who felt that the only distinguishing aspect of Muslim identity was religious practice, and that this new terminology was one more attempt to create something out of nothing.

The children in Gorazde were sometimes rather vague about Muslim religious practice. Sanela said she was a believer but was not sure what it meant. When I pushed her she said *I know that it's a belief in Allah, and we just believe in him.* She no longer bothered to go to mekteb, the religious school she had attended before the war. Children from more religious families, like Fikreta, were clearer. In mekteb Fikreta had learned that *we Muslims have to pray to God. For example people of other nationalities, they usually go to the churches and they also pray to God, like we go to mosque. I mean they do the same thing but in another way.* Fikreta had worked out who she was by looking at others who lived beside her and did things differently.

I finally began to understand why, in spite of all that had happened, many of the Gorazde families still felt they should live with their Serb neighbors once more. Part of being a Bosnian Muslim depended on living with others who were not. Differences were valued because they helped people to define themselves. Fikreta asked *How can we be alone in the house and not be with anybody else?* No one in the Muslim families wanted to live in a mono-ethnic state. Again and again I heard: *In the whole Bosnia-Herzegovina there is no life, life would be without any sense* if Muslims lived alone. "To be Bosnian was to have a feeling for otherness, for the different as part of the daily reality of one's most personal environment. It was this experience of the different that made it possible to be Bosnian," Ivan Lovrenovic wrote in his

cultural history of Bosnia. He also lamented that "the new territorial-
ization" and "the poison of chauvinism" had destroyed this "crown-
ing glory" of Bosnian social life and turned Bosnians into Bosniak
Muslims, Serbs, and Croats. Yet this feeling for otherness did not
seem to have completely disappeared in Gorazde.[13]

Some Gorazde parents told me that the war had made them more
aware of what being a Muslim meant and more curious about their
religious roots, but I had no sense that the war had created increased
religiosity or chauvinism in any of the children or their parents.
Those who were religious had always been so. Those who were not
had not changed. All the children said they believed in God, but for
the majority this did not involve much in the way of religious practice, such as regular attendance at mosque or mekteb. Senad, whose
grandmother had been a bula (a religious teacher), believed in God,
but I don't learn about it. He thought it excessive to have to pray every
day, five times a day. He also rejected the teaching in school that his
own religion was best: All people are the same, no matter what religion
they are.

For these families, actions like fasting for a few days during
Ramadan were ways of showing that they belonged to a particular
community. Hasan fasted because of the tradition. Hasan's mother
was pleased that there was now religious teaching in school, but this
had more to do with Hasan learning about his own customs than
with devotion. She had been ashamed when, as a refugee in Germany,
she had not known the dates of her own religious festivals and a German woman had. She wanted her son to learn the things she herself
could not teach him. Other parents thought religious teaching
should be confined to the mosque and not take place during school
hours. The reason for this again came down to sharing living space
with other groups. Islamic teaching in the schools would make it
difficult for children of other nationalities to come back to Gorazde.

This moderation contrasted with the new assertiveness of some of
Gorazde's Muslims. The Mufti (Muslim jurist and religious leader)

had tried to have a Serb woman, who had lived in the town through-out the war, dismissed from running the kindergarten. He gave me a variety of reasons, including *loose morals* and a father who had fought on the Serb side, but he was most upset by the idea of Muslim children being taught by a non-Muslim. He also made various pro-nouncements that the war might be related to Gorazde citizens' lack of godliness. Many families seemed uncomfortable with his behavior and distanced themselves from it. *Everybody has the right to believe what he wants,* said Narcisa. *People who believe in Islam should be treated no differently than Catholics and other religions.*

New female religious teachers (bulas) had arrived from Zenica and were giving classes in a private house. Fikreta had gone because she was curious. These new bulas wore headscarves, and she was irritated because they had told her she could not wear tight clothes and mini-skirts and should wear a scarf over her head. *I can pray,* she told me, *I can pray to God but I won't accept having that scarf over my head.* She preferred the *real mekteb,* run by locals, which she attended regularly. *There are some Arabians and their women are usually wearing those and . . . I don't like it. My mother wouldn't accept it either, and no one in Gorazde and no one in Bosnia wears those scarves.*

She was also unhappy with their teaching about other nation-alities:

> *They tell us that people who have other religions are not religious at all and that we shouldn't have any contact with them. But I don't think that is true. Like Serbs and Croats, that we shouldn't have contact with them. These people from Zenica, they're Arabi-ans you know, and they teach us these sorts of things, but in our real mekteb they only teach us about our religion and how to pray. Our real hodza in our mekteb, he teaches us about Suras, that's a kind of lesson from the Koran, and how to pronounce things. And in this Arabic mekteb they teach us about Christians and about Jewish people, and how they didn't respect these books God sent them.*

She did not argue when she disagreed with the bulas. *When I have to study these lessons, I just study them to get a good mark, but I don't try to keep them in my mind. My mother wanted me to go to the real mekteb and not to go to them anymore because they don't pray to God in the same way that we do.*[14]

Like the interviews, the children's written stories indicated that living in a specific and much loved place, being a citizen of a particular country, was more important than the ethnic or religious identity of victim or aggressor. Terms like *sacrifices for our Bosnia,* or *the good spirit of the Bosnian people,* or *our brave town, Gorazde,* were common. One fourteen-year-old girl wrote: *War is the worst experience that could happen to me and all the people in Bosnia. I heard that some people wanted a country where only one people would live and other people had to suffer because of that.*

The sense that their country was still inclusive came through even in the angriest of texts—as in this one from a fifteen-year-old girl:

And those who wanted the war are not human beings; they just look like human beings. Their hearts are made of stone and through their veins runs dirty blood. How could they do it? How could they ruin a country which belonged to them as much as us? The country had room for everyone. How could they kill the children of their friends, friends who sat beside them at school? Only wild people could have done this, those who lived in the forest, but what could be done? [. . .] I think that Bosnia-Herzegovina will be the same as it was before and that the people who deserved will live in it without those who have ruined and killed it.

Again the *wild people* are unidentified. The headmaster of the high school in Foca saw this Muslim habit of talking about unspecified aggressors, and of teaching children that Serbs from Montenegro and Serbia had fought in Bosnia, as profoundly dishonest, a way of denying that Muslims and Serbs had been equally involved in a civil war: *The graveyards are full of Serbs and Muslims born and killed in Bosnia.*

So Serbs were aggressors on one side of the street and Muslims who lived on the other were defending themselves? Who kicked Serbs out of Zenica? Dusan's father asked *How can I be an aggressor in my own country?* My unspoken answer was: only by refusing to share it with those who regard it as a common home. I could see that, from the perspective of the Muslims who wanted to rebuild this common home, talking about an unidentified aggressor, or using the term "Chetnik" in preference to "Serb," did make it possible to separate the cause of the conflict from local Serb neighbors, so that those *who deserved* could still be included in a joint state.

The problem was that young Serbs in Foca did not want to be included in the Bosnian state, and did not believe it existed. There were no fluffy edges to Serb children's sense of themselves. They knew who they were, and they knew they were not Bosnian. For many of them the war had helped in this crystallization.[15] Some parents lamented the loss of the old identity: Bojan's mother mumbled sadly *I was born in Bosnia and I am still in Bosnia.* She obviously did not like the topic much, and was almost whispering when she added that she was *Serb, I don't know what difference does it make. We say Serbs, it was Bosnia before . . . What do I know?* However her son Bojan told me confidently *I am Serb, because I am not other nationalities, it is important for everybody.* Ivana's mother said proudly *I am still Yugoslav,* but Ivana was sure she was Serb. Dusan had always been Serb. It was *not just my nationality, but also the nationality of my grandfather and great-grandfather.* Even those who had understood the complexities of the Dayton Agreement, and knew that Republika Srpska was an Entity within a country called Bosnia-Herzegovina, were quite sure they were not Bosnian. Vesna had called herself a Bosnian of Orthodox religion before the war. She was still *Orthodox,* but now a *Serb.*

Again, there was a small disaffected minority in Foca. They were all girls, and belonged to the group of children who were curious about the war and more open to their Muslim neighbors' returning. Helena did not care what nationality she was and did not understand the differences: *I don't know if there are differences between Muslims and Serbs; maybe in religion but not life.*

The distinctiveness of Serbian identity showed up most clearly in written stories. Many Serb children used a poetic and rhetorical style reminiscent of their own national epics, and quite absent from Muslim scripts. One fourteen-year-old boy wrote: *War [. . .] turned our dreams into nightmares [. . .] War is a monster who wanted to seduce people of different religions and bring them to bloodshed [. . .] Hostile warriors left trails of grief behind them [. . .] Instead of laughter there is grief, instead of a hand, an artificial limb, instead of a healthy body, many scars [. . .] I would like it if war never happened again and we could live in our Republika Srpska, which is small but dear in our hearts.*

Several raised questions of land ownership and origins. A fifteen-year-old girl wrote: *The Muslims were responsible for starting the war. I do not say this because I am a Serb but because it is obvious. They started the war because they wanted to create their own country in areas which were always ours. Everybody knows that Muslims come from Serbs, and they did not have the right to start a war and endanger our childhoods. They had no reason to do it.*

Even the youngest children set the Serb victory of achieving an "independent homeland" squarely in the context of the Serbs' historical experience: their victimhood through the centuries, their exploitation by others, and their strength and virtue. A thirteen-year-old girl put it this way:

> *War brought unrest to our hearts. Many people gave their lives defending their homeland. Serbs survived a lot of suffering, misfortune, and annihilation through the centuries. Many families left their homes to start a new life with bundles in their arms. Everything that happened and happens to us reminds us that history repeats itself. Is it fate? Only Serbian people could handle all this*

because they are used to pain and suffering. We got used to fighting for someone else's interests without thinking. We did not realize our own strength.

Sometimes Serbian identity was connected to a feeling of being misunderstood and isolated by the rest of the world: *The entire world is against* Serbs, wrote another thirteen-year-old girl, *but I don't understand, we are human too. I hope that we can prove it, truth and justice will emerge. Why does the world separate Serb children from others. We want peace love and joy; we don't want shooting and war.*

Vesna Pesic, a sociologist and politician from Belgrade, describes this kind of thinking as resentful nationalism. This is an identity built on frustration (at failed historic projects such as the re-creation of the old empire), feelings of inferiority and jealousy (from lagging behind Europe), and anger at the undeserved ill feelings of others, combined with selective blindness to behaviors which might have created resentment in the others. Sometimes this blindness was striking. Stojan's father asked me in amazement one day why Muslim children had any problem with reading Njegos, the nineteenth-century Montenegrin poet whose epic *The Mountain Wreath* celebrates the conversion—or massacre and expulsion—of Turks from Montenegro. The idea that lines like "No single seeing eye, no tongue of Turk, escaped to tell his tale another day! We put them all unto the sword" might be troubling to Muslims, whom many Serbs still called Turks, had not crossed his mind. Pesic argues that resentful nationalism is the basis of all identities in the Balkans. I could not find this symmetry in the Muslim community in Gorazde, and indeed it was this failure to think within a similar framework that generated some of the Serbs' anger and their frequent assertion that Muslims lied.[16]

The school psychologist in Foca suggested that children wrote in this way to gain approval, that it did not necessarily represent their true feelings. This may well be true. At one point I thought of working in Visegrad, and asked a group of children there to write stories. In this case the stories were written under the eye of their teacher and handed back to me. This one by a fifteen-year-old girl is typical:

> *Many Serb heroes are deep in their graves, deep in the black ground, proud because they gave their lives for their country. Certainly, it was not what they wanted. They wanted to walk freely around Republika Srpska. But they had to stop those who want to harm Serb people, someone like you. Serb Sarajevo is no more, thanks to people like you. You were not on the Serb side during the war and now you come to test fifteen-year-olds? Are you not ashamed? How dare you, how do you have the courage to come now in Republika Srpska, now when we do not need you? [. . .] Now we live in a collective center. Serbs do not trust anyone, especially those who were our enemies. Serbs, those proud people, now only believe in themselves.*

The hatred directed at me was fair enough, but in Visegrad story after story was written in a similar manner with little reference to personal experiences. Many used identical phrases such as an appended *P.S. First you bombard us, and then you test us.* It seemed as if strong suggestions had been made to the children as to what to write. I was not able to discover how much they believed their own statements, as I felt unwelcome and unsafe in Visegrad and did not return.

Social identity theory suggests that all identity is fluid to a degree. Mother, daughter, housewife, doctor, partygoer, churchgoer, citizen of a nation: we can be all or any of these and shift between them depending on the social role we need to fulfill and the situation in which we find ourselves.[17] In Foca the children wrote their stories in the schoolroom. They were unsupervised by their own teacher, but

writing for a stranger from the "aggressor country" probably increased the emphasis on national pride and defensiveness. When I
got to know some of the children and their families, the rhetoric disappeared and I discovered some of the very Bosnian moderateness
that I had found in Gorazde.

This was evident in religious practice. Foca, like Gorazde, was experiencing a religious revival. I attended packed church services on
various holidays with the crowd pushing in the door toward the
singing, incense, and light beyond the ancient painted screen. At
Easter I went to a mass baptism. The families and attendant relatives
were in their best clothes, one mother resplendent with bright red
hair and tight red short skirt, holding her baby in a blue flounced
dress. There were two more babies, some embarrassed-looking teenage boys, and a cluster of six- and seven-year-olds. The occasion had
a rather routine, businesslike feel: One priest wrote at a desk, while
the other sang. The children lined up with the sponsors behind them,
babies were held in their sponsors' arms. The priests took it in turn to
sing and chant at speed, questions were thrown out and answered,
the lined-up children were anointed, then had water splashed on
them, then were anointed again. People wandered in and out of the
church. I felt as I always did at Orthodox ceremonies: overwhelmed
by the mysterious beauty but, coming from a rather participatory
Protestant tradition, bemused by the passivity of the congregation.
There was a feeling of magic being worked, rather than of promises
and relationships being made.

When I told Dusan's father, who had always been a believer, about
the baptisms, he responded *Humph . . . it's kind of a fashion.* He liked
the idea that Serbs were returning to the church but feared it was not
real, and had less to do with piety than with the conformity learned
under communism. Dusan told me he was *not that religious but I believe in God.* Almost all the children expressed similar views. Some
were baptized, some not. For most, celebrations such as the family

saints' days *(Slava)*, Christmas, and Easter were important as traditions that showed one belonged to a family and an ethnic community. They resented the intrusion of politics into these matters.

The Serbian Orthodox church had played a significant role in the
mobilization of Serbs' anxieties about Islam before the war, warning
that it was caught between "two powerful religious internationals [Is-
lam and Catholicism]" and that "the national and ethnic survival of
the Serbs is in great danger." The same writer had called for "the expression of an exclusively Serbian nationalist ideology" and declared
that "Serbia must of necessity be formed within its ethnic boundaries." The church had added legitimacy to the use of force to achieve
such an aim. Another article in an official church publication just before the war had accused the "partisans of peace" of being "champi-
ons of treason and defeat" and of having helped "the evil forces that
are opposed to God (and by the same token to humanity)." "In our
present Armageddon," the article continued, "they are on the side
of the destructive Gog and Magog (the mythical personifications of
enslavement and tyranny)."[18]

The young priest who taught religious studies at the school in Foca
felt it was disrespectful to have destroyed the mosques, but pointed
out that some of them had once been churches taken over by Muslims. He opposed rebuilding them, just as he opposed Muslims' return to the town, for reasons of security. The president of the SRS assured me that there was no extremism or politics in the Orthodox
religion, and then explained how his party's symbol, the double-
headed eagle, represented the unity of spiritual and secular power. He
thought Milorad Dodik, the newly elected prime minister of
Republika Srpska, was *a Satan* for suggesting that religion might
be taken out of school. *Has the Orthodox church ever called for war?
No!* he said. *But Islam always calls for war. That is the tragedy of those
people.*

None of the children in Foca shared this disparaging view of Islam as a religion. They all said people had the right to believe and worship as they wished. Nikola's parents hoped that religion might have a role as a cultural alternative to nationalism, something enjoyable to express who you were, rather than identifying you with a political party. But they feared it was not working out like that. *The way they teach it, children are starting to hate it.* Nikola's father worried that religion might replace Marxism as the most onerous and boring subject in the curriculum. Jovan's father was all for getting religion out of school.

Children were not preoccupied with national issues in either town. Getting good grades at school, relationships with friends, sports, and the lack of things for young people to do in their town (particularly in Foca) were what concerned them most. When I first asked them to describe themselves in an open-ended way only two children spontaneously mentioned national identity. I had to ask about it directly to learn how they identified themselves.

In some children I could sense the tensions and contradictions created by a pluralist and inclusive upbringing followed by living in a community which lauded ethnic separatism. Divac, who had grown up in a mixed apartment block in Sarajevo thinking of himself as Yugoslav, held *Muslim separatists* responsible for the war. He missed his old life, and still did not understand why Muslims had wanted to destroy it. My suggestion that they might have felt uncomfortable in a Serb-dominated Yugoslavia was roundly rejected. *They wouldn't be minority if they were Yugoslav. They're supposed to be Yugoslav.* This is the argument the English have with the some of the Scots and Welsh over their reluctance to see themselves as "British." Even the most cosmopolitan citizens of hegemonic nations tend not to notice the degree to which the interests and values of a multinational country can become enmeshed with the interests and values of the most numerous and widespread group, if that group is their own. I had tried . . .

If Yugoslavs are mainly Serbs, I asked Divac, *you don't think that might be a problem for people who aren't Serbs?*

Why would it be? Because we were all Yugoslavs, in my opinion.

They would say "Look at how the Yugoslavs have treated Kosovar Albanians, who are supposed to be Yugoslavs but are not treated equally."

I don't know, I heard on TV that many Albanians came to our country without citizenship, they were just sent there without visas.

Never mind. The main point was that before the war Divac had had an idea of himself as belonging to something multinational and inclusive. Since the war this had disappeared. *Of course it's changed. It's not that I have a different opinion from before the war. I have to adapt to the surroundings [. . .] I didn't know that I was Serb. But we are not living in Yugoslavia any more. We are living in Republika Srpska.*

Is being a Serb an important part of who you are?

Now it is, he replied.

Just how much he had adapted became clear when I had switched off the tape and we were discussing how depressed and hard things were in Foca. He said he wanted to leave Republika Srpska and Yugoslavia as quickly as possible. *I will try to go somewhere, anywhere there is a better situation.* He asked me why the international community had been blocking aid to the town, and I explained about the failure to hand over indicted war criminals or allow Muslims to return home, and he suddenly changed. The easy-going, open young teenager, whose father had protected his Muslim neighbors, was suddenly an ardent nationalist talking to a representative of a NATO aggressor state, defending Serb pride from outside pressure and interference. *Maybe there are things we don't want to do. These people [Karadzic et al.] are national heroes for us. Maybe we prefer not to have people come back. If you make that choice then there is a price to pay. Maybe we prefer to pay that price.*

The war had not been caused by conflicting perceptions of national identity, but it had certainly created them in this younger generation. All the Serb children now thought of themselves as Serb, and half of them said if they could vote, it would be for a Serb party. But the war had also produced a feeling of not having "a country," confusion as to the nature of the state in which they lived, and alienation from their current home. Although most said they would fight for Republika Srpska if it came to another war, half of them did not want to live there or vote at all. Like Divac, they just wanted to get out. Many wanted to go to America if possible, because it was a *developed and modern* country, never mind that it was the enemy that had so unjustly bombed them.

As for the Muslim children in Gorazde, war had given them a country: Bosnia-Herzegovina. They too were prepared to fight for it in any future war, and unlike the children in Foca they wanted to live in Bosnia in the future. They also had a stronger sense of Muslim identity than before the war, but for them ethnic identification was not paramount. When I asked them whether, if they could vote, they would vote for a Muslim party, the majority said no, just a decent one.

"The Serbs began it. On 28 June, they shot the Austrian Crown Prince Franz Ferdinand and his wife Sophie . . . everyone says the Serbs want war in order to maintain their independence and Russia will support them." Thus began twelve-year-old Piete Kuhr's diary, on August 1, 1914. Piete was German and lived with her brother and grandmother in eastern Prussia, eighty miles from the German-Russian front. Her first few pages were filled with excited patriotism. She was moved to tears at seeing military uniforms brought out of storage. (Her grandmother had a different response, which reminded me of Amela's grandmother: "I have lived through this twice before . . . why can't people live in peace?") At school Piete learned it was her patriotic duty to stop using the French "adieu" and start saying "auf Wiedersehen." "The girls are pleased that Germany is entering the field against its old enemy France. The most pleased of all are the teachers. We have to learn new songs that glorify war." She wrote these out:

> God save our precious fatherland
> Our ancient swords serve as of yore,
> Lasting as long as iron ore
> To save us from another's yoke
> Preserving the heart of German folk.

On August 5 she wrote:

> In our geography lesson we were again concerned with Serbia. I myself had quite forgotten where exactly its frontiers ran and had difficulty pointing it out on a map. We now have a great hatred for this little country and shout "down with Serbia!" No one in my class can say what flag Serbia has or what its inhabitants are like, for example what religion they have. I said in school today, "Princip is better looking than Archduke Franz Ferdinand." I couldn't have done more to stir the hornet's nest if I had said that our Emperor Wilhelm was a traitor.[19]

Piete had no real concept of who the enemy was until the conflict began. I watched a similar process at work in Britain during the run-up to the Falklands War in 1982, when suddenly the public, which had taken no interest in the horrors inflicted by the Argentinean junta in its Dirty War upon its own population in the 1970s, was preoccupied with the evil nature of the "Argies," and eager, as a popular newspaper headline said, to "Bash" them.

The social psychologists Muzafer and Carolyn Sherif conducted some famous experiments with eleven-year-old boys in the 1940s and 1950s. In one, children who had camped and played together for a week were then divided into two groups in a way that deliberately cut across the friendships formed. The researchers discovered that even with such an arbitrary division and no previous history of conflict, the new group identities overrode all previous relationships. Before the split 60 percent reported that their best friends were among those who later were in the other group; only 10 percent still claimed those friendships after the separation. Those who tried to sustain friendships were ostracized, branded traitors, and sometimes physically abused.[20]

The need to categorize ourselves and feel we belong is so deeply embedded that even when groups are newly created on a completely random basis and participants are not acquainted with members of either group, they tend to value the members of their own group and devalue those of the other. In a different experiment, Henri Tajfel gave participants the chance to maximize material gain for their own group, or to gain less but increase the differential between their own group and the other group. Most participants chose the second option: they would rather that their own group gained more at the expense of the other than that both gained more overall. Overt conflict exacerbates such tendencies but does not cause them. Once separated and placed in competition, the eleven-year-olds in the Sherifs' experiments rapidly developed group identities, insignia, and codes of conduct, as well as derogatory stereotypes about the other group.[21]

There was no need to resort to any history of ancient antagonisms or supposed warlike habits to explain why two communities in the Drina valley, who had lived intermingled and closely together for almost forty years, and who were then separated by war, became antagonistic to each other. My surprise was rather that in both communities, two years after the war, one could still sense the significance and impact of that joint life. At times I felt quite bewildered as to where I was. It was not just the similar arrangements of furniture within the rooms, the almost identical clothes, the same rituals and courtesies of hospitality. It was also the phrases the families used when they talked, their aspirations and their values, their moderateness regarding excesses within their own religious communities. When I asked parents what values mattered for their children, they always gave me the same lists: *not to lie, not to steal, to respect elders, to value learning, not to abuse or mistreat others, whatever their beliefs or the color of their skin.* I had the sense of living in a common moral community with many shared values, where differences had only recently come to symbolize danger.

War creates its own dynamic, and the Serb leaders clearly hoped that their campaign of terror would lead to reprisals and create the inter-ethnic hatred that had not previously existed. The justification of "mutual animosities" would then become a self-fulfilling prophecy. Tell people to go to war because their neighbors are planning to kill them, expel those neighbors with such brutality that some will strike back with equal nastiness, and then express astonishment, as Karadzic did, that "the international community should want people who hate each other to the point of extermination to live together again."[22]

War had created a sense of threat on both sides. For Serbs it had made sharing territory and daily life with Muslims almost inconceivable for the present. Reconciliation with Muslims was seen as a weapon that the West continued to use in its war against Serbs, forcing them to live with people who hated them after they had sacrificed so much to free themselves. War crimes trials were perceived as another one-sided injustice because the majority of defendants were Serb.

One night I drove Gordana, a young Serb friend who worked for the UN in Foca, to a party in Gorazde. These staff members of international organizations appeared to me to be the main hope for Bosnia. Unlike the children I interviewed, they were old enough to remember good friendships with the other side, and unlike those children's parents, they were young enough not to have done any fighting themselves. Most were university students; many had been abroad. They moved easily between the communities, with access to all the media and all opinions. When Gordana came to my flat to change for the party I sensed an edginess, and at my answer to a seemingly innocuous question about Gorazde, she suddenly launched into an angry attack. I and the West would never understand, she asserted, because we relied on video and newspapers and these were manipulated, and who did I think had started the war? Serbs had been totally bewildered at the beginning, not understanding why there was shooting, and the JNA had taken away all the weapons so that Bosnian Serbs had to buy them back to fight and were treated like "shit" by Serbia, and Dayton was a complete disaster and tragedy for them—*and what about the concentration camps?*

What concentration camps, what were their names?

I can't remember, but you must know our history—and we were back in the Second World War. There was no arguing with her. All this while she changed into party clothes and did her hair and complained about the cold.

I HATE Muslims for what they did to us! Why did they start this? You know why I want to get my apartment back in Sarajevo? So I can sell it and leave! That's what we all want, we DON'T want to live with them and they don't want to live with us and anyone who tells you differently is lying. When they say they don't hate us, they are lying.

Gordana, why is it so important to prove to me that they hate you?

Because it's true, and the worst thing is they come from us, they are Serbs.

Are you sure you want to go to this party?

Yes—are you sure you want to take me?

Of course.

So we went, and she ate and drank and seemed comfortable with her Muslim colleagues from Gorazde. At one point she argued with Sean, an American friend who worked for the UN High Commission for Refugees, about why the United States thought it should be World Policeman.

It should be, Sean said, *but unfortunately it isn't. Because it's the most powerful nation. If it lived up to its responsibilities, the war would have stopped far sooner.*

And why, Gordana countered, *isn't Izetbegovic at The Hague?*

He's an incompetent man but not a criminal. Karadzic was responsible for Srebrenica. That happened, you aren't responsible but your leaders are.

Izetbegovic had concentration camps, he shot soldiers with snipers.

None that I know of, and sniping is a legitimate act of war.

If you take Karadzic to The Hague you are saying we are all guilty.

On the contrary, Gordana, I interjected, *the point of arresting him is to release others from guilt. What I want to know is why you support him.*

Because he was our leader. The Germans supported Hitler. This was certainly an interesting parallel.

But now they're ashamed of that support, I replied.

But it took twenty years and we will need that time.

It's not the justice of your cause, the right to autonomy, but the brutality with which your leaders pursued it that was the crime. Anyway, I added, *now you have your territory.*

Yes, we have "Africa," they have "Europe." They have the cities.

But Muslim people mostly lived in cities before, said Sean.

Yes, exactly, and why? Because the Turks gave them power and wealth, and us nothing! We were back with the Ottomans.

But that doesn't make driving them out of the cities or bombing them in the cities right, does it? I asked.

In Srbinje we put them on buses, they were not hurt.

But Gordana, they had the right to stay, I responded.

How could they stay? They would have been killed. Just like the children, Gordana saw busing people out of their hometown as a humane action.

I was so often told that Muslims hated Serbs and that they lied when they said otherwise that I began to realize that the Serbs needed to believe this, because only the existence of this Muslim hatred could justify and neutralize the forced expulsion of their Muslim neighbors. It was possible to find hatred and similar distrust in a few of the Muslim families, but war had not extinguished their desire for a joint life, even if it had made them feel life together could not be the same. The tragedy was that the Dayton Peace Agreement, through its inability to undo the logic of separation that had led to war in the first place, was continuing the de facto partition.

David Shipler studied Arab and Jewish communities in Israel in the mid-1980s. What he found regarding children's perceptions of one another makes depressing reading. Jewish children had stereotyped images of Arabs as fearsome, violent, strong, duplicitous, and cowardly. They also thought them fanatical, brutal, and primitive. (These stereotypes were reminiscent of some Serb writings about Muslims.) These images were reinforced by school textbooks. For example, a text about Arabs and Islam, produced by the Israeli ministry of education, focused on war, thievery, and conquest rather than on Arab contributions to medicine, science, or architecture. A picture of a line of Arabs riding camels was captioned: "An armed group of men. It is possible they are heading for a robbery raid." Bedouin women were described as unfeeling: those "who lose their sons or husbands in battle receive the hard news without weeping or cries." (Some Serb women had similarly complained to me of the unfeeling nature of Muslim grief, because of the lack of tears, while some Muslim women had told me that Serbs were *hysterical* and *exaggerated* their feelings.) Children's literature emphasized Arabs' hatred of Jews and their wish to destroy Israel.

Shipler points out that all these images were reinforced by the absence of personal contact between Israeli Jews and Arabs since 1948, when Arabs disappeared from most Israeli lives except as hired labor. A 1980 survey found that 51.6 percent of Jews thought the majority of Israeli Arabs (Arabs who were Israeli citizens living within the 1967 borders) hated Jews. Many Jewish children favored expulsion of all Arabs. Shipler quotes an Arab teacher and politician's description of a typical discussion class: "What you hear in the questions is terrible. For example 'why do you have to settle here? This is our country; you have to be expelled outside the country. You have a lot of land, and we have a very tiny piece of land. This is for Jews, so you have no right to stay here and if we let you, you have to thank us for that.'"[23]

Arab stereotypes of Jews showed a remarkable symmetry, the most prominent being "the aggressive, brutal Jew, who embraces violence without remorse." The stereotypes became more pronounced as contact between the two groups decreased. Israelis were seen as Zionist aggressors, and their supposed plan for an enlarged Jewish state was emphasized. Literature and schoolbooks were full of nostalgia for the lost homeland, praise for Arab military resolve, and descriptions of Jewish cowardice. For example, a junior high school textbook said Jews were able to fight only when they were protected in fortified villages or shielded by war planes.[24] Shipler's book is even more pertinent today in light of the renewed conflict between Israel and the occupied territories. It can be seen as warning about the possible consequences of "solutions" based on partition, ethnic separation, and failure to confront the difficult issues raised by forced expulsion and refugee return.

Yet this bleak picture is not the only possibility. Piete Kuhr's grandmother ran a Red Cross soup kitchen at the railway station as the First World War dragged on. Piete encountered the full horror of war as the wounded, dead, and dying poured through her town on troop trains from the Front. A prisoner-of-war camp, with its ever extending graveyard, brought home the suffering of her "enemies" on the other side. By the end of the diary her patriotic fervor had been transformed into empathy for others of all nationalities, a profound hatred of war, and cynicism toward those responsible: "We have clearly perished from a surfeit of victories. And to what purpose, to what purpose? How can a child understand it?"[25]

I found that same hatred of war, the same wish for it never to recur, and the same profound cynicism about political leaders in every child I interviewed and in almost every story the children wrote. The empathy for the other side was less visible, unless expressed in the most general terms of sympathy for all the children in the world. If the goal is to create empathy and trust for certain others, there is no substitute for lived experience of those others. Separation and silence, like uncharted waters on medieval maps, leave a space where myths can flourish: "There be Dragons."

part three

Psychosocial
Consequences

8

War and Well-being

During a particularly severe air raid in Bristol, England, in May 1941, several high-explosive bombs hit the children's hospital. Dr. Frank Bodman, who was on duty at another hospital nearby, rushed over to assist with the evacuation of the young patients. Later he described what he saw: "Soldiers were crunching through a litter of broken glass, fallen plaster, and blown in blackout material picking children out of cots and beds, and tucking them under their arms, running down the steps and dumping them pell-mell into a lorry. The hospital was in darkness and the only light came from the fires raging in the city below. A very heavy barrage was in progress and heavy high explosive bombs continued to fall quite close to the hospital."

Fifty-four children between two and twelve years old were transferred to Dr. Bodman's hospital that night. None had suffered any physical injury in the raid, but the severity was such that Bodman noted: "I still feel a little frightened myself when I recall it." After some months Bodman decided to see how the children were doing. He traced all but three of them. Seven had died of infectious illnesses, including meningitis and diphtheria, an indication of the physical vulnerability of children in war. But, to the doctor's surprise, only five of the forty-four children he contacted had any lasting psychological symptoms that could be attributed to the raid.

Most of the children had been disturbed for the first few weeks after leaving the hospital, with responses that differed according to age. All but one of the youngest infants were quite untroubled. The toddlers were jumpy when sirens sounded and ran to safety. Slightly older children had a period of pretending nothing had happened and then started discussing it either with their dolls or in their games. Those aged seven to eleven found the raid exciting and interesting, and the oldest children also showed concern for younger ones. Those children who experienced further raids were untroubled when they occurred. The few children with persisting problems were all young (between one and five years), and most were no longer living in dangerous areas. Their problems varied: they wet or soiled themselves, continued to scream or jump if they heard a siren or saw a gas mask, had bad dreams at night, or were frightened of the dark. Bodman believed his findings demonstrated children's extraordinary toughness and flexibility in threatening situations.[1]

Anna Freud and her colleague Dorothy Burlingham, who ran a nursery for infants in north London, echoed Bodman's emphasis on resilience. They noted that children as young as two had some understanding of what was happening: knew that bombs knocked down houses and killed people, understood why one had to take shelter, and could even judge how safe a shelter was according to its depth. What children found difficult to understand and accept was being separated from their mothers. Although Freud had expected "traumatic shock" in response to air raids, something similar to the war neuroses of soldiers who served in the trenches of the First World War, she saw none. Like Bodman, she noted children's calmness and curiosity. She also made a careful delineation of what she regarded as normal fear and anxiety. This wore off if the child was allowed to ignore the threat and was not reminded of it by over-anxious caretakers. Indeed, she noted that after a week or so many children were bored or irritated by raids. She believed that the "quiet manner in which the London population on the whole met the air raids" was "responsible in one way for the extremely rare occurrence of 'shocked' children."

There were some disturbed children. Most of these were children whose mothers were extremely anxious, such as the five-year-old whose mother made him get dressed and stand beside her, holding her hand, as she trembled at the door whenever there was a raid. Or they were children who had lost fathers and for whom raids seemed to serve as reminders. But the most distressed and disturbed children were those who had been sent to the countryside for safety while their families remained in the city. "The war acquires comparatively little significance for children so long as it only threatens their lives, disturbs their material comfort, or cuts their food rations. It becomes enormously significant the moment it breaks up family life and up-roots the first emotional attachments of the child within the family group. London children, therefore, were on the whole much less upset by bombing than by evacuation to the country as protection against it."

Separation from the mother, even if she was not a very competent one, appeared to be far more damaging than living in the unhygienic squalor of bombed-out buildings and the London underground. "Our own feeling revolts against the idea of infants living under the condition of air raid danger and underground sleeping. For the children themselves during the days or weeks of homesickness this is the state of bliss to which they all desire to return."

Freud also paid attention to how children coped. Regressing to the behavior of a much younger child with thumbsucking and bed-wetting was common. Children played war games without fear, in imitation of their daily experiences, and Freud predicted that they would shift to peacetime games when the war was over. Their make-believe battles were different from the compulsive repetitive play of a child whose father had died. Like Bodman, Freud noticed that most of the children did not talk about their losses, or their frightening experiences, for months or even a year; then they might suddenly recount the events as if they had happened yesterday: "In all these instances speech does not serve as an outlet for the emotion which is attached to the happening. It is rather the other way round. The child begins to talk about the incident when the feelings which were aroused by it have been dealt with in some other manner."[2]

In 1949 Dr. Charlotte Carey-Trefzer followed up more than two hundred children who during the Second World War had attended the Great Ormond Street Clinic in London with any form of war-related distress. She noted that while air raids produced "the greatest number of reactions," it was evacuation without parents that created "deeper and more persisting damage." Like Freud, she found that the persistence of children's reactions to air raids related more closely to their mother's reactions than to the seriousness of the raids. For example, Sylvia was nine when her house was hit by a bomb and the whole family were buried while in bed. "The parents made no fuss; they all got out without major injuries. After that Sylvia showed general anxiety and was backward at school." However, the condition cleared up of its own accord after the family was rehoused. When Sylvia was seen eight years after the event, she had done well at school and had a good job. Sonja, in contrast, was four when a bomb fell behind her house. Her mother, always a nervous woman, was scared stiff, and Sonja wet the bed and stammered from that day on. When she was seen again her mother was still "highly strung," distressed by all that had happened in the war, and Sonja was "spoilt and self willed" and still stammering and wetting the bed.[3]

It appeared from these findings that children largely overcame the shocks and stresses of war if they were in the company of their mothers or other family members who were coping well. Children's own first-hand accounts of the Second World War seemed to confirm this. Dirk Van der Heide was a twelve-year-old schoolboy when the Blitzkrieg began in Rotterdam in 1940. His diary shows excitement and curiosity rather than terror:

> The air raid shelter was full of people, all our neighbors and some people I didn't know . . . Keetje [younger sister] began to

cry and father whispered something to her and kissed her and
she stopped. Finally she went to sleep in his arms. We waited
about two hours. At first most people thought the noise was
only practice. All the time people kept running outside and
coming back with news. It was war all right and the radio was
giving the alarm and calling all the time for all men in the re-
serves to report for duty to the nearest place. The radio said this
over and over. It was very exciting. The bombing kept on all the
time, boom-boom boom, and everyone said they were falling
on Waalhaven, which is only five miles away. [Later I] got up a
game with several other children playing soldiers and bombers.
We took turns jumping off the high back steps holding umbrel-
las and pretending we were parachutists but we had to quit this
because the grown ups said it made them nervous.

As the war continued, and as people he knew and loved began to
get killed, Dirk recorded his sadness and how "awful it is to watch
people standing by their bombed houses." He began to be afraid, particularly one night when his mother was absent: "I did cry some
while the bombing was going on but so many other little children
were that no one noticed me I think. I just got into bed with Keetje
and hid my face. I was really frightened this time." Then he learned
that his mother had been killed, and later the same night there was
another raid. Overwhelmed by his sense of loss, he found the next
raid much more frightening:

I can't believe mother is dead and that we will never see her
again . . . I cried almost all night and I am ashamed of what I did
in front of everybody. I tried to run away from Uncle Pieter after
he told me about mother getting killed. I tried to get out in the
street to fight the Germans. I don't know what all I did. I was
crazy. I was alright until the bombs started to fall around mid-
night and then I couldn't stand it. I know I yelled and kicked
and bit Uncle Pieter in the hand but I don't know why. I think

I was crazy. I went to sleep later but I don't know what time it was.

Dirk and his sister and uncle then made a terrifying escape through minefields, across the Channel to England, and when the Blitz started there, to New York. He recorded his nightmares about running away from bombing, his fears on the boats because he could not swim well, and his misery at the occupation of Holland. In school in New York he found it hard to concentrate and got poor marks. A doctor told him that he was nervous because of the bombing, but that he would get better with time. "Sometimes when airplanes go over I want to run and hide. One night when it was raining I woke up and heard the rain on the glass and was frightened. I thought I was back in Holland and that what was striking the window was pieces of bombs."

Though his uncle wanted him to forget the past, Dirk knew he would never forget about the war, "or forget the Germans and how Mother died." But in spite of his experiences and his acknowledged fear, one has no sense that Dirk regarded himself as badly disturbed or sick. Moreover he made it clear that the reactions of others were important to his well-being. He wrote of the moment when the battleships that had accompanied their boat to New York turned and left: "When the boats all turned back we could see how frightened everyone was. That's what made us frightened. We weren't frightened before." Then a Zeppelin appeared and accompanied them into the harbor "and people have been watching over us ever since and there haven't been any bombings. Not one. And that is why Keetje and I are happy now."[4]

The emphasis on children's resilience began to change in the 1960s and 1970s. Some psychologists writing about the conflict in Northern Ireland argued that children were facing psychological genocide, or that constant exposure to violence was producing a "lost generation" who would continue with violent and antisocial behavior when peace returned. Others argued that one had to consider context when looking at children's behavior—that, for example, although in England truancy was associated with later delinquency, high truancy rates might mean something quite different in an area where parents were afraid to let their children go to school. (In fact the rates of delinquency and crime were lower in Northern Ireland than in the rest of the United Kingdom and there was no indication that they were rising.) But while these authors argued about the long-term behavioral consequences of living with violence, there was still agreement that other psychological effects, such as fear and bedwetting, were short lived, particularly if the parents were coping well.[5]

In the 1980s the tone of the discussion changed: professionals began to talk about lifelong psychological scars and enduring symptoms in large numbers of children. Elissa Benedek captured this shift in mood when she wrote in the mid-1980s of "an inability for professionals to accept that traumatic events, caused by fellow humans, in the lives of children might color and shape their lives for years to come." Gone was the admiration for stoicism and lack of complaint that characterized the authors of the Second World War. Enter the new world where those who could not acknowledge their own pain and the hidden pain of others were in unhealthy denial.[6]

The shift seemed to be the result of a number of converging developments in psychiatry and the wider world. These included the "discovery" of post-traumatic stress disorder (PTSD) and its establishment as a legitimate diagnosis in the third edition of the American Psychiatric Association's *Diagnostic and Statistical Manual of Mental Disorders* (1980). The disorder was defined by four key components: a precipitating event, which had to be outside the range of normal human experience, such that it might produce an abnormal reaction in anyone; recurrent memories of that event; physiological arousal such as jumpiness and increased alertness; and avoidance of memories of the event through an emotional shutting down called numbing. Remembering could take a number of forms: nightmares, vivid and intrusive thoughts, or the feeling of reexperiencing the event as if it were happening again (flashbacks).[7]

PTSD was the only disorder in the manual for which there was a specific precipitant that had to be present before the diagnosis could be made. Its inclusion was in part the result of powerful advocacy on the part of psychiatrists working with returning veterans from the Vietnam war. They felt that the standard classifications of personality disorder, depression, anxiety, psychosis, and substance abuse did not properly encompass their clients' experiences but left them stigmatized, alienated, and even more vulnerable to "self-medication" with drugs and alcohol. Those advocating the inclusion argued that in fact PTSD had always been around. Charles Dickens, for example, had suffered "rushes of terror" and what today would be called flashbacks after surviving a serious railway accident. The "shell shock" and "combat stress" of the world wars, and the more recently discovered "survivor syndrome" in which some Holocaust survivors found themselves depressed and anxious, cut off and emotionally constricted, with frequent nightmares, could all be reframed as PTSD.[8]

PTSD appeared at a time when biological psychiatry was gaining importance. The discovery of effective medications for previously untreatable mental conditions led to calls for more rigorous, standardized methods of research to establish the existence of specific diseases and the validity of treatments. PTSD lent itself easily to formulation by means of a symptom checklist: patients who could check off the appropriate number of boxes had the disorder; those who could not did not. Meanwhile the new cognitive psychologies provided explanatory scripts both for the failure of memory processing and for its treatment. The cognitive model suggested that the brain, unable to assimilate terrible events, somehow became stuck in replay mode, continually revisiting the events. This state of responsiveness to remembered catastrophe was painful, so the mind tried to shut down, hence the emotional numbing and forgetfulness. The attempted repression was not always successful; flashbacks and intrusive memories could break through, especially if there were triggers to the memory such as particular sights or sounds, hence the avoidance of such reminders. Therapy would depend on helping the patient confront the memories and assimilate them.

The newly defined affliction of PTSD began to frame both public and professional responses to disaster. Meanwhile, increasing media coverage of deadly events both publicized the diagnosis and allowed people far from such an event to feel emotionally connected to it. In Britain, when a crowded football stadium in Bradford caught fire in 1985, millions watched the fire on television and identified with the families of those who died. The emergency services used the term "post-trauma stress" for the first time and set up an outreach program to offer clinical help to survivors. Within a few years the term was well established, and media reports of catastrophes routinely included the phrase "professional counselors are in attendance." This sent two messages: first, help was at hand; and second, the televised distress was a matter for professional assistance. The professionals were available: a new field of "traumatic stress" studies had emerged with its own society, journals, and scientific papers; and there was now a "social movement" of specialists—psychologists, social workers, and psychiatrists—who wanted to both understand and assist the victims.[9]

Globalized television brought global disasters. Now not only the shocked survivors of stadium fires or sinking ferries but the civilian victims of war moved into living rooms around the world as staples of the TV news. This was particularly true of the media-accessible Balkan wars. Civilians were increasingly the deliberate targets of late twentieth-century conflicts, and PTSD became a recognized medical consequence of civilians' exposure to violence.

By the mid-1990s PTSD was regarded by Western professionals and public alike as a serious psychological disorder, and as the most likely response to a wide range of traumatic and stressful events. The suggestion was that it was often unrecognized, even by the sufferers themselves, because of repressive reactions in the victims and avoidance of distress on the part of carers. This needed to be overcome, as PTSD required early intervention involving some kind of re-exposure to the traumatic event, through talk or play, in order to prevent life-long damage. Children were considered to be among the most vulnerable: UNICEF stated in its yearbook for 1996 that millions of children had been psychologically traumatized by war in the previous ten years and that (without treatment) "time does not heal trauma."[10] By the end of the 1990s most large humanitarian agencies had trauma programs. In most conflict and post-conflict areas of the world one could find mental health professionals using symptom checklists to assess the level of pathology, training local residents to identify PTSD, and setting up counseling services to encourage the working through of feelings. Psychological trauma and its treatment often appeared to take precedence over other medical and material problems.

"Surviving under what is arguably the most draconian embargo in modern times, trauma which could usually be expected to lessen with time is intensifying because of hunger and deprivation. Iraqi children have given up playing games because the games remind them of dead playmates," Felicity Arbuthnot wrote in the *Guardian* in 1994. Note that she did not suggest that the lack of interest in games might be due to hunger, although she continued: "In July 1993, the UN Food and Agriculture Commission noted with deep concern the prevalence of several commonly recognized pre famine indicators." Having pointed out the damage that sanctions and consequent malnutrition were doing to Iraqi children, she ended, not with a plea to lift sanctions or to provide more food aid, but rather with "All Iraq's children need counseling so that normality and childhood can be restored."[11]

In Sarajevo during the siege in 1994 there were seven NGOs running counseling programs. *You know 80 percent of our psychological problems would disappear tomorrow,* a weary social worker told me one day, *if you could persuade your government just to lift the siege of the city.* Unfortunately, counseling programs are much easier to achieve than changes in political policy. A focus on individual psychopathology allows for spurious professional neutrality, creating the illusion of attending to need, while avoiding advocating other social and political interventions that might have a direct impact on the collective mental health of the community.[12]

In recent years a chorus of dissent has arisen challenging the hegemonic position of PTSD in defining the well-being of survivors of political violence. The voices are disparate and not always in harmony with one another. Some come from within the psychiatric profession itself, arguing that the diagnosis lacks specificity and has not as yet proved to have a distinctive biological profile or effective treatment. They challenge the need for what they argue is just a repackaging of aspects of other diagnoses, such as the ruminations of depression, or the arousal of anxiety and panic disorders, or the avoidance that occurs in phobias. Others worry that the preoccupation with PTSD and trauma programs leads to neglect of other serious mental health problems in war-affected areas.[13]

Anthropologists and historians have suggested that PTSD could be seen as a culturally specific response to the needs of a particular group at a particular time. In many periods and places, moral responsibility for disaster and catastrophic evil could be placed outside the individual by means of explanations based on witchcraft or religion. In the secular world of Europe and America today, they point out, PTSD has a significant role to play in creating moral order. It allows victims to identify and place the source of suffering outside themselves, and to be compensated. For those whose victimhood is questionable, the diagnosis can be transforming. Thus for Vietnam veterans returning from a war that their own community regarded as morally dubious and in which they themselves may have been perpetrators, the diagnosis turned them into soldier/victims, just as de-

serving of compassion, treatment, and compensation from the state
that had sent them to war as the victims of natural disasters or terrorist actions.[14]

Meanwhile, the diagnostic concept has expanded. The fourth edition of the American Psychiatric Association's diagnostic manual
(1994) no longer requires the events to be outside the range of normal human experience. Now, simply, the suffering individuals should
have experienced, witnessed, or been confronted by a catastrophic
event that threatened them or others they knew with death or injury
or damage to their physical integrity, and they must have reacted
with a subjective feeling of intense fear, helplessness, and horror. The
new criteria allow for an even wider use of the diagnosis, and the dividing line between what is appropriate human responsiveness and
what is pathological has become even harder to determine. The word
"traumatized" is on everyone's lips after every event from the loss of a
pet to an earthquake, but no one is clear about what it signifies.

This is even more the case when humanitarian organizations ex-
port the concept abroad, particularly to countries disrupted by war,
where families and communities have broken down and normal culturally protective practices such as appropriate mourning and burial
of the dead cannot take place. Never mind that in the local culture
the manner in which intense feelings such as fear or sadness are expressed may be quite different from that in the West, or that ideas of
how to deal with pain and suffering may not involve the ventilation
of feelings or the sharing of intimate histories with professional
counselors. In this situation people will borrow what is on offer, especially if the framework is one that will gain significant attention
from aid-providing organizations. PTSD has become a signifier not
just for the whole realm of psychological suffering after a disaster, but
for suffering as a whole.[15] This was brought home to me at a conference in Sarajevo in 1996, when a psychiatric colleague, visiting for the
first time, mildly suggested that rates of PTSD might not be very

high. *How can you say that?* a local doctor responded in rage. *Have you any idea what we suffered in this city?* It was as if to suggest that residents did not have PTSD was to impute that they had not had terrible experiences, or were not sad, angry, grieving, and suffering.

There is no doubt that symptoms of PTSD can be identified in a wide variety of situations all around the world. Yet one cannot assume, just because symptoms are present, that they have the same meaning to each person experiencing them in every situation.[16] Indeed it seems rather strange to assume that children who survived the sinking of a ferry boat would make sense of their experiences in the same way as children who lived through ethnic cleansing or bombardment. Nor does it seem likely that war experiences will have the same meaning to children whose families are on opposite sides of a conflict.

All these children might experience intrusive recollections of the events, might have nightmares and difficulty concentrating in school, but some might regard these symptoms as "an understandable response to tragic occurrences," as the child psychiatrist Steven Weine discovered when he interviewed Bosnian teenagers who had survived ethnic cleansing and emigrated to the United States. Although these young people had vivid and intrusive memories, "they did not view having these memories as being abnormal or pathological but as an understandable response to tragic occurrences." Nor did they regard themselves as victims of isolated singular traumatic events but of a collective assault on their people. They were enjoying their new lives, liked by teachers and others, and doing outstandingly in school. The political meaning they gave to their traumatic experiences, and their sense of collective identity, meant they did not regard their symptoms as a problem.[17]

Psychiatrists working in the occupied territories in Palestine found that the most common symptoms in children exposed to house demolition and shelling were "identifying the event as 'extremely stress-ful,'" difficulties in sleeping and concentrating, and "avoiding re-minders" of these sorts of events. These children were also frightened of high, dark, and closed places, afraid that things would collapse, as well as frightened of things they knew could not hurt them. Children living in safer areas had more "symptoms of anxiety." Most com-monly they felt alone even when in company, they worried much of the time, and they worried when going to bed at night.

Might these responses be defined as the "normal fear and anxiety" reactions observed by Anna Freud in the London Blitz? The research-ers thought not. Although in studies of the impact of the earlier Inti-fada these same authors acknowledged that high rates of symptoms dropped dramatically in peacetime, by the time of the study quoted above, they regarded these high symptom rates as indicative of clini-cal psychopathology.[18] On this basis they would certainly have diag-nosed Dirk Van der Heide as having severe PTSD. We do not know how the Palestinian children themselves made sense of their fears and feelings. Might not staying awake, and being afraid of high, dark, closed spaces and collapsing walls, be entirely appropriate, and in-deed possibly lifesaving, responses when your home is at risk of be-ing demolished by a tank? It does not seem surprising that children find such events stressful and have trouble concentrating, or that others living in safer communities but watching what is happening to their neighbors on TV feel lonely and worry more than usual, espe-cially at night. Is it helpful to define such responses as mental illness?

What is significant is that a substantial proportion of the Palestin-ian children in this study had relatively few symptoms of psycho-pathology, even in the middle of a prolonged conflict, living under curfew, subject to daily deprivations, rarely able to attend school. Fig-ures vary in different areas around the world, but in most studies conducted after conflict, 50–80 percent of children do not have many psychological symptoms. The presence of a new diagnosis, more "scientific" methods of measurement, and an emphasis on vulnerability and illness rather than resilience and coping has not removed the old question, posed more than fifty years ago: Why do some children who live through terrible and horrifying events come out unaffected while others suffer badly?[19]

One thing that matters as much in today's conflicts as during the Second World War is family. The discoveries of Freud and Carey-Trefzer have held true: having family around you helps, if the family members themselves are coping.[20] But to some questions there are still no consistent answers. Do older children find it harder to cope, or do they do better than younger children? Do boys suffer more than girls, or less? Does being exposed to more violence make children more likely to be unwell (the so-called dose effect)?

As soon as one pays attention to where and how a child lives, contradictory findings begin to make sense. For example, the first Intifada may have given girls from a normally restrictive and patriarchal society a chance to take on new roles and gain status, and this may have actually improved their mental health. Boys, in contrast, may have suffered from the lack of structure, rules, and supervision, and so may have had more behavioral problems. Younger children may have tended to stay home, and therefore to have been more protected.[21]

Meaning matters. Psychological trauma cannot be looked at as a mechanical event, equivalent to a bullet hitting bone, where caliber, velocity, and bone strength can predict the amount of damage. Children are not the passive recipients of experience. They are actively engaged in making sense of their environment, and acting to change it, from an early age. They gather meanings from what is around them, first from their parents or caretakers and then from the world beyond—friends, school, community—as well as from their own previous experiences. War touches every aspect of children's social world, including their history and values. The changes in sense of identity, feelings of trust and security, and connection to others that I found in the Bosnian children may have a profound impact on well-being. They may not manifest themselves as "symptoms" that can be counted, but rather as "ways of living" that have to be observed and discussed with the children themselves.

9

Day after Day

War is no longer declared,
but rather continued. The outrageous
has become the everyday. The hero
is absent from the battle. The weak
are moved into the firing zone.
The uniform of the day is patience,
the order of merit is the wretched star
of hope over the heart.

—Ingeborg Bachmann, "Every Day"

I heard some shooting when I woke up one morning. I asked my mum "What's happening?" and she told me that the war had started [. . .] When it got dark, me and my family ran away to a safer place. When we got there my father had to go and fight against the Chetniks [. . .] He visited us just one night. They told us that my father had been killed a few days later. That was so hard for me, and also the house we lived in didn't have any windows or doors [. . .] A shell hit the kitchen one day when all of us were inside. There was so much dust we didn't know where we were. But anyway we stayed in that house. There were thirty-one of us living there. Eight shells hit the roof of that house. There was a basement where we hid. We stayed four months and then we came back home. That was the happiest day of my life. The war went on for another four and a half years. Peace coming made no difference to me. But I was free to go to school.

—Fourteen-year-old boy, Gorazde

I feel very sad, because I have seen frozen children in deep snow.

—Thirteen-year-old boy, Gorazde

War, unlike plane crashes and hurricanes, continues day after day. In Bosnia it went on for four years, and many children experienced a whole series of catastrophic events, one after the other. We know from children's accounts of other wars that different kinds of events have quite different effects.

Krystyna Stankiewicz, who lived in Lodz, Poland, began a diary in 1941 when she was five and a half and kept it through the next four years. There were bombings, round-ups, and shootings of civilians, but as a small child in a kindly, extended middle-class family she was scarcely touched by these events and recorded them in a matter-of-fact manner: "22.6.41: We had a boat ride on the Vistula. We have started a blackout because of the War. We are frightened of bombs." Her main preoccupation was food. "26.10.43: Twenty people have been shot. We are laying in stores for the winter." But then her mother was arrested (carrying money for the resistance). "19.1.45: Mummy will not come back till after the war: the Germans have taken her to Germany. We miss her terribly and I cry all the time." Krystyna became depressed and irritable, although she went on getting good marks at school. The theme of missing her mother came up in every diary entry until the war ended and her mother was released.[1]

R. J. Street, who was a teenager in London during the Blitz, recorded in his diary the excitement of his first air raid: "The gunfire was very heavy, and when it was some way off we watched it and saw it disperse the planes. It was raining shrapnel and after the raid there were scores of children scouring the place for souvenirs." One month and 110 raids later, after four raids in one night, he wrote:

> I told mum to duck and she dived under the table, but I did not have time to do so, so lay flat on the floor to be out of the way of the glass, but the first landed some way off, and we were ok. I got under the table for the second, which whistled even louder. And landed 150 yds away, it must have been a big one . . . The continual strain and all these bombs near me and those 2 while I was

out made me let down the good reputation of my fellow Londoners and I was horribly sick. I was not very well for some time after.[2]

If a child loses his home, his father gets killed, and he is crowded into inadequate shelter and repeatedly shelled, a symptom checklist cannot sort out the specific effects of these different events. Yet in discussion children can make subtle distinctions between different feelings and explain how these fade, change, or endure over time. I wanted to see if children did have symptoms, so in addition to asking children to write stories, I gave out symptom checklists measuring trauma, depression, and anxiety to 334 children aged thirteen to fifteen, more or less equally divided between Gorazde and Foca.[3] I then chose forty children, equal numbers with high and low levels of symptoms in each town, and had long conversations with them and with many of their parents and teachers. (The school psychologists assisted with the mechanics of the selection process so that I could avoid knowing whether a particular child had high or low levels of symptoms when I did the interviews, so that I would not be biased toward looking for distress in some children.) In this way I gained a picture of children's well-being both in symptomatic terms and on the basis of their own and their parents' understandings of how their experiences had affected them. I also used nonverbal tools such as asking children to draw a lifeline, and I administered a questionnaire to record the quantity and details of their violent experiences.

The first surprise was that equal numbers of children in both towns felt unwell two years after the war, no matter how well-being was assessed. Given that Gorazde had suffered far more violence during the war than Foca, it appeared that interpretations of experiences were just as important as the dose effect.[4] Second, the girls had higher symptom scores than the boys in both cities, yet when well-being was assessed on the basis of interviews there were no gender differences. Girls were not sicker; they simply found it easier than boys to acknowledge symptoms in questionnaires. In almost a quarter of the children I interviewed, checklists and interviews produced contradictory results. This suggested a problem with trying to define well-being simply in terms of the presence or absence of symptoms. You could end up labeling children as sick who thought of themselves as well, and missing children who did feel unwell but did not express that feeling in symptomatic terms.

Their perceptions were subjective and retrospective. Sometimes the importance and meaning of an event shifted from one conversation to another, as did the amount of detail recalled, suggesting that children's current lives and concerns were important in framing their understanding of their war experiences. However, some distinctive patterns emerged.

Losses

The greatest disaster that could happen to children was to have someone close to them injured or killed. Death and injury, including extraordinary near misses, came up again and again in the written stories and were often the most precisely recalled events. More than half (27) of the children I interviewed had lost a close friend or relative during the war. Many had fathers who had been injured, most of them on the front line; the children had enduring and vivid memories of being told about these events. Sometimes they could recall all the details of a relative's injury or death as if they had witnessed it (see Dusan's account of his brother's death in Chapter 2).

Very often these losses were multiple. A fourteen-year-old Serb girl had lived in Sarajevo at the beginning of the war, then her family had fled to Foca because of the shelling. She wrote in her story: *I sat in the car and cried. I was looking at my house for the last time.* Then she heard that an uncle (her mother's youngest brother) had been killed. *Everyone was crying, especially my mother, I was with her, we cried to-*

gether. Her father joined the army, and later he came to see them in Foca.

> *He was in a good mood. I remember he taught me how to sing some Serbian songs, as if he knew it would be his last night in his apartment. The sun shone the next day. I was in my room getting ready for school. Suddenly someone was banging on the door. Mother opened the door and saw my uncle was crying. He said to her "R. is dead." It was my father. I heard my uncle's words. I fell on the bed and started to scream. I cried as much as I could. My mother cried also. Our neighbors asked what happened. My uncle told them. We went to the funeral. My mother and grandmother fainted and it seemed to me that everyone was spinning around me. When the funeral was over we went home. I did not leave home for three days. A week passed. One rainy day I was returning from school. A friend of mine ran up to me and told me my mother had gone in tears to my aunt. I dropped my bag and started to run as fast as I could. I arrived. Everyone was in mourning clothes. I asked my mother what had happened. My uncle had committed suicide. I asked her "But why?" Mother told me: "Because of your father." Those were our worst moments.*

In the Gorazde stories there are frequent accounts of shelling and shooting, but almost always this is background detail to the loss or injury of someone the child knows. The stories bring home the relative significance of these events. It is the loss that is upsetting and remembered. A thirteen-year-old boy wrote:

> *My friend and I were playing marbles; our parents went to my grandma. We had only two marbles and we played. The bullets whizzed around us, but we didn't want to leave the game because it was interesting. We played for half an hour and then we came in-*

doors because the shooting was very strong. One shell hit our building a few minutes later and the mother of one of my friends was wounded and her father was killed. The second and third ones hit my room where my bed and my comic strips and other games were. When I came into the bathroom I saw my friend lying down without his hand. Then I went out and called some people to help him.

Five of the children I interviewed had lost immediate family members, and four of them were actively grieving two to six years after the event. They responded and coped in very different ways. Sanela remembered the exact hour when her uncle called and told them her father had been killed by a grenade. She went to the hospital with her family and saw that he was dead, but at first she still thought he would come back, so she was not upset. It took two weeks for her to understand. After that she cried a great deal and was very sad. She stayed indoors all the time, watching the funeral from a window. Later she visited his grave, but the visits had to stop when Serbs took the territory.

The sadness was enduring. When I interviewed Sanela six years after her father's death she still felt it intermittently, although she could not always pin down the cause. Sometimes she forgot he was dead and then remembered suddenly. Sometimes she felt he was watching her. Although she could conjure up happy memories of her father, which she found comforting, she also had frequent unpleasant dreams about both him and the war. She dreamed of people being killed; that would wake her suddenly. The dreams frightened her and sometimes stopped her from wanting to sleep, so she would watch TV until she felt better. Her appetite was poor, she could go two or three days without eating, and she sometimes felt frightened without any reason.

Sanela talked freely about these difficulties, and in spite of them she was doing very well in school, with consistently high grades. She had friends and was able to talk about her father with them and her family, although she did not always want to. She found that the best way to feel better when upset was to visit a friend and play on the computer. Her mother, despite complaining of loneliness and worries about money, came across as a warm, practical woman who had made a cheerful home.

The atmosphere in Edin's flat was quite different: immaculately tidy, sparsely furnished, and cold. His father had been shot in the first weeks of the war and their own house completely destroyed by shelling. Edin's mother initially refused to allow him to be interviewed, worried I might label him as disturbed, when she felt he had *no problems*. She herself seemed immensely sad and very tense. Any remarks about her loss were brushed away with a reference to fate and the will of God.

Edin was polite, nervous, and monosyllabic in interviews. He was almost in tears as he described how his father had been shot by a sniper on the line early in the war. They had all cried when his mother had told him, and he had been unable to sleep. He had gone to the funeral, and they were able to visit the grave, although that made him cry, and his mother had said *If you cry you won't go*. He still cried whenever he thought or talked about his father, but he tried to avoid doing this as it made his mother cry and he wanted to do anything he could to stop her being upset.

He was now the man in the family and had responsibilities. He had also lost a cousin his own age and his grandfather, both from shelling. He missed all of them. Like Sanela, he sometimes forgot his father was dead and thought he might come walking in, and he too had comforting memories. Sometimes he felt angry. He insisted he had no problems, although he was doing badly in school, and his marks worried him a bit. His way of coping was to play the accordion his father had bought. He had avoided it at first, then found he enjoyed it and was quite good.

Helena's father was killed in the first weeks of the war (see Chapter 6). Immediately after his death she asked her mother to promise never to marry again and then did not talk about her father again. This was in spite of her mother's encouragement to do so, and in contrast to her little sister, who mentioned him a lot. Tense, argumentative, and perfectionist before the war, Helena cried for weeks after the death, and became irritable and difficult, refusing to help in the house, saying her house was in Sarajevo. However she was getting top marks in school.

She cried when she talked to me about what had happened, and told me she preferred not talking, as she was a very private person. Her mother respected this but worried about her, and was still very depressed herself. She felt very isolated in Foca and worn down by the need to work hard and appear strong for the children. She too cried through our interview, saying she wished she had more real friends in the town.

Dusan had suffered the most recent loss; his brother had died in the last year of the war. His feelings of sadness, emptiness, and desire to identify with his brother are described in Chapter 2.

The sadness of these four children was compounded by their parents' feelings, and in the case of the two boys, by a need to take on new roles in the family to compensate. The two who had talked about their dead relative with friends or family were managing best. Although they cried when discussing the death, they were otherwise cheerful and articulate and open about their feelings. Helena's desire for privacy seemed in part a way of differentiating herself from her mother, but it came at a price, as did Edin's stoicism. None of these children regarded their feelings as indications of ill health; they viewed them as what should be expected when you lose someone you love, and a familiar home, in a war. All felt they were slowly improving with time.

Interestingly, Dusan and Helena both denied having any symptoms whatsoever when filling in the symptom checklists. For Edin, however, the safe space of an anonymous checklist was the only place he felt able to express how bad he felt. Besides appearing unwell throughout our conversations, he had the highest symptom scores of any boy in Gorazde, with marked feelings of depression and PTSD— yet he insisted to me that he felt fine.

Do you feel that you shouldn't have symptoms and that's why you say you don't? I asked.

Yes, he answered very quietly.

All four felt they were coping. They had found ways to deal with sadness when it overwhelmed them, mostly through the distractions of physical and intellectual activity, games, and friends. They all wished that there were more recreational activities for young people in their towns, and that their parents had easier lives, but they all rejected offers of additional psychological assistance, and although I regarded all four as unwell it is unclear that giving them a pathological label such as clinical depression or PTSD would have benefited them in any way. On the contrary, it might have further stigmatized them at school at a time when they were all desperate to fit in. It seemed more important to reinforce the normalizing strategies that three of the families had adopted, of open communication if it was wanted, and respect for privacy if not; and to encourage such strategies in the one family where they were lacking.

Witnessing Death and Injury

One fourteen-year-old Serb girl wrote of being captured by Muslim soldiers with her family (the site was not named but was almost certainly Josanice). She woke up to find her house on fire: *What is the feeling when you wake up and find you are burning and dying?* She and her family got out, but she saw her best friend lying with her throat cut, alongside the friend's younger brother and sister. She could see they were not quite dead. The soldiers took her family's money and released them after some hours. Whenever she was reminded of the event she dreamed that *I am in their hands but this time they won't let me go . . . then I wake up with a wet face.* However when awake she rarely cried because she felt her own losses were small compared with those of others. Even so she often saw *pictures, sounds, voices crying, pictures of dead bodies [. . .] The graveyard reminds me a lot, those pictures on the monuments . . . names . . . But I don't complain. I have my mother, father, brother, the most important in life. I have those who love me, but I would erase the memories if I could.*

Children who had witnessed death and atrocities usually continued to have vivid and intrusive memories. Elvira in Gorazde had bad dreams almost every night. She lived in the center of town where the bombing had been intense, and she had seen a number of people die. Three soldiers who had taken shelter in the anteroom of their basement were hit by two grenades:

> *They got stuck on the door because they were rushing forward looking for help, so there were three of them, you know, on the door. And my mother just got close and she didn't know whom she would help first. And the man she was laying down next to S, his face it was totally gone. He was probably turned toward the door, so he got one piece off on his face. And when he started bleeding the blood came right out on us. And my mother just threw something like a blanket over us, so we could not see that. And he was asking for water and my mother wanted to give him water. She got lost again because she didn't know how to give him water because this man didn't have a mouth anymore [. . .] Later my father arrived and they brought a car for this guy. They couldn't put him on the wheelchair because he was completely full of holes. He was really screaming and we really got scared.*

That same night another neighbor was killed in the same spot: *I came down to the basement with my mother and I was holding a candle for her, and this woman was asking my mother to take her belt away because it was too tight around her waist, and when my mother tried to do that, this woman didn't have a stomach at all.*

On another occasion a grenade narrowly missed Elvira and hit three of her friends. Two died instantly. She stood frozen staring at her third friend until a car came to take them away. *She didn't have her leg and her head was completely bloody. I couldn't see which part was which mostly [. . .] I just stood and she cried. I heard "Help me, Father, it hurts here, it's painful here and there."*

She told these stories calmly, saying that she had never cried, at least in the daytime. Yet she continued to dream about these events almost nightly and wake up afraid and in tears. Often it would be the same event but with mother, brother, and sister in the place of those who had actually died. She was frightened of the dark, and her mood was very up and down, depending on how she was getting along with friends and at school. She also had some of the highest scores on the symptom checklist.

Elvira and the Serb girl had had experiences of a particular intensity that seemed to contribute to painful and enduring symptoms and resulted in both children feeling unwell. Strong sensory stimuli such as smell, sight, and sound are thought to be associated with more intrusive traumatic symptoms.[5] But not all children regarded intrusive memories as indications of illness. Nina could not forget the frozen dead man she had passed on her journey over Grebak. Narcisa had memories of the mutilated bodies she had had to step over in the street. She wrote: *Now, when it's peace, I always see the picture of the cut-up bodies when I pass by this place. I think that I will always have that sight in my memory. I hope that we will never have war in our country again, because this war was enough. The consequences of the war will never be wiped out. Four years of suffering and worry are over but we shouldn't forget them!*

Both Nina and Narcisa regarded their memories as isolated occurrences that were decreasing over time and had no impact on their general well-being. Narcisa clearly also felt she had a duty to hold on to some of the memories because they might inoculate her against future war. Many children in both towns wrote of the wish to forget and the difficulty of doing so, but Gorazde children also wrote of a duty to remember: *I remember a lot of things from the war which I wish to forget but my conscience does not let me,* one wrote. And another: *I am trying to forget everything, and also, I am trying to remember it in some way [. . .] Although I do not tire myself with memories, because I want to know about everything else happening in the world, because I lost enough time in four years.*

Shelling

The greatest difference between the two towns was in their responses to shelling. Gorazde had been shelled intermittently for four years and at times the bombardment had been so ferocious that residents had to stay in their basements for days. Yet most children in the town did not regard shelling as their worst experience. They seemed to go through the same cycle of adaptation that Amela experienced (see Chapters 1 and 2).

The initial reaction was of curiosity or even excitement. This was followed by fear as they learned that the explosions could kill and injure. Almost all the children I talked to remembered being frightened during the early stages of bombardment. Elvira told me *I didn't know what it was, at all. And later when I was a bit more grown up, we wanted to go out; we just didn't want to stay in the house. But when some people died in our basement, then we got scared.* Later the children felt more confident: *When we heard the sound of the grenade flying above us, we just kept playing because we knew it was flying over us, that it was not going to . . . but when they fired the grenades—you hear when they fire it—and when you don't hear that sound any more you just lie down, because you don't know then where it's going to fall.* And finally there was the boredom that had reduced Narcisa and her brother to counting the grenades (Chapter 2). This indifference often put children at risk, as when Nina and her sister, wanting to collect water in town in spite of the danger, were nearly hit by a shell. Feeling vulnerable partly depended on how intense and close the bombing was and how personally exposed they felt. Nina was most frightened when two shells landed close to her in the fields; Elvira saw soldiers and her friends killed before her eyes.

Many of the children found the shelling toward the end of the war more frightening, because by then they had heard stories of what happened to Muslims in towns taken by Serb forces. In 1995 most of them had some idea of what had happened in Srebrenica. Nedjad told me *All of them were saying they would take Gorazde as well. I thought the same. I was sure that Gorazde would fall. I was afraid, really afraid that they would catch us and the same thing that had happened in Srebrenica would happen to us.*

How did you cope?

My brother and I stayed in our room. He's older, and he kept telling me "It never will happen, not to us." But I was sure he knew . . . that would be the end. Mother told both of us "It will never happen." She told us in any case whatever happened we wouldn't be separated, we would stay together.

As in the London Blitz, children felt safest in shelters with people they knew, with people who did not panic, and when they had games to distract them. One mother told me it had been hard to get her children to understand that if they were caught in a raid it was better to take cover with strangers than to try to run home. As children still often tried to get home, parents would go out to find them and make them safe wherever they were. How parents themselves coped mattered. Armin's mother said that during the 1994 offensive she had lain awake every night, terrified that the town would fall. *I just thought how I will kill first the children and then myself because I didn't want the Chetniks to take us alive.* She knew her children were aware of her fear: *They noticed the difference and they knew everything.* Armin told me *We got used to it. But I was always on guard.*

Some children never grew accustomed to the shelling and remained frightened all the time. Either these were children like Edin—who had already lost his father and who said *It was awful; it was very bad; I was afraid; it was always hard*—or they were like Iris, who shared her home with relatives who had escaped from Foca. Her aunt, who had been detained for a year, told her terrifying stories of young girls being raped. Iris lived one street from the Serb line in Gorazde and endured periods of intense shelling throughout the war. Every new bombardment felt threatening: it would kill her directly, or the town would be taken. Unable to sleep, she imagined that Serbs would come into the basement to slaughter them, or that something undefined but terrible would happen to her. *Nothing was as bad as that. I mean you were waiting all the time, you were so tired, and finally you lay down, and then you heard grenades again . . . I really longed for sleep.* It was no better at school: *you went to school if the shelling was less. There were sandbags under windows as some kind of protection. But the lessons were so short I didn't have time to learn anything. All I could think about was whether I was going to stay alive.*

She described one raid:

> *It was a Bosnian-language lesson and I was actually answering a question, when by chance I heard something coming down. I don't know why we thought the bags on the windows would help us, but . . . we all just jumped through the door of the classroom. You can imagine how it was with the whole school rushing out of all the classrooms. There was panic and screaming, crying [. . .] You didn't think of other people in these moments, you just thought of yourself, how to save yourself [. . .] We just lay on top of one another: all the other pupils were on the floor. You know how it feels: you hear the glass breaking in town, the shooting, grenades, then you just shake because of all those explosions [. . .] I prayed, and I tried to hug myself, to make myself feel better. I didn't think of talking to anyone. I cried a thousand times, I could lose my life a thousand times.*

In contrast, Foca was bombarded only briefly at the end of the war, when NATO's aerial attack destroyed the town's bridges. The bombing began abruptly and continued for a few days. Many of the children in Foca did regard this as their worst experience, but not all were frightened. Those who believed the bombing was targeting them were scared; those who understood that the bombing was aimed at military targets were not, even if they did not know why they were being bombed. Jovan took refuge with his parents in the cellar. *I didn't know exactly what it was for, and I still don't know. I didn't feel so secure, but I don't know how to explain, I wasn't scared [. . .] We didn't think they would bomb civilian targets, I knew I wouldn't be hurt because they didn't have anything to shoot at here. They were just destroying bridges and some military buildings.*

Nikola's apartment was close to the bridge, and a piece of shrapnel flew in through the window close to his head. *I didn't cry but I was out of it. I closed my ears, I didn't talk at all.* He believed they could *all be destroyed.* A fifteen-year-old girl wrote: *Everyone was in a panic and they did not know what was happening.* Not surprisingly, she was *screaming and crying.* She went on: *My fear was so great it took over my body bit by bit. Our building had no shelters, so we were terrified and expected the worst.* However, as in Gorazde, even in this short period children adjusted. The same girl added: *The other days were also awful, but not like the first. It was as if we got used to it and it became part of our life.*

Most of the children who believed the NATO air strikes would endanger them had parents who shared this belief. Helena's mother told me she was terrified because she was convinced they would bomb people as well as bridges. Helena had the same fear: *I thought they would drop bombs on the lines and the Muslims would come into our country. They would send us away somewhere.* Bojan's mother was scared, his grandmother was crying, and his aunt was worrying about her nephew out in the town. Bojan grew more and more frightened as the night went on. There were also some children like Svetlana, who was accustomed to her mother's chronic anxiety and so was unaffected by it. It was almost as if her mother's worry about the bombing made it less threatening, because her mother worried about everything.

Most children used forms of distraction to cope with the bombardment. They played with toys or friends, or talked. Like the children in Anna Freud's nursery, they were uncomfortable only if their parents drew their attention to the shelling, as Amela's mother did on occasion (Chapter 2). But some, like Iris, found the shelling impossible to ignore. In the first year Elvira coped by blocking her ears, humming, and rocking herself. Similarly, a thirteen-year-old girl wrote:

> When there was shelling I had to cover my ears with my hands and everyone made fun of me because of that, but even if I tried not to, I couldn't stop. It was as if I had some radar that connected to the shells, so that I had to put up my hands and cover my ears whenever I heard the whistling. I know it's strange but even now I can't listen to the sound of planes, the sound of a helicopter, or thunder, I have to cover my ears. It's automatic.

Being Uprooted

The effects of evacuation and displacement depended on where children went, why they went, and with whom they lived. Few of the Foca children were separated from both parents, because in that town evacuation was organized in advance of the fighting. Children usually traveled with their mothers to relatives in villages or to Montenegro or Serbia, so that it felt little different from holiday or weekend trips in the past. Only children like Ivana and Tatiana, sent away from their parents to relatives in Belgrade, missed their families and found it hard at first. *The worst thing that happened to me was being separated from my parents,* Tatiana told me. *When I was in Belgrade I couldn't wait to come back, I missed them so much.* But after a time the pleasures of living in a big city compensated for the loss, and both girls found it difficult to return to Foca.

In Gorazde the war took families by surprise, and many children suddenly found themselves left with grandparents. Fikreta wrote about how it felt:

We stayed at our grandparents' house for four years. Our parents couldn't visit us because the roads were controlled by the Serbs. I cried often because there was a lot of shooting there [Gorazde], so I was afraid something could happen to my parents. We spoke to our parents after a long time by an army radio operator. When I spoke with them I started to cry as soon as I heard their voices. Days passed, I was sad, and nothing could make me happy.

Living in relative safety and being with her grandparents could not make up for her fears about her parents' safety.

Senad, in contrast, was sent with cousins and an aunt to Spain. He found the journey and his life there so exciting and interesting that it compensated for missing his parents. On arriving in Barcelona, he felt like a hero: *When we came out of the airplane people had gathered as if they expected some president, and they all applauded us and waved to us and we waved to them. Everything was so comfortable. Then we caught a bus, and there were so many people in the street, trying to see what was happening, as if it was someone very important.* The Spanish took trouble with their housing and food, keeping groups of Bosnians together. Senad was fascinated by everything and made Spanish friends. He kept in touch with his parents by ham radio. The hardest time was when he thought they were in real danger. He cried after Srebrenica fell: *We prayed to God not to have the same thing in Gorazde, because we really wanted to see our parents again.* Nina, evacuated with her mother and sister, found parting from her father incredibly painful, but still thrived in her new life in Germany.

Two years after the war a third of my interviewees were still displaced inside Bosnia, and their feelings about this depended very much on the security and attractiveness of their current accommodation. Svetlana was simply waiting for the next eviction, and missed her old home in her village a great deal. Milica and Radmila both liked their new homes in Foca much better than previous village life. This was partly because of their conviction that "Turks" now hated them so much that they could not live together again (see Chapter 6). It was also because city living meant no sheep to mind, friends nearby, and a short walk to school. For Divac, the provincialism and unfriendliness of Foca contrasted unfavorably with Sarajevo, and the insecurity of his family's accommodation made things worse. Even so he insisted that he had adjusted and would not want to return to the city. Surprisingly, with the exception of Helena, it was native-born children in Foca who seemed less well. It was as if the displaced Serb children were determined to make the best of it and, perhaps, to show me that leaving the Federation had been good for them.

In Gorazde, Samir had no desire to go back to the now half-destroyed house in which his family had been like prisoners. He preferred sharing one room with his family in a collective center until they could get something else. He said he had horrible memories every time he went near their old house. Sanela, though, wanted to go home to her village in Republika Srpska, perhaps in part because it was closer to her father's grave.

Domestic Events

Even horror is relative. Some children were quite clear that particular events in their personal lives far outweighed the misery caused by the war. Amela's life with her violent and alcoholic father meant that the coming of war was something of a relief, because her father went away. She regarded 1994, when Gorazde suffered the worst offensive, as *the best [year] in my life*, because her father was on the front line, while she used her wits to help take care of the family and developed a close friendship with her mother. It was her father's return and his continuing violent behavior after the war ended that resulted in her attempt to kill herself by taking her grandmother's pills. Nina regarded her parents' separation at the end of the war as *more catastrophic* than the siege. For a brief period she lost weight, cried all the time, and had suicidal thoughts, none of which had happened in that first terrifying year of war.

Children made clear distinctions between the different and sometimes contradictory feelings produced by different events. All of
them, in both communities, saw death or injury of family members
or friends as the worst thing that could happen. The impact was
enduring, and was exacerbated if the child witnessed the event.
Shelling frightened most of the children. But the fear was less if the
bombardment could be interpreted as nonthreatening and if it became routine.

In Gorazde, where the whole community had been exposed to sustained violence, there did appear to be a dose effect: children who
had experienced more violence felt less well two years later. In Foca,
where there had been less violence, the dose effect was if anything
reversed. The displaced children, for the most part, had been more
exposed to violence in places like Sarajevo, but it was local children
who felt worse two years later. Children's personal interpretations
were more important.

For all the children, their subjective sense of safety seemed to
matter more than the objective threat or how often danger occurred.
Aerial bombardment that is intense and unexpected may feel much
more frightening, even when of brief duration, than shelling that has
become the background to daily life, unless one is reminded of one's
vulnerability by a direct hit. Domestic violence and the breakup of
family relationships can directly disrupt a child's security in a manner that more objectively dangerous events do not.

There were specific patterns of responses. Losses, especially of
close relatives, were more likely to result in persistent sadness and depression. Bombing and seeing someone injured or killed produced
immediate fear, nightmares, and intrusive imagery in some children.
Yet these "traumatic" symptoms did not provide a guide to longer-
term well-being. There were children like Nikola, who were extremely frightened during the bombing yet had no symptoms and
felt quite well two years later. Narcisa's flashbacks of bodies in the
street were fading with time, and she felt happy and secure in her
current life and did not regard such memories as an indication of ill

health. Samir, who felt more insecure and fearful about the future, interpreted his memories in a more negative way and did see himself as unwell.

Children's memories of events and responses to them were not fixed. They shifted according to individual mood, what was going on in the community, and what purpose children thought the narration served. Ivana presented the NATO bombing as frightening in her written story: *I wanted to sleep, but it was impossible, because planes were buzzing the whole night. I was really scared so I got close to my mother. I was wondering What will happen to us? Will we stay alive? I lost my grandmother in the war, so I was afraid I might lose somebody else from the family. I didn't close my eyes until almost dawn.* But in her interview she did not mention the bombing at all; instead she focused on her Muslim friend Asra, and on witnessing Muslims being forced into prison. When I asked directly about the NATO bombing she said *I was not afraid then, I knew they wouldn't bomb us.* However her mother believed she had been frightened and remained affected, and told me she still had a slight startle reflex to planes. I was with Ivana one day when NATO planes were flying overhead and saw no reaction at all. When I commented on the planes, she shrugged and laughed, saying they were boring.

Jovan told me that one of his most disturbing experiences was seeing dead bodies in the river, and that the picture came into his mind whenever he passed a particular spot on the bridge. In his first interview he said they were Serb bodies. A few weeks later he told me he thought they were Muslim bodies and clearly found this in some ways more upsetting, remarking spontaneously: *I saw people who are not my nationality, I'm talking about dead bodies. But it stresses me when I think how somebody could do that.*

I am not suggesting that there is one true version of events in either Ivana's or Jovan's case; rather that the details and emotions children remembered as significant two years later depended partly on the circumstances in which they were asked to remember, and who was asking. Ivana, when asked by a stranger from a NATO country ("the aggressor") to write about the war during class, understandably emphasized the negative aspects of the NATO attack on her community and remembered the moments of fear. Many of her classmates did the same in their written stories, often using the formal and rhetorical language of adult public discourse. In interviews, as Ivana got to know and trust me, she focused on more personally significant events, such as her Muslim friend's experiences, and she remembered amusing details of the bombing. Jovan's ideas about the identity of the bodies in the river seemed to shift as there were arrests of war criminals in the community for actions against Muslims and as there was more discussion in Foca about Muslims returning.

In exploring the effects of the children's experiences of war, I had discovered two things. First, specific events could produce quite specific feelings, but were hard to relate directly to longer-term psychological ill-health (except for personal bereavement). Second, there was some kind of dose effect, evident in children in Gorazde, but there had to be other reasons for feeling less well in a post-conflict society, because in Foca the least exposed, native-born children were the ones who felt less well. I would have to look at the way in which the children made sense of the conflict as a whole.

10

Making Sense of Madness

Why were they attacking us? I always asked myself why. What reason could there be for this war which has given us so much pain and a scar on the heart that will never heal? I always ask myself that.

—Fourteen-year-old Muslim girl, Gorazde

Why was the war so cruel to us? Why did we have to experience this fate? These are the questions of the youngsters who lost their happy childhoods and their parents. We survived this war which left only graves, ruins, and sad memories. We try to get back to a normal life and to forget all the terrible things that happened. Why does it have to be that way? We still ask the same, same questions, even when we know they are difficult questions to answer and that no one tries to do so.

—Fourteen-year-old Serb girl, Foca

In 1942 seventeen-year-old Ina Konstantinova ran away from her home near Moscow to join a partisan unit and work as a saboteur behind German lines. Formerly a rather moody and restless girl, she wrote in an undated diary entry that year:

I have found my niche; here I am among friends. I am at peace with myself, and I'll definitely return victorious, but should something happen to me—believe me, I'll die honorably. This is how we all feel. Already many hardships have to be endured, but you should see me running about carrying out assignments . . . In short "life is beautiful and wonderful!" Today the Germans carried out as many as four air raids against our village. The bombing was awful and their machine guns gave us a good thrashing. The bombs exploded about 70 meters from us, and bullets whistled above our heads (I lay in a ditch). But you see—I survived. Consequently nothing will ever happen to me; I believe this wholeheartedly.[1]

In contrast, fourteen-year-old Yitskhok Rudashevski, confined in the Vilna ghetto with his family, wrote in his journal for June 24, 1941:

Our hearts are crushed witnessing the shameful scene where women and older people are beaten and kicked in the middle of the street by small bandits . . . Tears come to my eyes: all our helplessness, all our loneliness lies in the streets. There is no one to take our part. And we ourselves are so helpless! . . . We are so sad, so lonely. We are exposed to mockery and humiliation. A new feeling of terror frequently overcomes the few neighbors of the yard. They are looking for weapons. The courtyard is full of Germans. There is a ring, the door is torn open and all hearts are pounding. Germans in helmets rush in, their weapons resound. Meekly the cupboards and drawers are opened to them. Cruelly they fling everything apart, fling, throw, go away and leave behind them a sad house with things scattered all over. We stand around with pale faces. We calm ourselves only when we learn that they have left. The mood becomes worse from day to day.

But Yitskhok's mood changed completely when a school opened and he joined a club that did "ghetto research" to document the details of ghetto life. On October 5 he wrote: "Today we go to school. The day passed quite differently. Lessons, subjects . . . There is a happy spirit in the school. Finally the club too was opened. My own life is shaping up quite a different way." And on December 10: "I decided not to trifle my time away in the ghetto on nothing and I feel somehow happy that I can read, develop myself and see that time does not stand still as long as I progress normally with it . . . I do not feel the slightest despair."[2]

Both Ina and Yitskhok died in the war. When Ina's unit was surrounded by German troops she sent her comrades toward safety and covered their escape with machine-gun fire. Yitskhok and his family went into hiding after the Vilna ghetto was liquidated in 1943, but they were discovered and murdered in the slaughterhouse at Ponar.

What comes across from these young people's writing is their ability to endure horrendous and terrifying events because of their capacity to actively engage with those events and give their own lives meaning. Ina can find life beautiful while being shelled, and can deny the obvious risks because she has an active role in confronting the perpetrators. Even within the meaningless, brutal, and squalid confines of the ghetto, Yitskhok's helplessness and despair lift when he is able to study and decides to record and make sense of what is happening around him.

Being able to give meaning to one's experiences appears to be protective, both when terrible events are occurring and afterward. A comparative study done in 1969 of Israeli children living in two kibbutzim showed that those who had been exposed to bombardment were no more anxious than those whose kibbutz had not been shelled. The researchers believed that this was true not just because children had accustomed themselves to shelling and so no longer saw it as threatening but also because of their perceptions of their own role in confronting it. The Israeli media had portrayed them as brave and heroic, and this praise, combined with the kibbutz ethic of mutual solidarity, lessened their anxiety.[3]

Situations and the meanings given to them can change. In the late 1980s and early 1990s, black youth living in townships in South Africa were exposed to extraordinary amounts of violence on a daily basis. According to surveys done in Alexandra Township in both 1987 and 1992, more than 74 percent had witnessed an assault and more than 67 percent a killing. Many had been subject to arrests, evictions, and intimidation. Yet when residents were interviewed and asked if they saw the violence as a problem, their answers changed from 1987 to 1992. The majority of young people interviewed in 1987 did not see it as a problem, while in 1992 the majority did. All regarded the violence as something abnormal, but in 1987 the youth saw it as positive because it was part of the liberation struggle with "clear political objectives and thus imbued with transcendent meaning." In 1992 they "no longer saw the violence as having a clear political objective" and felt unhappy because they saw the state as having deliberately stirred up internecine violence. It was the changing political context and the way young people interpreted what was happening in their community that determined how distressing they found the violence to be.[4]

Many researchers, working in different parts of the world, have found that active engagement in or ideological commitment to political struggle seems to protect children from some of the psychological problems that can arise from exposure to political violence. In the first Intifada of the late 1980s, Palestinian children who participated often showed greater stress at the time of involvement, because of their greater exposure to the violence. However in the period of peace that followed the Oslo accords those children who had participated had more self-esteem and looked back on the violence as less significant, while those who had been passive had more psychological difficulties. Developmental age played a role as well. Palestinian adolescents, who could view themselves as freedom fighters, coped better with police attacks than younger children who lacked the cultural knowledge to adopt an ideological position.[5]

When it came to interviewing the children of Gorazde and Foca I expected to find something similar. I thought there might be a relationship between the different ways children made sense of what had happened to them and how well they felt. I thought perhaps those who had the clearest, most "ideological" views, and who could provide themselves with explanations for the conflict, would feel better than those with none. But it was not that simple.

For a start, the majority of children had no overt ideological position. In both cities *I hate politics* was a common response, and children had a very negative view of politicians. When I tried to get Svetlana to tell me what the word "politics" meant, she responded *Awful [. . .] nothing [. . .] it just disturbs people.* Nikola said *Somebody always wants to destroy somebody. In my opinion it is not good, I don't like politics, and I am not interested in that.*

Many children showed very little interest in questions like *How do you make sense of what's happened?* or *How will you explain this war to your own children?* They did not want to talk about the meaning of the war at all. As discussed in Chapter 5, either they did not know and did not want to know, or they had explanations but made clear when they shared them with me that the topic was boring. In both towns it was the children who kept their distance from the conflict and avoided looking for explanations who felt psychologically well and secure. They were focused on their personal lives, good marks at school, friendships, sports, and the latest videos. The children who were curious about what had happened, who asked questions and did try to make sense of it all, were the ones who felt less well. Perhaps not surprisingly, this engagement in a search for meaning also had other costs. The engaged children disliked politics, but this did not stop them from being "politically sensitive." They were much more knowledgeable about current events than the distanced children, and more worried about the prospect of a future war.

The parents of the engaged children reported that they picked up on items of the news and asked questions like *Does that mean the war will start again?* In interviews these children also spontaneously mentioned current local or national political events that concerned them. In Gorazde this included issues like the city becoming an open town and the rumors that Gorazde might be "given up" to Republika Srpska if there was a partition of Bosnia. In Foca it was worry about the possibility of war in Kosovo, or the fights within the Republika Srpska political assembly. I had the sense that these young people were spending at least part of their time scanning their environments on the lookout for threats.

These distinctions between distanced and engaged children and the relationship to psychological well-being were true for both towns. However (as noted in Chapters 5 and 6), there were other characteristics of both the distanced and engaged children that seemed to relate to the community in which they lived. In Gorazde whether children were distanced or engaged was associated with how much violence they had experienced. The distanced children were those who either had been in a safer part of the enclave, and thus exposed to less shelling, or had actually been out of the country as refugees. In Gorazde the refugee children were also among those who could be seen as least patriotic. They were not interested in fighting for their country in another war, or necessarily in living there in the future. Distancing in Gorazde also allowed for a more dispassionate, less partisan view of the conflict than that held by their more engaged and less well contemporaries. Distanced adolescents attributed responsibility for the war more evenly to both sides, and they had no problem with the idea of Serbs returning to live in their town. What worries they did have centered on school and exams; they were mostly less aware of current political events, felt safe, and did not worry about another war.

Nedjad, for example, who had spent the war in the relative safety of a small village where there had been little shelling, was one of the few Muslim children to express complete empathy for Serb children in his written story: *I know many children from Republika Srpska who lost their dearest. They will suffer forever as well as children in BIH.* On two separate occasions I asked him how he explained the war and each time his response was *Hmm . . . I don't know.* Nor was he interested in finding out. Although he acknowledged some symptoms in the checklist, he was one of the children for whom that method of assessment appeared to be misleading. It was clear in interviews that he was completely well, enjoying his life, doing well in high school, and planning to go to university.

In contrast, the children engaged in searching for meaning in Gorazde were those who had experienced the most violence. They tended to regard Serbs as more to blame for the conflict, a few of them were more ambivalent about Serbs coming back, and they felt much more anxious about the prospect of a future war.

Samir, whose story of his family's imprisonment in their own house is told in Chapter 1, had had some of the worst experiences. On the checklist he acknowledged having numerous symptoms, such as feeling frightened without reason, tense, panicky, and nervous, feeling sad, tearful, and worthless, having recurring memories of the imprisonment, feeling very jumpy, and avoiding places that reminded him of his experiences. In interviews both he and his parents said he had become more fearful, withdrawn, and lonely since the war. They were concerned enough to be seeking help.

When I asked Samir how he made sense of the war, he was engaged and animated. He saw Serbs as responsible for the conflict: *Everything started because Serbs hated Muslims [. . .] Serbs hated Muslims too much [. . .] they wanted to have Bosnia [. . .] so that Muslims wouldn't be there. They wanted to have only Serbia.* At a later point he told me he was confused about Serbs and politics and there were things he still could not understand. He wanted to know *Why did they hate? Why did they want that? Why did they want to rule?* Being able to answer these questions would help him come to terms with his experiences. He was uncertain how he would respond to Serbs who came back to live in Gorazde, and he felt a bit insecure because it had been made an open town.

In Foca I could not distinguish between distanced and engaged children on the basis of how much violence they had suffered. They had all experienced significantly less violence than Gorazde children. However they did differ in their attitudes to the return of Muslims and in their ideas about who was responsible for the conflict. In contrast to Gorazde, it was the psychologically well and distanced children who were most against Muslims returning and most convinced that Muslims were primarily responsible for the war. It was the less well children, those who were searching for explanations, who were more evenhanded about responsibility and more open to the possibility of living with Muslims again. Radmila and Liljana illustrate the contrast.

Radmila had not had a good war. She had fled with her family from a mixed village near Gorazde, been caught between the lines, moved back home repeatedly, and been frightened by NATO bombing (see Chapter 6). However, she reported no symptoms on the checklist, felt completely well now, and appeared to be so, enjoying her life in the farmhouse near Foca. She had no interest at all in the reasons for the war.

Did you ever wonder yourself why it happened? I asked.
No.
You didn't think about it?
No.
Do you have any explanation?
No.
Do you wonder at all?
No.
What do you think the war was for?
I don't know.

Radmila was convinced that living together again was impossible because Muslims hated her. But she had no worries about the possibility of a future war. She did not think about it.

Liljana's war experiences were not as bad as Radmila's. She lived with her father's extended family in a large house built by her grandfather. Both her parents worked in business. She spent the first four months of the war in Serbia with an aunt. Her worst experiences of the war were worrying constantly for her father on the line, missing *friends who left,* and *bad living conditions.* The NATO bombing frightened her as her home was close to the bridge. They all spent a night in the cellar and then retreated to the woods for the second night. Fortunately, no one in her family was killed.

Two years after the war I found her to be one of the most unhappy girls whom I interviewed. She could not sleep and had frequent bad dreams, although these were not about the war. She said she ate too much, cried all the time, was worried, irritable, tense, and restless, and thought quite often of ending her life. She felt that these symptoms had nothing to do with her experiences in the war but arose from her life now: the atmosphere and living conditions in Foca, the stress of her first year in high school, where her marks were poor and the workload felt overwhelming. She thought she had got in with the wrong crowd of new friends. In her story she wrote eloquently of her wish to understand what had happened, her sadness at missing her old friends, and the current mood of the city:

> *War. Why war? I was always wondering that, but I never got an answer. Maybe I never understood why something awful like that happened, because I was still a child, but I know that it marked me in some way. Four awful years, spent in fear, pain, grief for those we lost and for the nice childhood I never had. Wishing for fun, company, games, joy in everything that makes life beautiful, but unfortunately there was none of that. God, I'm wondering why is the world so cruel, why dark forces made our destiny and brought the greatest misfortunes to children who are not guilty of anything.*
>
> *It was very difficult to part with best and dearest friends who*

had to go somewhere else and to leave their homes. Even now, after the war, it is not so nice or great. We all miss many things, we're all somehow depressed, tense, nervous, but it's like that and we have to carry on living. The most important thing is that people didn't die for nothing, and the rest will come with time. Even I know that to get back to the better life before the war, it will take a lot of time.

She would have liked some explanations. When she was young she had pestered older people and eavesdropped on her father's conversations when he was home from the line, but she had not understood what she heard. *Now nobody is giving me answers,* she said, and she had stopped asking because of the fatalistic view that *What happened happened. We can't change anything.* But it was clear from her story and our conversations that she puzzled over it all. She read voraciously, *serious books* such as Vuk Draskovic's *Noz* (The Knife) that she hoped would provide explanations.[6] *I want to read to find out how was it in previous wars, how people felt, how they survived.* She watched television and had discovered that *The war is over but nothing is solved. Everybody wants to come back to where they lived before. A lot of people died and it seems it was for nothing. Because there was a lot of talking and it seems that we will still live together again. Not now, but maybe in a few years.*

Like many of her contemporaries in Foca she felt this made the war itself meaningless: *A lot lost their homes, and in the end it seems to be for nothing, to live together. What was the purpose of the war?* Given the sadness she had expressed about friends who had had to leave, I pushed her on this topic, and like Vesna (Chapter 6), she was clearly ambivalent and uneasy about the contradictions in the situation. Her explanation for the war was

We all wanted to be in power. Muslims wanted their power. They wanted us to be under them. Not in the real sense like it was before once under the Turks. In one way they wanted to be in power to

*have authority. And just in one way we wanted the same. But I
think the other nationality, Muslims, wanted that more, Croats,
and because of those political conflicts, war came. They just could-
n't agree with each other, and that's why we decided to live separately. So that everybody could rule their own people.*

But she felt that separation was *not good,* and when I asked what
should happen to those who wanted to come back she paused for a
long time and then said *If they think it will be better for them, it's their
decision. Whoever wants to, he can come back, but in that way, we will
all be mixed again.* She thought people who had lost someone would
mind.

Would you like your old friends back?

Another long pause. *Yes, I would . . .*

So it's a contradiction, I started to say, and she interrupted: *Not so
much . . . because a lot has changed. But I would like them to come back.*

Even though she thought the lessons for the future were clear—
*There is no need to create hatred between people because they are all
people of flesh and blood, it doesn't matter that we are different nationalities*—she was very pessimistic about anyone being able to learn
from experience. And while she hoped people would come back, she
knew *We won't be happy.*

Will you be happier living separately? I asked.

I don't know, no.

So you're stuck then?

Exactly.

It is worth noting that after I discussed this same theme with
Vesna, who expressed similar confused ambivalence about the forced
separation and living together, she became slightly physically unwell.
She and her mother talked with me about whether this might have
been a result of the interview, because Vesna had not thought or spoken of these matters before and the conversation had upset her. They
then decided it was a "summer allergy." As she recovered quickly and

wanted to continue, we did meet again without ill effects, although I avoided difficult topics in the second interview.

My findings contrasted with those of many studies of children in other countries: in Bosnia the children who avoided looking for any meaning and distanced themselves felt psychologically more comfortable than those who tried to make sense of things. Looking for meaning was associated with psychological distress. So what was going on?

For the children described at the beginning of this chapter, the search for meaning led to active participation in the conflict and to greater self-esteem. In the ghetto in Vilna, Yitskhok Rudashevski began to feel less helpless and frustrated when he found an active way to challenge his circumstances by documenting them. Ina Konstantinova was active in the war as a partisan, with every minute of her life taken up in pursuit of a goal. South African and Palestinian children have lived through years of low-intensity conflict where active engagement means actual participation in demonstrations. In contrast, the war in Bosnia was a prolonged high-intensity conflict, in which children had little opportunity for active participation except in sharing the tasks of basic survival.

In both towns the children had to endure long periods of anxiety about close relatives on front lines and about the threat of being attacked. In addition the Gorazde children endured actual shelling and siege for nearly four years. After the war, both groups of children lived in relatively unstable political environments: Gorazde was a Muslim island within the Serb-controlled Entity; Foca was at odds with the international community monitoring the peace accords and suffered the consequences. The presence of the UN Stabilization Force (SFOR) throughout the country was a constant reminder of the war.

Both groups of children also lived with the legacy common to all post-communist states: disenchantment with and alienation from politics, and a belief that politicians are corrupt and self-serving. And they were old enough to remember that the upsurge of political activism in their country in the early 1990s had been a prelude to war. They had no models of effective democratic political activism, or clear targets against which to act. Families on both sides talked of feelings of unimportance and powerlessness.

In this context it was not surprising that activism and ideological commitment did not present themselves as effective means of coping. Rather than searching for the meaning of a conflict they could not control, many children focused on friendships and on personal achievement, such as good marks at school, sports, or music. Meanwhile the unwell children, who were engaged in looking for meaning, paid the price of a certain political sensitivity and awareness of threats to their security. Because of their powerlessness in the face of these threats, this sensitivity led to feelings of discomfort, which led to more alertness and more discomfort. Children who are sensitive to their political environment without being able to take action can find themselves as many described: sad, anxious, and restless.

Other studies have found that looking for an explanation of stressful events does not always prove helpful. In the fall of 1980, at a school soccer game in southern Illinois, a lightning bolt hit the field, knocking down all the fifth- and sixth-grade players and killing three. Steven Dollinger, a psychologist at Southern Illinois University, decided to look at the children's explanations of the disaster, and how these explanations related to their emotional upset. He expected that certain kinds of meanings might be more protective than others. What he actually found was that those who gave any explanation of what had caused the disaster were much more upset than those who gave none. The content of the explanations did not seem to matter. Some blamed chance, some an act of God, some the team itself for wanting to play in poor weather. It was those who stuck with "I don't know" who had fewest emotional difficulties. Dollinger speculated that there were two possible ways of understanding these findings.

First, that the search for meaning follows from the degree of upset: those who were the most upset were those most in need of explanation. Alternatively, that the meanings themselves led to becoming upset. Both theories made sense to me in southeastern Bosnia.[7]

In Gorazde, where children were exposed to years of shelling, it looked as if being more upset resulted in a greater need for explanations. Some (though not all) of the children who suffered more of the violence felt unwell; consequently they were more engaged in trying to make sense of what had happened. They thought about questions such as "Why did they want to kill me?" "Why can't I go home?" and "Who was responsible for destroying my home?" There were no easy answers, and plenty of nagging questions. Why were those identified as war criminals still at liberty? When could Muslims with homes in Republika Srpska safely return there to live? Posing unanswered questions does not bring psychological relief. In addition, their political sensitivity and insecurity made the prospect of living with returning Serbs, some of whom they saw as the aggressors, more alarming. Not surprisingly, they were more ambivalent about doing so, and more partisan in attributing blame. The Gorazde children who had been more protected from the violence were less troubled and more secure. They felt more distanced from the conflict and did not need to look for explanations, because the war had caused them less distress.

Seeking explanations had a different significance for children living in Foca. Here it looked as if it was the search for meaning that led to distress, rather than the other way around. For some children, searching for meaning increased their sense of victimhood and isolation. In some stories the writers explicitly stated that the feeling that the world was against them had made the bombing of the town particularly traumatic: *The world was on their side and that's why many people from Republika Srpska are traumatized by NATO bombing.* Similar feelings echo through the unhappier texts:

Now I am here in Srbinje but I don't feel good. I am with Serb peo-
ple, our brothers, but nothing can change my childhood. The war
stole everything I had; it took my lovely cousins and uncle [. . .]
Why did war happen? That question will never get out of my head.
And I still wonder does Bil Klinton know how it is for us and what
he did to us. The whole world is always against us, everybody is on
the BIH side. They were always on their side, during the war and
now when it has stopped. They simply want to destroy us Serbs.
They want to eradicate us.

This girl's essay ends on a note of proud and lonely bravado, telling
the world to leave us alone, because no one will *choke* the Serbs and
God is our only hope. However, she will *never forgive anyone* or reconcile herself to the fact that she *cannot go home* to Sarajevo. One has no
sense that her ideological commitment to the Serb cause has helped
her come to terms with her losses. Instead, her interpretation of
events has increased her feelings of abandonment and threat.

For some in Foca, trying to make sense of what had happened in
the town led to an awareness of injustice. These "engaged" children
were more open to the possibility of living with non-Serbs again, and
less partisan about who was responsible for the war. But their search
for meaning also exposed them to uncomfortable truths about their
own community, which contributed to their psychological discomfort. So Liljana felt *stuck* because Muslims' return would make non-
sense of Serb suffering in the war, but she also missed her old friends,
was unhappy with her new ones, and felt as a basic principle that
people should be able to live with one another. Svetlana had no explanations for what had happened, but she wanted some. She did not
blame anyone, missed her Muslim friends, and wanted them back.
She too had been nervous, restless, and irritated since the war ended.
She told me that things were not right because of *changes here since*
the war. I didn't feel like this before.

Children who chose to ask questions about what had happened in

Foca had to make sense of the sudden disappearance of large numbers of people; visible destruction in a town that was not shelled; parental silence; large spaces where mosques had stood that nobody mentioned; sudden arrests by international troops; and the depressing, stagnant nature of the community. These questioners were mostly children who had been born in Foca, and all made frequent references to how unpleasant the town had become. Marko told me *It's not as it should be,* although he could not explain why. Tatiana, who had spent much of the war in Belgrade and had looked forward to returning to Foca, said *Everything is going wrong.* She disliked the atmosphere in town. At school she was so stressed by the workload that she thought of abandoning everything. Many native-born children identified living in a neglected and isolated community, worrying about school marks, and missing friends as their worst problems. Possibly there was greater pressure to do well in school in Foca, because scholastic achievement compensated parents whose side had lost the war and gave children a way out (through university) of an unhappy living situation.

While the search for meaning in Foca could result in children's developing more moderate opinions, such views had a cost. They put these children at odds with the dominant public discussions in the town, where both political leaders and popular opinion as expressed in the local media accommodated themselves to (and even celebrated) the results of ethnic cleansing. Those children in Foca, like Susana, Milica, or Radmila, who avoided examining such issues avoided any such conflict and had better individual psychological health. They were enjoying their lives and doing well at school.

Near the end of my time in the Drina valley, in the summer of 1998, Samir and his family decided that he should visit a traditional healer, a well-known woman who lived in a large apartment block near his house. She agreed that I might come with the family to learn about her methods, and so I spent an afternoon with Samir and his parents in her small, overheated apartment while she *took away his fear*. It was overheated because the stove was full on in the middle of summer in order to melt a fist-sized lump of metal. Once it was molten she cast it into water and examined the pattern it made: a complex web of loops and whirls, all tangled together. *That indicates a great deal of terror*, she told Samir. Samir, wrapped in a blanket and sweating profusely, held the water and the iron and looked at the mountains outside the window while she said prayers over his head. Afterward he drank some of the water, and the remains were cast away in a particular place far from his home. The session took an hour. At no point did his therapy involve any discussion of what had caused the fear. It was simply named and symbolically removed, both digested and thrown away.

When the session was over Samir looked different. The tension had gone from his face and he seemed genuinely cheerful and relaxed. These feelings continued over the following weeks, and when I repeated the symptom checklists he was almost symptom free. He felt much better. He was not frightened anymore. He said that if some of the fear came back he would just return to the healer. A Serbian girl in Foca, who had suffered nightmares and sleeplessness after the NATO bombing, also wrote of seeing *a woman who helped me and got rid of the fear,* which suggests that the tradition was common to both communities.

None of the other unwell children wanted individual psychological assistance, although I offered to put them in touch with professionals in their towns. What they thought would make a difference was better living conditions, stable places to live, or the possibility of returning home. They wanted more things for young people to do, like computers, movies, and clubs. They wanted to see their parents less stressed by poverty, unemployment, and grief. They wanted old friends back, more understanding and supportive teachers in school, an end to corruption, reparations, the arrest of war criminals, and security. The children knew that their recovery did not depend on individual therapy but was intimately bound up with the recovery of their social and political communities. These responses and choices have made me question the conventional approaches of the humanitarian aid community toward war-affected children.

It would be unwise to make generalizations on the basis of a study of a small group of children in one war zone. However there are possible implications that deserve further thought.

First, trying to understand the psychological impact of a war only through a symptom checklist may be misleading. It may result in the unnecessary pathologizing of children who are well, while those who feel unwell but cannot express this as "symptoms" may be missed. The only way to find out which symptoms matter is to ask children, and to spend time with them.

Second, war is long and complicated, and different events will affect different children in different ways. The dose effect—how much and how long—does seem to matter when the violence is severe and prolonged, but so does the children's interpretation of what is happening: How threatened did they feel? Were they frightened for their own lives, or for someone they loved? But overwhelming fear and the appearance of traumatic symptoms at the time of an event do not necessarily predict longer-term psychological distress. A researcher working in the Bosnian city of Tuzla at a time when the city was regularly bombarded found that 94 percent of the 364 displaced children he examined met criteria for PTSD as set out in the fourth edition of the American Psychiatric Association's *Diagnostic and Statistical Manual of Mental Disorders*. However he suggested that in that particular context high levels of symptoms might be adaptive.[8] I also found that children who had been badly frightened during shelling or bombing were fine two years later. The enduring impact seemed to be more closely related to how personally disruptive the event had been: What had happened to their family and friends and the landscape in which they lived?

Thinking in terms of personal disruption helps to explain the enduring effects of loss. Children who lost fathers and elder brothers had their whole worlds torn apart. This was especially the case in Bosnia, which is a patriarchal society in which families organize around male leadership. Young boys like Edin were pushed into more adult roles and given no space to grieve. Girls like Helena felt completely cast adrift. It also makes sense of the very varied effects of displacement. Local Foca teenagers, who wanted to get away from homes they no longer recognized, felt more unwell than those determined to adapt to new circumstances. Radmila was happy to start afresh in an attractive new house with her family around her. Tatiana was miserable returning to a town that had changed beyond recognition. The disrupted past was closer because the reminders in the form of uninhabited ruined buildings and empty spaces could still be seen.

Third, for some children there are some things worse than war. Again thinking in terms of personal disruption may explain why. Divorce and domestic violence can completely undermine a child's immediate world, while, as Amela's experience showed, war may actually be a liberation from abuse.

Fourth, the difficulties of living in a politically isolated and materially neglected postwar community such as Foca may well outweigh the effects of bombing and shooting. Two years after the war ended there were more unwell children in Foca than in Gorazde, although Gorazde suffered much more violence during the war. The facts that most of these Foca children were more alienated than their contemporaries in Gorazde, and that half of them wanted to leave the country, suggest that the misery created by ethnic cleansing affects not only those who are driven away but also those who remain behind. The disruption of the town, the arrival of large numbers of new people, combined with a change in its name, left many local families feeling like strangers in their own community. Foca-born young people like Liljana and Svetlana made clear their sensitivity to this mood.

Fifth, the fact that for some children, in some situations, distancing is an effective means of coping challenges widely held assumptions about the psychological impact of stressful events. It suggests that we might do well to pay more attention to avoidance as a constructive rather than pathological coping mechanism.

Much therapeutic endeavor today is based on the premise that all stressful experiences should be explored and reexamined in order to be assimilated. Some of those working with children have suggested that all children exposed to stressful events should be encouraged to reexamine the events at an early stage, and that in order to "foster mastery" of the associated distressing emotions the therapist should "overcome the efforts of the child to avoid and deny" what has occurred. Children can then be helped to a more realistic understanding of the event, reassured about their own responses, and educated as to what may occur in the future.[9]

Although the term is not always used, this is one form of "debriefing," a method of front-line psychological assistance that has become increasingly fashionable in recent years. In their essence, debriefing methods involve group work in which all those exposed to a stressful event are seen shortly after its occurrence. There is encouragement of emotional ventilation and exploration of what happened to gain understanding, combined with the provision of information and social support. This approach has been used indiscriminately with whole communities exposed to a particular event, on the assumption that it will avert later psychological disability.[10] Results with young people have been mixed: with some it has increased their distress; with others it has been shown to decrease unpleasant intrusive symptoms. However, a growing body of research suggests that debriefing is ineffective, and in some circumstances harmful, resulting in an increase of distressing symptoms. This may particularly be the case with those whose coping methods rely more on avoidance.[11]

There is some research suggesting that more avoidant methods may be protective. Hanna Kaminer and Peretz Lavie studied long-term coping mechanisms in Holocaust survivors who had either been in concentration camps or spent long periods in hiding. They found that one group rarely talked about their experiences even with their close families. They had not forgotten these experiences, but they avoided thinking of them and had successfully repressed the unpleasant feelings of helplessness, anxiety, and depression they had felt at the time. This was particularly evident in sleep. They slept well and found it hard to recall their dreams. They were well adjusted, had a positive outlook on life, were neither defensive nor easily aroused, had few physical illnesses, and were doing well in work and personal relationships. Those in the less adjusted group, meanwhile, were flooded with memories in the form of traumatic symptoms during the day and nightmares and sleep disturbances at night. They were more anxious and depressed and had far more physical complaints. They were also much more sensitive to their daily environments, particularly any aspect that could be seen as threatening. The researchers suggested that the ability to seal off memories of past atrocities and limit remembrance could be adaptive and that therapists should explore this possibility.[12]

Displaced people in northern Angola, who have suffered four decades of war, advise those in their community who are bereaved and suffering to "abandon the thoughts and memories of war events and loss," accept the inevitability and universality of death and suffering, and get on with making a new future through the creation of new families. Bosnian Muslim culture similarly encourages stoicism in the face of disaster and loss. I was often told by more religious families of the importance of not expressing too much distress about death, as this might upset the dead. Mourning is expressed through formal and gender-divided rituals.[13]

Nerma and her mother invited me to a tevhid to say prayers with other women for Nerma's grandmother a month after she died. I had seen few tears but watched Nerma spend a whole day cheerfully scrubbing her grandmother's house in preparation. Avoidance may sometimes have a cost. One man told me that he had never cried over his twelve-year-old daughter's death because parents' crying over children filled the grave with tears and prevented the children from being happy in Paradise. For the same reason he preferred not to talk about his loss. This man suffered from intermittent chest pain, and we agreed that his heart "ached with grief," but he wanted me to find solutions other than the ventilation of emotions, solutions that did not run against the grain of his faith.

I should make clear that distancing is not the same as the clinical concept of denial, in which the conscious mind actually denies that events have happened. Kaminer and Lavie pointed out that the well-adjusted Holocaust survivors were not denying their experiences and had not forgotten them. Similarly, none of the Bosnian children who distanced themselves from the conflict denied the events or pretended that painful aspects had not taken place. Most of them volunteered quite detailed descriptions of their personal war experiences, and were animated, and sometimes visibly moved, in doing so. However their normal choice was to avoid seeking explanations for the past. In addition, all were actively engaged in normal life, had plenty to say about it, and were functioning well. This was quite different from one of the children from Gorazde who had been exposed to a great deal of violence and could be described as "in denial." Although he had been in Sarajevo during the siege and his father had been injured, he was unable to remember any detail of his war experiences, and he was withdrawn and monosyllabic throughout the interviews. He insisted he was all right, but he had done badly at school since the war because of poor concentration and was seen by friends and teachers as not really coping.

My clinical experience in the Balkans also suggested that, if given the opportunity, the majority of children are good at judging for themselves which approach is right for them at a particular time. I worked with five related children after a horrifying massacre in Kosovo in which nineteen of their relatives, including their mothers, were machine-gunned in front of them and they themselves were left for dead. Over three years I watched them successfully piece their lives back together. Each child chose a different method of coping. One needed to talk about the massacre at length and replay the whole experience. One wanted to tell the story to a journalist, but did not want to repeat it again. The others had no symptoms and did not want to discuss the subject at all. Two years later all of them wanted to tell their story when asked to give testimony to the International Tribunal, and when they saw that their accounts could contribute to gaining justice for their relatives. This family taught me that even children who are related and have shared a horrifying experience will not deal with their grief in the same way, yet the differences need not impede their recovery.[14]

The same children will use different methods at different times. The majority of the Bosnian children told me that they used distraction such as play or talking with parents and friends while actually in the shelters. Israeli children exposed to Scud missile attacks in the Gulf War used similar methods.[15] Nina and Elvira distracted themselves when bombs were actually falling, but also kept detailed diaries of events, another means of emotional processing. Some children threw their diaries away after the war; some kept them as a record which they reread.

Anna Freud noticed that children who had endured the Blitz usually did not talk about the events until they had emotionally processed them in other ways. Most children will find appropriate ways to express themselves when they want to do so if they are given a chance. Imposing discussion and exploration of events on a child who at that moment wants to avoid a topic may be as harmful as being unable to listen to a child who wants and needs to talk. This is not to suggest that those children who become trapped in an unproductive repetition of events, as revealed in their play, or dreams, or stories, should not be assisted to find a way out; rather that early indiscriminate intervention may prevent the emergence of more appropriate and natural methods of coping. Those children who are engaged in the search for meaning are clearly looking for their own recovery. The question is how they can be best supported in doing so. Social and political interventions that rebuild their social world may have a far greater impact on emotional well-being than individual psychological ones.

There is also a need to recognize that both these methods of coping—searching for meaning and distancing—can have personal and collective political consequences that can be positive or negative depending on the environment. In the autumn of 2003, the Kosovar children were the first Albanian witnesses prepared to face one of the alleged perpetrators in a war crimes trial in Serbia. We traveled to Belgrade together, and while staying in the city the children made friends with the Serb hotel staff and the security police who protected them, and they told me how amazed they were at the kindness of everyone. Their search for meaning and justice had begun a process of reconciliation.

However a commitment to a transcendent meaning in political struggle can lead not simply to the sacrifice of one's own life but to a willingness to kill others, as exemplified by Ina Konstantinova, engaged in sabotage behind German lines in the Second World War, and by the young Palestinian suicide bombers of the second Intifada. The ideological training for suicide bombers includes mythohistorical interpretations of the past, the destruction of empathy, the fostering of hatred of the other, and encouragement to value martyrdom, with its promise of both material (for the bombers' families) and spiritual rewards.[16] When the quest for heroic meaning is taken to the extreme, it can have horrifying consequences.

Disengagement from the search for meaning in Gorazde allowed children to acknowledge the role of their own side in the conflict and to feel more open to reconciliation with former enemies. In Foca, in contrast, the children who used distancing could avoid contradictions and maintain better individual psychological health. They came across as well adjusted to their environment, but some of them, like Susana, also demonstrated a disturbing lack of empathy. Avoidance and silence on issues such as what had happened to their classmates left unchallenged their implicit beliefs that ethnic cleansing was a defensive necessity and that security rested in living in an ethnically homogeneous mini-state. Neither of these beliefs seemed likely to promote the rebuilding of inter-communal relationships within the country, the long-term stability of the region, or their own security and well-being as individuals. Paradoxically, in Foca it was unwell children, who questioned the accepted version of events, who offered the best hope of communal recovery. But how easy was such a quest to sustain? And at what cost to themselves? Four years later I went back to find out.

11

Crimes and Punishments

There were Serbs living in a nearby village [who] did not want to go any-where. They got along with others well [. . .] Then the VRS told my father that they would destroy our village, so Father said "Well we can take that Serb village." He wanted to use them as hostages if the Serbs from the front line started shelling. He planned to do that. But he would not kill and torture the Serbs in that village [. . .] I don't know. Father had to do it, he had no choice.

—Fifteen-year-old Muslim boy, Gorazde

Prosecutor: You knew, in fact, that none of those procedures in place for detaining these people legally were ever followed, isn't that true?

Krnojelac: And that is why, excuse me, I begged and asked not to be there and to be taken out of the KP Dom, so as not to be held responsible for it . . . I was not pleased at all when I saw 2 people, my neighbors until then, the Muslims, at the KP Dom. I was not pleased to see them there, nor did I want to be the one who would be their superior. That is why I asked to be withdrawn immediately.

—Milorad Krnojelac, former warden of the KP Dom prison, 2001

I have now come to the belief and accept the fact that many thousands of innocent people were the victims of an organized, systematic effort to re-move Muslims and Croats from the territory claimed by Serbs. At the time, I easily convinced myself that this was a matter of survival and self-defense. In fact, it was more. Our leadership, of which I was a necessary part, led an effort which victimized countless innocent people. Explanations of self-defense and survival offer no justification . . . Why did I not see it earlier? And how could our leaders and those who followed have committed such acts? The answer to both questions is, I believe, fear, a blinding fear that led to an obsession, especially for those of us for whom the Second World War was a living memory, that Serbs would never again allow themselves to become victims. In this, we in the leadership violated the most basic duty of every human being, the duty to restrain oneself and to respect the human dignity of others. We were committed to do whatever was necessary to prevail . . . In this obsession of ours to never again become victims, we had allowed ourselves to become victimizers.

—Biljana Plavsic, pleading guilty to crimes against humanity, 2002

I returned to the Drina valley in the summer of 2002 and moved back into my old apartment looking out over the river. The view was much the same as before apart from a widened footpath and a factory at the end of the road. The house had been newly plastered and the only shrapnel scars left were in the stairwell and a tiny reminder in my bedroom door. The biggest change was in Nerma herself. She had undergone that magical "duckling into swan" transformation that occurs between fourteen and eighteen. She looked stunning, had acquired a handsome boyfriend and a place at Sarajevo University to read economics, and was spending every night at the international rock festival that was taking place in the town that week. Everyone was on the street: whole families filled cafés and promenaded back and forth across the river, munching snacks and greeting friends. I went out partying with Lejla, my old interpreter, and Ana and Jelena, two sisters from Foca. All of them worked together for the International Police Task Force in Gorazde. It felt as if things were changing at last.

The houses next door to Nerma's were still empty shells, but these were now a minority. Changes in the property laws had made it easier to evict temporary occupants, and the slow trickle of returning Serbs had become a steady stream. Almost a thousand families had registered to come back, and many were in the process of rebuilding their houses with help from international donors.[1] In the suburb of Kopaci, two hundred Muslim families had taken matters into their own hands two years earlier and had camped out on the Inter-Entity

Boundary until the international community had bullied the reluctant Serb local authorities into giving them back their homes.

The Balkan world as a whole was changing. After the war and the
NATO air strikes in Kosovo, Milosevic had been thrown out of power
in Yugoslavia in a popular uprising and handed over to the International War Crimes Tribunal at The Hague by his own people. Vojislav
Kostunica was now president of the Federal Republic of Yugoslavia,
and although an ardent supporter of Republika Srpska's right to independence during the war, he now apparently accepted the integrity
of the Bosnian state. Negotiations between Serbia and Montenegro
made it look as if the term "Yugoslavia," as well as the federal presidency itself, were about to be consigned to history. The other Balkan
architects of Dayton were no longer on the stage. In Croatia, Franjo
Tudjman had died and been replaced by the moderate pro-Western
Stipe Mesic. Within the Federation, the nationalist SDA had lost
heavily in the 1998 election to the moderate Social Democratic Party
and Alija Izetbegovic had retired, although hard-line nationalists retained allegiance among the Bosnian Croats and the Bosnian Serbs. It
looked as if the entity structure itself might be weakened by a new
constitutional court ruling that had declared the dominance of any
ethnicity, in either Entity, unconstitutional and discriminatory. Political structures at every level would be obliged to have representatives
from all three constituent peoples. Local administrations would be
obliged to hire returnees according to national quotas, based on the
population of the last prewar census.[2]

Meanwhile the pursuit of international justice continued steadily
at The Hague, if somewhat more erratically on the ground in Bosnia.
The Tribunal had shifted its focus from camp guards to political and
military leaders and had indicted two former Bosnian Serb presidents, Momcilo Krajisnik and Biljana Plavsic, for genocide, crimes
against humanity, and violations of the laws and customs of war. The
indictment stated that in order to "secure control of various municipalities of Bosnia and Herzegovina which had been proclaimed part

of the Serbian Republic of Bosnia and Herzegovina, the Bosnian Serb leadership . . . pursued a course of conduct involving the creation of impossible conditions of life, persecution and terror tactics in order to encourage non-Serbs to leave the area, deportation of those reluctant to leave, and the liquidation of others." Krajisnik had been arrested in his pyjamas and awaited trial. Biljana Plavsic had handed herself over voluntarily.[3]

The slow-burning fuse of agony over Srebrenica was approaching some kind of resolution. Forensic examinations of mass graves had so far revealed more than two thousand bodies, the majority of whom appeared to be civilians killed in execution style. There were many more gravesites to be examined and every indication that the rest of the seven to eight thousand men and boys missing since the fall of the town were dead. General Mladic and Dr. Karadzic remained at large and occasionally visible. Karadzic had been the object of a number of bungled arrest attempts. He reputedly lived somewhere in the mountains near Foca. General Radislav Krstic, commander of the Drina corps, which had organized the transport for the forced expulsions of twenty-five thousand women and children and had assisted in some of the executions, had been tried and sentenced to forty-six years for genocide.[4] A memorial meeting had been held in Srebrenica that July. No politicians from Republika Srpska had attended.

There had been more arrests in Foca. My friend Gordana had been on duty in the International Police Task Force station in early 1999, when without warning French Stabilization Force (SFOR) officers had tried to arrest Dragan Gagovic as he was driving five little girls home from a karate tournament. There was an exchange of fire that ended with his death, and the children were taken into safe custody. Gordana found herself alone in front of the station, facing a large crowd of angry parents led by a drunken Tuta, the paramilitary gang leader, holding a grenade. She tried to explain that the children would be released very soon. The crowd, incited by Tuta, weren't interested in explanations and broke into the barricaded station and severely beat up the international monitors, who narrowly escaped with their lives. A local police officer managed to save Gordana, who hid terrified at home for the next three weeks, receiving threatening phone calls.

Tuta had blown himself up and injured two Germans when they tried to arrest him in October 2000. At The Hague Dragoljub Kunarac and his colleagues, on trial for their mistreatment of Muslim women in Foca, had received sentences of between twelve and twenty-eight years in the first convictions that defined rape and enslavement as crimes against humanity.[5] Krnojelac, Foca's former primary school headmaster who had been warden of the KP Dom in the first year of the war, had been arrested in the summer of 1998 and sentenced to seven years for aiding and abetting persecution, inhumane acts, and cruel treatment.

I wanted to see what had happened to the children. Did they know anything about these events, and did it matter? How had they grown up? Had they all recovered? How did they feel now about living with former neighbors, and what were their hopes for themselves and for their country? I managed to find more than half of the original forty children, ten in Gorazde and twelve in Foca.

I bumped into Samir and his family by chance. They had just moved into their new house on the steep hill above Gorazde's armaments factory. After nine years of sharing, all the children had rooms of their own. They made me coffee in the spacious living room while I admired their sheep, which were visible in the small orchard. They had finally got some help from donors and rebuilt the grandfather's destroyed house. Samir was unrecognizable. The shy, nervous, slight boy had grown into a fit, muscular youth. He was training as a welder, but his real interest was sports and his main worry and frustration the lack of work and decent training opportunities in Gorazde. He felt as if he had lost too much time and had not achieved anything, such as his ambition to be a football player. He dreamed of going to Germany, or at least Sarajevo, to work and train, although not permanently. He liked Gorazde, but it was a dead end. He now had a girlfriend. The fear and insecurity, sadness, nightmares, and flashbacks had all gone. He avoided going to the old house alone, because if he did the memories of the family's imprisonment there returned and made him *feel bad in his soul.* Yet he no longer felt bothered about whether the neighbors who had imprisoned them would come back. *I wouldn't pay attention. They can come back.*

The ones who hurt you? I asked.

Yes, but you can forget all that. I don't need them punished. I don't think about the past, just the future. I want my children to have a good one.

He did want someone punished: *the ones who gave the orders.* He thought The Hague was *too good* for Milosevic. Anyway he had heard that only Serbs who were *not afraid* stayed in Gorazde; the others returned just to sell their houses.[6] *I would like to live together, why not? There are good and bad people whatever nationality. If it's a good person, why not be friends?*

National elections were a month away and Samir was now eighteen, but he was not interested. *There are so many lies on our side. They promise much, but they steal and nothing changes.*

So what kind of politician would you like? I asked.

Someone who thinks of our well-being. There is still no party that can connect us. There has to be one that can connect people, connect Serbs and Muslims.

Sanela was still living with her mother and sister in a flat formerly occupied by Serbs. No one had reclaimed it. Sanela no longer wanted to go back to their village. She enjoyed life in town too much. She was getting top marks at medical high school and planned to go to Sarajevo to train as a physiotherapist. She felt no ill effects from the war. She still missed her father and felt sad at times like the anniversary of his death, but found it harder, as she grew older, to remember him clearly, although her mother sometimes talked of the nice life they had had.

She was more ambivalent than Samir about her Serb neighbors' return. She was glad Milosevic was at The Hague. He was *disgusting* and deserved to suffer as they had suffered. *But I can't forgive them; it doesn't make me feel better. Probably other children who lost someone feel the same thing. I can't get over it. I have nothing against them. They can return but I don't feel comfortable with contact. It would be better if they said "Yes we did it," but whether I would feel easier I don't know. I really didn't have a chance to talk with them. I haven't seen anyone I knew. I prefer not to think about it. I don't think about it.* Yet she still followed documentaries and the news. *It's hard but I still do it. I want to understand the war.*

What is your understanding now? I asked.

They wanted a Greater Serbia. They failed and that is their loss.

Are all Serbs guilty?

There are good ones, but they're rare. They had an awful attitude to Muslims and I don't think it's changed.

Narcisa had decided studying law was boring. *Someone else can do it.* She had discovered a facility for math and had her future mapped out: do an economics degree at Sarajevo, marry her boyfriend, travel, and then come home and set up a business with her parents. She loved Gorazde and had no wish to live anywhere else; it was where all her family and friends lived. She noticed she was more emotional than before the war, but she had always been an intense person; she did not see herself as unwell. Recently her mother had become ill. This had got them all talking about their experiences in Visegrad, and she thought her emotions were related to that. Thinking about the place made her uncomfortable. In spite of this she felt much easier about Serbs coming back than before. She and a friend had admired a new boy at school and gone over to talk to him. *When he said his name was Goran I had no reaction like . . . oh he's a Serb.* They had become friendly. They did not discuss the past. *I don't see him as responsible. I had thought I would be bothered but I wasn't. I think it's going to be good, there are some chances.*

It was the Serbs' leaders she held responsible, and to some degree her own as well, although she thought *Muslim and Serb behavior was very different in the war.* She had just seen a documentary about Srebrenica on television which had upset her: *When they ran out of bullets they started burying people alive.*

All the young people I reinterviewed in Gorazde felt well. Their concerns and worries were the normal ones of relationships (almost all of them were in love) and future careers, exacerbated by the almost nonexistent work prospects in the town. Nina was already studying German in Sarajevo and hoped to be an interpreter. She had come to terms with her parents' separation, although her mixed feelings of love and anger toward her father still caused her confusion. Senad was going to Madrid to do computer studies. Nedjad wanted to teach history. Armin wanted to be a crime investigator. Elvira planned to be a pediatrician.

Most were not worried at the thought of living with Serbs again, and like Narcisa had already had positive experiences. Elvira, though, shared Sanela's ambivalence. She had met an old friend, a Serb, the previous summer. *She said to me "Look what they did to us, how they separated us," as if she didn't blame Serbs, as if she was from a completely different planet! As if Americans had done it! She asked for my phone number, I told her openly I did not want contact. She cried and said "Am I guilty?" I said I was not accusing anyone, but her father did these things, then I left the room.* Elvira had not seen the friend since. *I don't mind if they all return but I don't want contact with them.*

They were all disillusioned with politics and politicians, and most of those old enough did not plan to vote. Narcisa thought all politicians were corrupt, self-interested, and untrustworthy. The few who did intend to vote wanted *tolerant* non-National parties that were *for all Bosnians.* Nedjad felt Bosnia was becoming a *state of old people.* He wished the older people who had conspired to make the war would just get out of the country altogether.

My first impression of Foca, as I drove in over the brand-new bridge across the Drina, was that it had undergone a similar renaissance. There was a bustle in the streets, new rows of small boutiques, and new cafés. The international organizations, which had evacuated after the Gagovic incident, had come back more than a year earlier, bringing Muslim employees with them. I had been told that Muslim families had returned to live in some of the surrounding villages and even in the town itself. However, as in Gorazde, the festive feelings of a warm summer day masked the reality that unemployment ran at 75 percent. The main employer, the state-run wood-processing factory, had burned down the previous year, and more than fifteen hundred people had lost their jobs.[7] Rumors abounded that the fire had been deliberate, set on a Saturday when the works were deserted. Headmaster Mojevic thought it was not unrelated to the sudden emergence of a number of small private firms doing the same work.

Not much had changed in Mojevic's primary school, Sveti Sava. Dust and sunlight filled the unpainted empty corridors, and the picture of the saint still hung above Mojevic's chair. The Biljana Plavsic calendar had gone and a large map of Bosnia-Herzegovina covered half of one wall. *This is Bosnia*, Mojevic said, *and whoever thinks differently is wrong.* He wanted to tell me about the projects for inter-Entity cooperation in which he had been engaged, including joint holidays on the coast with Federation children and the setting up of a mixed sub-school in a village where Muslims had returned. He had finally left the Serb Democratic Party, fed up with its corruption and its failure to work with the international community in helping the town. *When dirty water is up to my ears I get out.*

We had a drink on the terrace of the newly painted Hotel Zelengora. The refugees had all moved out. The headmaster's own house in Ustikolina had been rebuilt, and his sister went there often.

He stayed away, feeling he might not be welcome. He lit a cigarette and apologized to me, saying he had quit but the old accusations of war crimes had resurfaced and got him smoking again. As before, he was anxious to tell me his version of events. This time it was a complicated story of how he had convinced a fellow commander that forcing Muslim detainees to dig trenches on the front line was illegal and had gone to rescue them. On their return journey to the KP Dom prison, other soldiers had taken them out of his hands, and while he had run to a phone to check orders, *a tragic accident* had occurred: they had all been killed. He was incensed that he should be accused of their deaths, he who had once gone to prison himself for four days for protecting Muslim prisoners. *A great writer from Montenegro said "It takes courage to defend oneself from someone else, but greater courage and humanity to defend someone else from oneself."* His conscience was clear. *If war started again, I would again be with my people.* In spite of his own anxieties, however, he thought things in Foca were getting better. *Those who wanted little states are now in a minority.*

Svetlana and her family had been evicted again. It took me some time to find them, living in a farmhouse left empty by fleeing Muslims just outside the town, which they shared with a widow and a disabled child. All of them were facing eviction in the next fifteen days and had no idea where they were going. They were very upset about this uncertainty and about Svetlana's uncle's sudden death earlier that week. Although their previous flat had been reclaimed by its Muslim owner, who had promptly sold it, the original owner of this house had not filed for repossession, but the municipality was evicting them anyway *and giving the property to someone else,* said Svetlana's father. He thought the municipality used the new laws to suit itself. Their old house was still in ruins and no one had offered assistance to rebuild it, although some neighboring Muslim returnees had received assistance for their houses. The municipality was supposed to provide alternatives for homeless people, but said it had none. He had actually helped build the flats that now housed the displaced people who had lived at the Hotel Zelengora, but they would give him one only if he paid half the mortgage immediately. How could he possibly do that on their tiny wages?

Svetlana was feeling pretty miserable at that moment. She wanted to scream and shout because everything was so awful. She felt particularly bad for her father. *He suffers a lot but he cannot cry. This week he won't eat at all.* There had been other problems as well. A few weeks earlier two men had stopped a car beside her and tried to grab her while she was walking home alone. The appearance of a neighbor had frightened them off. The incident had brought back familiar feelings. She had flashbacks and felt anxious much of the time. *Before that happened I wasn't afraid of anything and could go anywhere; now I am really scared to go anywhere alone when it's dark.* We sat under laden plum trees looking down on the river and she said it was a pity that I had come just now, because before all these things happened she had been having the best time of her life. She was learning to be a cook; she had made new friends and had really begun to enjoy her life in Foca. *It's different with lots of friends, just totally different.* Like Sanela in Gorazde, she had no wish to return to village life: *I can't even remember much about the village now.*

Unlike Sanela, however, Svetlana was no longer curious about the war and just thought it was stupid. Regarding the Milosevic trial, she did not want *to listen or to say anything about it.* She had heard there was some kind of killing at Srebrenica, but *I really don't have an opinion. I don't want to think about it.* She personally had no problems with Muslims returning. She had seen quite a few families in Donje Polje, the Muslim section of town, and had a Muslim friend who had come back to Foca to take exams, because it was easier than in Sarajevo, so she had helped her get textbooks. But Svetlana had lost her unequivocal wish to return to the way things were before.

They want theirs and we want ours. We can't live together because

Muslims say Serbs were Muslims before and Serbs say Muslims were Serbs before [. . .] I would be afraid if I had to go to a Muslim area.
    Why?
    That's a stupid question. Because they are Muslims and we are Serbs and we were at war. Because maybe they would hate me because I am a Serb.
    So how does one get past the fear?
    I don't know, I'm not sure. It would be good if all Serbs and Muslims went back to their homes, but the reality is that the Muslims get more help than the Serbs. If we were treated equally it would be better. It was not a topic that interested her much. As before, politics bored her, and she was not going to vote. *In this country we voted a hundred times without getting anything. I really don't see the point.*

I could not escape the feeling that Svetlana had distanced herself from the questions that had bothered her four years earlier, and that this distancing had contributed to her feeling more at home in the community.

Some of the other Foca young people seemed to have made a similar adjustment. Tatiana, looking radiant from a holiday on the coast, also told me that the previous year had been one of the best of her life because of making new friends. She still hated *Foca . . . the way they think and gossip. In this town you have to watch how you walk, how you cross the street, whom you talk to . . . I could never stay here; it's not good for young people or their careers. They don't like foreigners, don't like different cultures. I like different cultures and nations. People make barriers around themselves to keep the outside world out.* She was eager to escape and had taken a year off from school to earn the money, working as an interpreter for French SFOR. She planned to go to France after a year at Novi Sad University in Serbia.
    Why not Sarajevo? I asked.
    My father is not a nationalist but he wouldn't like me to go there, although it's probably better than Novi Sad. He wouldn't like his golden

princess in the Muslim part of Sarajevo, it would lead to gossip and it's too risky.

This had nothing to do with any personal animosity toward Muslims, she told me. She had been very pleased when the father of a Muslim friend had greeted her in the street, and she felt sad that the girl herself had still not been in touch. *Probably because I wasn't here. I don't believe she doesn't want to see me.*

Regarding the return of Muslim people in general, she never discussed it. *I am indifferent,* she told me with a shrug.

It was such a contrast to her stated outlook that I commented: *You seem very detached?*

I don't have anything in common with the people returning. We live in our own apartment; we didn't occupy anyone else's apartment. There are more important things to think about.

She was not sure if she remembered the mosques in Foca, although she thought it was *stupid* to have knocked down something that had been there five hundred years.

What if there was an attempt to rebuild them?

I am indifferent. They will build it or not.

As to what had happened to Muslims in Foca or elsewhere, she had little information or curiosity. She was not sure if she believed any of it. *I don't know, I can't say it's impossible. It's possible of course.*

What about Srebrenica?

I don't know anything concretely; I heard a lot of people were killed.

Do you think it's true?

Maybe . . .

Stojan also was eager to get out of Foca. He had no ill effects from the NATO bombing, had done well in high school, and planned to go to Belgrade to be a construction engineer. He did not see himself coming back. *There's no future here* in Foca. *Everyone wants to go.* He had given up basketball for lack of a team, but he still enjoyed his life. When I asked how he felt about his old neighbors and friends coming back, he said he didn't remember them, but *it isn't a problem.* His father had been given a new flat by his employer, so they had moved out of the neighborhood. He did not think many would come back to town, only the elderly. He didn't remember so much about the war. As for those things that supposedly had happened in Foca, most people thought it was lies and he agreed.

But you told me you saw houses burning, I remarked.
Yes, that's not a crime, one house burning.
But the whole of Donje Polje?
True, but maybe the people who did it were angry.

He had not heard about any other crimes. *I am a patriot,* he explained.

As in Gorazde, the majority of the children I reinterviewed in Foca had grown into healthy young adults. Dusan had recovered from the death of his brother. He thought of him quite often but it was with pleasure rather than pain. Ivana wanted to go to Novi Sad to study psychology. Divac's family had sold their flat in Sarajevo. He still enjoyed visiting the city even though he found the *Muslim domination too strong.* He would have liked to study literature, but doing economics in Pale had more prospects. Jovan fantasized about traveling to Greece but had chosen to study dentistry in Foca to earn enough to help his parents. Muslims coming back did not affect them very much, as very few were returning to the town itself. They did not think about it.

There were exceptions. Helena, whose father had been killed in the first month of the war, had not had a good time since I saw her last. Her family had been evicted from their apartment and had to live in a collective center out of town but had now found temporary accommodation in one room for the three of them while they waited for a flat. Helena would have liked to go back to Sarajevo, but that house had been sold. *I don't want to stay* in Foca, *but who asks me.* She looked exhausted, admitted that she was sleeping and eating poorly, and said she felt tense and miserable. Occasionally she even had thoughts of suicide, although they were just thoughts. Her grades had fallen to average and she no longer enjoyed high school, but she still read avidly at home. She had no idea what she would do next or where she wanted to go. *New Orleans,* she joked. *Good bars, good music.*

I wondered to what degree her unhappiness was related to missing her father. She felt sad whenever she thought about him, but said she did not think about him very often. Much of the misery seemed to be related to living in Foca, which was *awful and depressing.* She had some good friends, but could not talk to people in general; given her rather different opinions from her contemporaries I was not surprised. In spite of not having lived in Foca during the war, she was much better informed than many others about what had happened in the town. She had heard that *a lot of Muslims were killed by Serbs, especially women and children,* and that *a big crime was committed against Muslims in Srebrenica.*

Sara still missed her Muslim best friend: *I used to dream she was here, every night.* She no longer worried about people coming back. *Muslims could be better friends for you than Serbs [. . .] maybe before I had some anger and hatred, now I know Serbs did some similar things to them also.* She had heard that *Serbs had occupied the town, imprisoned Muslims, and forced them to go away.* It made her feel awful. She had visited Sarajevo recently and loved it. In Foca she felt trapped and hopeless, afraid that she would not get the grades necessary to escape.

Young people in Gorazde shared the continuing ignorance about crimes committed by their own side. They knew nothing about Josanice. Elvira responded to hearing about the massacre of elderly Serbs and children with the same indifference that I encountered in Foca when discussing Srebrenica. Her reaction was unusual, however. The others in Gorazde were shocked and upset that they had not known. *Do you want to know about it?* I asked Narcisa. *No, just as they don't want to hear about Srebrenica, but yes, it's important. It should be on our Bosnian TV.*

The Wounds of War

"The world has only just begun to realize that left untreated, the psychological wounds of war can be most damaging, as children grow up unable to function normally, often driven to perpetuate the violence they have experienced," states UNICEF's yearbook for 1994.[8] The implication—that those who suffer most will inflict their suffering upon the next generation—did not seem to fit the children I watched grow into young adults in the Drina valley. In their stories only a very few children in both cities wrote of the desire or need for revenge. In my first interviews I gave the children the hypothetical moral dilemmas beloved of social psychologists, and was impressed by the maturity of their answers.[9] Almost all expressed principled objections to lying and stealing. These things were wrong because they damaged others, trust, and one's own good name; but they would put these principles aside in order to save a life, even the life of a stranger. Conflict situations such as someone occupying your desk or using your things should be verbally negotiated, with or without help from authorities. There were no ethnic distinctions in these responses.

Four years later, although some of my respondents felt anger toward those they perceived as the main perpetrators of the war and ambivalence about contact, these feelings did not manifest themselves as hatred for their contemporaries on the other side or a desire for revenge. It was striking that some of those who had suffered most, like Samir, Narcisa, Helena, and Sara, were the most open to the renewal of relationships. Apart from Helena, most had recovered remarkably from the war, although some like Svetlana had been very disturbed by new events. They all had the same worries and concerns over studies and relationships. Most were making "sensible" career choices, opting for security at the expense of other hopes. They all showed the same deep attachment and sense of responsibility for family. They all were frustrated with small-town provincialism and talked in identical terms of their alienation from politics and their suspicion of politicians.

Yet the wound to the community seemed wider than ever. Individual psychological health seemed to be sustained, at least in part, by means of damage to collective understandings. Bosnia-Herzegovina played football against Yugoslavia for the first time that summer. The match received massive publicity. Foreign dignitaries and the political elite from both Entities attended the match in Sarajevo. Some hoped it would be seen as a symbolic acknowledgment of a mutual recognition of statehood. But the Yugoslav team captain walked onto the field with his hand in the Serbs' three-finger salute.[10] The more numerous Federation fans, mainly Muslims, whistled and jeered through the Yugoslav national anthem (once the anthem of the old Yugoslavia), waved the wartime Bosnian flag, and shouted provocative slogans such as *Allahu akbar* (Allah is the Greatest) throughout the match. Fans of Republika Srpska (RS) and Yugoslavia, who for their own protection had been carefully segregated, waved Serb nationalist flags and shouted *Raso Raso* (the nickname of Radovan Karadzic). Both sides shouted *Ustasha* when unhappy with a decision of the Croat referees. The players themselves were sportsmanlike, and the more experienced Yugoslav team prevailed. When Yugoslavia scored, the RS politicians joined in the applause, guiltily stopping at the horrified glances of their Muslim colleagues in the VIP box. After the match, Yugoslav and Serbian fans and the police who tried to protect them were badly beaten up by supporters of the BIH team. Far from healing wounds, the match had highlighted the wide gulf between the Entities and the degree to which Bosnia was not yet a unified country.[11]

Nikola had gone to the match and rooted for Yugoslavia. He could not imagine anyone in Foca doing otherwise. Dusan too was delighted at the victory. He continued to resent the West's attempts at *forced reconciliation* and still hoped for independence for Republika Srpska. *No one can issue a document stopping Serbs from liking Yugoslavia.* He did not believe people wanted to live together, otherwise there would not have been a war, and he was glad to see so many house exchanges.

Although most of the Foca young people now knew that Republika Srpska was part of Bosnia-Herzegovina, and traveled without fear in the Federation, none saw Sarajevo as their capital. As their university choices indicated, they oriented themselves eastward toward Serbia. Stojan still preferred to be a Yugoslav, even though the term was on its way out. Jovan thought that if the Entities disappeared he could always go to Serbia. Even Francophilic Tatiana, who was *indifferent to all of this* and wanted to get out of the Balkans altogether, did not want anyone to call her a Bosnian in case *they could think I was a Muslim.*

Why not say Bosnian Serb?

Serb is simpler.

I reminded her of her preference for the term "Muslim" as a little girl. *I wouldn't like that now. Simply, I am not a Muslim and I want them to know what I am. It's not so important, I'm not a nationalist. But if someone asked me what I was, I would say.*

The Bosnian government's attempt to substitute the term "Bosniak" for "Bosnian Muslim" had not helped. It made many in Foca feel that yet again Muslims were trying to prove that Bosnia was "theirs." *We always lived together in this area, so why do they now want to prove they were here first?* Mojevic asked me.

Helena had supported Bosnia in the football match. She thought it really strange that people in her apartment block had supported Yugoslavia, and had even supported Romania when the Bosnian team played against that country. *It is our country,* she declared. Sara felt the same.

In Gorazde, Iris thought football matches brought out primitive behavior in everyone. Senad was furious. He had watched a Federation/RS match where *all the Serbs were wearing Karadzic T-shirts and shouting "We love you, Karadzic, you are our greatest hero" and they wore those hats with the skull and crossbones. It's the symbol of a massacre. They are more like Nazis.* Members of the Bosnian Party for Democratic Action (SDA) were *like Nazis* as well, bullying people into religious observance. He hated the new Islamic Center in town. *The guy who runs it has a beard now, but he sold tobacco and alcohol during the war instead of defending the city.* I had been in the Islamic Center myself to use the Internet. It seemed to be largely occupied by small boys playing Counterstrike on the computers, talking loudly over the Arabic reading of the Koran piped over the speakers.

The other young people I talked to in Gorazde were more sanguine, feeling quite unbothered by and uninterested in the occasional covered young woman or bearded young man who had appeared in town. Most were still believers but no longer attended mosque or mekteb. Nedjad thought people had stopped supporting the SDA. They saw themselves as Bosnian first and Muslim second. Narcisa completely agreed with Headmaster Mojevic about the word "Bosniak." *I hate the term, it's stupid! Our history professor said it's our national name. I am a Bosnian, like the Serbs and Croats. They're trying to create differences between people. They talk about getting along and forgetting everything and then they make up that name. None of my friends use it.* Like the others in Gorazde, she hoped the Entities would disappear. *It's not called "Muslim Bosnia," we all live here.*

Another event brought the differences home to me. On September 11, the first anniversary of the destruction of the World Trade Center towers, Bosnian TV ran a documentary about New York. I watched it with Nerma and her brother Rijad, both of whom wept most of the way through. *If you experience something that is not good you always pray to God that no one else suffers like this,* Narcisa said of the September 11 attacks. She had been horrified and upset on the day itself, imagining how the victims felt, and angry at the way Osama bin Laden had *misused and misrepresented Muslims and Islam.* Most of the others in Gorazde felt the same. In Foca rumors abounded: that it was the Mafia, or President Bush himself, prepared to sacrifice his own in order to launch a war near Russia, or possibly Karadzic had arranged it. Sara, Helena, and Ivana simply told me *It was awful.* Most of the others had *no special feelings* and were not upset, although they felt sorry for ordinary people. Divac was pleased, just as he had been when Yugoslavia beat the United States at basketball. They all hoped the Americans would get the message that they should stop interfering in the affairs of other countries.

Memory and Forgetting

It was not just that most young people in Foca and in Gorazde continued to have contradictory views about their identity, the nature of their state, and their relationships with the rest of the world. They appeared to be dealing with memories of the past in quite different ways. In 2002 I gave all of them the same health measures I had used previously. For the most part their lifelines showed increasing well-being and optimism. All the symptom scales, except Helena's and Svetlana's, showed a marked fall. They all explained the small number of residual symptoms as part of their normal repertoire for coping with daily life. However, there were significant differences between the towns in the parts of the trauma questionnaire that dealt with memory and avoidance.

Often high scores in these two areas go together. When people have specific painful recollections, they try to suppress them or avoid triggers to the memory, like Samir avoiding his old house or Narcisa avoiding Visegrad. But I found that although young people in Gorazde had more intrusive recollections, flashbacks, and nightmares than their contemporaries in Foca, they had less avoidance, and their avoidance scores were lower than in 1998. For the most part they did not avoid the places, thoughts, and feelings associated with traumatic events, or find themselves unable to remember them. Nina told me she still had the same dream every month: of Serbs coming after her in a helicopter or a plane, shooting or bombing. She would try to escape; once she got killed. She said she was not bothered by the dream. Armin said he regarded his flashbacks of the siege as normal. This made sense given that four years earlier some children in Gorazde had felt an obligation to hold on to their memories to some degree, in spite of the discomfort the recollections caused.

In Foca, in contrast, some avoidance scores had actually increased, although all the other scores, including those referring to intrusive memories, had fallen. Jovan no longer worried about whose dead bodies he had seen in the river. He told me he was forgetting a great deal. Ivana had some memories of Muslim apartments being looted: *It was awful to see. I can't remember it clearly. The best thing is to forget everything that happened. I have almost forgotten.* It seemed as if in these young people the symptoms of avoidance and forgetfulness referred to the war as a whole rather than specific traumatic events. Nikola had no particular memories that troubled him, but gave himself the highest possible avoidance scores. Thinking about the past was *negative*, and he was trying to *forget everything*. He became quite irritated with me in the interview, saying he never discussed questions about what had happened.

Are they important questions? I asked.

No, I don't think so. The most important thing is to have a sports hall, we don't.

Marko was not irritated. I had got into the habit of interviewing the young people in Foca at a café with a terrace overhanging the river. In the early evening the mist rises, hiding the water and giving the valley a translucent, ethereal feel. In spite of the chill Marko lingered after I finished my questions, asking me to tell him more about the book I was writing. I mentioned how children in Gorazde had responded to four years of shelling.

Who was shelling Gorazde? he asked in a surprised tone.

Well, it was besieged throughout the war, by Serbs, did you not know that?

Yes, he had known. His father, like most Foca fathers, had been on the front line there, *and I think we took the town. Well, not completely, but almost.*

Then he asked me what I thought about Foca. I told him that it was hard to see people in the town struggling, that my perceptions were also colored by listening to the experiences of those who had lived here before, and that the ruins in Donje Polje made me sad. He nodded impassively, seeming neither bothered nor curious.

How do you feel about the destruction here? I asked. He shrugged. His indifference made me push a little further. *Does it make you sad?*

No, he said blandly. *I am not sad. I am not bothered.* And he smiled his charming smile.

I thought about this knowing and not knowing. It was almost as if the war had been a football match and the knowledge retained was about what *our side* had won or almost won, whereas the knowledge avoided or dismissed was about what winning or almost winning had cost. As a child Marko had felt the town was *not as it should be.* Now grown up, he no longer noticed such a problem, or if he did it had no effect on him.

As I said in Chapter 10, this distancing practiced by the young people is not the same as the clinical concept of denial. Stanley Cohen has tried to rescue the word "denial" from the clinicians and classify it in more literary terms. He describes three kinds of denial in political contexts: literal (the facts themselves are not true), interpretive (the facts have been misunderstood), and implicatory (the facts are known but their moral or political consequences are regarded as minor or nonexistent).[12]

I had seen all these kinds of denial in defendants from Foca on trial at the War Crimes Tribunal at The Hague. Kunarac and his colleagues argued that there had been no attack on non-Serb civilians in Foca—that their suffering was unfortunate "collateral damage" incurred during a legitimate military operation. The defendants did not deny having had sexual intercourse with a number of Muslim women and girls. However Kunarac argued that a woman identified as FWS-50 could not have experienced severe mental pain or suffering when he had intercourse with her as she had been raped on previous occasions by other perpetrators.

Radomir Kovac, one of Kunarac's codefendants, believed his victims had consented to intercourse because they did not continuously and forcefully resist throughout the act and because, he claimed, he was in love with one of them. Moreover they could not be considered to have been enslaved in his house, when they had the key and could have escaped at any time. He did not clarify where teenage Muslim girls could have gone, with no money and only the clothes on their backs, in Serb-controlled Foca in 1992.[13]

Krnojelac did not deny that abuses had occurred in the KP Dom, but claimed that as *prisoners of war* the prisoners were *legally detained*. He argued that the prosecution had misunderstood his position. As warden he had had no authority over or responsibility for prisoners detained by the military. He had worn a military uniform at work because he had nothing else to wear after his house burned down. The prisoners who had sent him requests for help had done so because he was an old friend, not because he was their boss. His desk was arranged so he could not look out and see the prisoners, and he did not remember "ever casting a deliberate look" into the yard. "Whatever I learned, I learned from other people. I did not see anything with my very own eyes. It was known that people were brought in but I did not see anything with my very own eyes. I would have to remember had I seen it, but really, I had so many other obligations." He even denied some of the assistance prisoners said he had given them, because admitting it would have implied that he had known about their plight. The judges did not accept these arguments and stated that the combination of knowledge and a failure to act, when he had some power to do so, made him guilty of aiding and abetting the principal offenders.

In the dock Krnojelac came across as a mild-mannered, inoffensive man, certainly not a nationalist ideologue. He was married to a Croat and had Muslim neighbors who still spoke well of him. The defense and prosecution psychologists described him as completely normal, if somewhat passive and lacking in initiative. He described himself as someone who would feel duty-bound to finish assigned tasks to the best of his ability. Yet even if one does accept his defense of lack of responsibility, as did all my Foca respondents, the question remains as to *why* he did not stand up and look into the yard to see what was happening to the good neighbors he knew were there. The implication is that he felt it had nothing to do with him.[14]

Personally I and my family have no connection with those things, Jovan told me. He was right. None of this *war generation,* as Divac described them, those whose childhoods were consumed by the conflict, had any responsibility for the horrors that occurred. Their wish to distance themselves seemed in many ways sensible, and even a key to their personal resilience. It did not seem surprising that by 2002 far more of the young people had adopted this strategy than before. The possible consequences of not distancing seemed evident in Helena.

Yet this aspect of their resilience left me worried and depressed. I was glad to see them happy and well. But I felt, as I had four years earlier, that the cost in empathy was high and that underneath the detachment, the implicit understandings that had led to war in the first place remained unchallenged and intact, even in those who said they rejected nationalism. Tatiana was sure that *Serbs had suffered the most.* When I asked if the people who were driven out had suffered any injustice, she assumed I referred to Serbs evicted from Muslim-owned apartments because of the new property regulations, which she felt were unfair. When I said that I meant Muslims driven out during the war, she gave me the explanation I had heard from so many in Foca: *Someone had to go. If they had been organized like the Serbs were organized, Serbs would have had to go. Muslims were planning to organize themselves and if they had succeeded the Serbs would have had to go.*

So Serbs were organized?

No, Serbs were not organized, it's only by accident that Serbs took the town. Foca will always be a painful point for Muslims because of that stupid journalist who said lots of Serb soldiers came from Serbia and that Muslims ran away.

Sitting in a café in Nuremberg while attending the war crimes trials in 1946, the journalist Martha Gellhorn had a conversation with a young German. He told her that Germany "made War because England was ready to attack her. The Allied bombings . . . were not correct; they could not be forgotten: what did innocent women and children have to do with War?" He could not explain why Germany had bombed Warsaw, London, and Coventry first. "Talk about the concentration camps was exaggerated and propaganda; he had seen people returning from 'protective custody' . . . fat and sunburned . . . It was wrong to kill the Jews, it was a mistake. On the other hand you could not help hating them because they never did any real work . . . Now Jews were returning to this town, and German families had to give them back their houses and sit in the street. No one spoke to Jews." At the end of the war, he continued, "people hated Hitler, because he had lost the War," but now they could see that he had not been so bad.[15]

Others who had been children during the war later remembered "the collective silence" that followed in the postwar period. Families never discussed the war at home. Hitler and the Nazi years did not exist at school. History stopped in the previous century. Dan Bar-On, a psychologist who interviewed these children in middle age, thought this emotional and physical distancing beneficial. It allowed them to approach the truth in their own way when they were ready. Not all of his interlocutors agreed. "That's why you have this situation where one guy believes it and the other one doesn't. Hitler just didn't exist. We didn't learn anything except that the War started. That was all . . . that was a big mistake because as a result nobody—well very few anyhow became concerned about the matter."[16]

The silence after the war in Germany followed a war that had definitely come to an end, and in which one side had been defeated. It was *Stunde Null* (zero hour), as the Germans called it, and everything had to start over.[17] I had no such sense of history having stopped in Bosnia in the summer of 2002.

On the contrary, the conflict seemed to be continuing, not only on football fields, but in classrooms, where an education agreement brokered by the international community allowed the continued teaching of entirely divergent histories and separate languages.[18] Divac told me *Serbian and Bosnian are not the same,* although he had grown up speaking the same language as his Muslim neighbors. The war also continued in the offices of petty bureaucrats—such as those who told one of my friends, when he finally got his home back in Kopaci, that if he wanted electricity he had to apply on the other side of the country in Banja Luka—and in the speeches of politicians. Kostunica, Yugoslavia's president, declared the week I arrived that Republika Srpska was "part of the family, temporarily separated from the Serbian motherland" (although he later claimed he had been misrepresented and had only meant unity within the European Union).[19] *This war after the war is worse than the real one,* muttered my friend. The war was also being fought through memorial sites: Foca mourned its dead with a phallic monstrosity by the new bridge surrounded by flags and fountains; Gorazde maintained one of the Serb tank positions that had bombed the town, adding swings to the defunct military hardware so that children could play among the guns.

And the war continued in Foca's museum, once Tito's temporary headquarters in the Second World War, now containing a large memorial room dedicated to the recent conflict. Here a wall plaque informed the curious that Serbs "were among the most chosen nations in the world." In this area they had always "fought for survival" and been obstructed by the great powers; "the aim of Serbs west of the Drina had been the preservation of Yugoslavia as a country where all Serbs lived . . . The Muslims advised by the great powers started the War against the Serbs. In Foca they had started sniping from the minaret." Now Serbs were "again under pressure" because the international community "wanted to remove the Statehood Republika Srpska had gained by political and military means and make it disappear into a unitary Bosnia-Herzegovina." The Hague was yet another proof that "those who began the War are not yet satisfied with its results."

This is really stupid, Ana said at the museum, almost refusing to translate in her exasperation. She had been fourteen when the war began, and she found our interviews with young people in Foca perplexing because her own memories and experiences, which remained clear in her mind, were somewhat different. The war started for her the day she went to school and found it closed with some twenty bewildered Muslim children and only a handful of Serbs in the yard. They were all sent home. Her mother's boss was amazed that their own family had not *left already.* Ana had spent most of the war evacuated to Montenegro, completing high school and university there.

She had come home intermittently to an increasingly alien town. The first time was just after the fighting ended, when she was horrified to see the house opposite hers burning, and even more upset when her Serbian friends said *Well, it's nothing, a house being burned . . . nothing.* She found it odd that they all now seemed to have video players when no one had owned one before the war. That was the moment when she realized Serbs were stealing, and she felt awful. The municipal authorities had issued a telephone number citizens could call if they saw anyone looting, and once when she and friends saw two Serb ladies going into an abandoned Muslim apartment they called the number, but nothing happened.

The Serb authorities drove around town with a loudspeaker telling Muslims they had to stay indoors and could not even go shopping, so her mother went to buy essentials for their neighbors. Their best Muslim friends hung on to their house in Donje Polje for some months but finally had to leave because of death threats. Her father helped them pack in tears, unable to speak. He also argued with others in their apartment block to allow their Muslim neighbors, women and children, into the shelter during the fighting. He was threatened with court action for protecting Muslims.

Her parents cried each time they visited her, telling of neighbors arrested or forced out. Her grandmother, once a partisan herself, was devastated. Ana spent much of that first summer in Montenegro listening to accounts on the radio of Sarajevo being shelled by *Serbs, Chetniks, killers, and monsters.* She felt sickened and miserable that her father could be seen like that when she knew he was not. He had simply felt unable to abandon home, country, and identity. Ana knew the reports were true because her aunt had stayed in the city and her uncle had been injured by a Serb grenade. *It was the worst period of my life, just sitting in the house listening to the news. For three months I destroyed myself, didn't eat didn't sleep . . .*

I puzzled over what made Ana so different from the Serb children I had interviewed. She was older, and had had a longer period of shared life with Muslims before the war, including her own Muslim best friend and her parents' close friends and neighbors. Indeed, because her family were not churchgoers, her first experience of visiting a religious building was a school trip to the Aladza mosque when she was eight years old. She had thought it beautiful. Also, she came from a Serb family who believed in and lived the Yugoslav ideal of brotherhood and unity: partisans on one side, a grandfather on the other who had donated money for the building of mosques in nearby villages. Like Nina, Ana had been proud to be one of Tito's pioneers.

But many of Ana's Serb contemporaries had had similar experiences and did not share her views. Perhaps two differences were most significant: first, she and her family were inoculated against Milosevic and his propaganda because one of their relatives knew him and had suffered at work from disagreeing with him; second, they had relatives in Sarajevo whose first-hand accounts of wartime events challenged the official version.

Ana's depression in that first year of the war again indicated the cost of empathy and openness for young Serbs in Foca, and her mental health during the war was certainly helped by learning to distance herself. She turned off the radio after that first summer, got into the local high school in Montenegro, made sympathetic friends, and immersed herself in her studies. When she returned to Bosnia she accepted a job in Gorazde, where she had friends of several nationalities (a number of Serb translators now worked there), and felt no need to identify with Foca's Serb community. So accurate remembrance carried little cost, although she was aware that many in Foca saw her as a traitor.

Trials and the Truth

One afternoon I found myself caught up in the largest SFOR convoy I had seen since the end of the war. Tank after tank was followed by dozens of armored personnel carriers with soldiers in full battle gear. Helicopters buzzed overhead. The apparent aim was to destroy Karadzic's support network of safe houses. Dusan's father thought it a bad joke. *I know where Radovan is,* he told me. *We all do. Ninety-nine percent of Serbs support him.* He and his wife were in a militant mood, furious at attempts to *divide Serbs* by strengthening the border between Bosnia and Serbia. *September 11 is only a warning, we are going to destroy America with the help of Saddam Hussein.*[20]

A Serb-Arab alliance? I asked in some bewilderment. *Is any frontier worth going back to war?*

Should we allow Bosniaks as a minority to tell Serbs what to do?
Dusan's mother responded. *The only thing left free so far is that we
don't have to attend mosque!*

Tatiana was deeply upset by the helicopters and angry at the International Tribunal for *making stupid actions in Foca, hunting a person
who does not exist.* She did not think Karadzic or Mladic was guilty.
*Some crimes were committed by real psychopaths and they couldn't
control them. Normal men would not have done it.* Most of the others
felt similarly. They were *patriots, and nationalists, fighting to create a
country for Serb people.* Milosevic also had their sympathy and support. He too was a *patriot,* unable to control the irresponsible actions
of others. They admired his ability to defend himself and felt he had
been betrayed by his own people. Dusan thought the trial was a circus. *Ordinary people don't support handing him over.*

Summing up the case for the prosecution in Radislav Krstic's trial
at The Hague, the prosecutor Mark Harmon expressed his regret that
a certain witness for the defense, a well-educated Serb journalist, still
"could not believe" the facts of what had happened at Srebrenica, despite overwhelming evidence. He went on to argue:

> Purposeful ignorance of these terrible deeds and an unwillingness to confront them in a responsible way can only create fertile grounds for future misunderstandings between Bosnian
> Serbs and Bosnian Muslims and may poison the future for the
> people of Bosnia who deserve a respite from the ethnic strife
> that has characterized this conflict. The nations of the world
> created this Tribunal in an effort to ensure peace in the region,
> and part of our mandate is to ensure that evidence of crimes is
> objectively presented, tested in a court of law to ensure that the
> wrongs committed in the former Yugoslavia do not go unpunished, and to permit future generations to have access to the objective record of these events so that they may be inoculated
> against the calculated deceptions that thrive in the milieu of

chauvinism, blind ethnic pride, and ignorance. The truthful record of these events can assist in the recovery of the victims and also in the future reconciliation of the peoples of Bosnia.[21]

In passing judgment on Krstic, Judge Almiro Rodrigues emphasized the importance of individual attribution of guilt because "to associate this evil with Serbian identity would be an insult to the Serbian people and would betray the concept of civil society."[22]

The hope of those who set up the International War Crimes Tribunal was that trying the architects and main perpetrators of war crimes in the former Yugoslavia would relieve societies as a whole of collective guilt. In Gorazde it seemed to be having the desired effect. Residents were universally delighted to see Milosevic in The Hague, although Senad felt he was *too comfortable* and wanted him to suffer. The arrests and trials of the major criminals made it easier for Samir, Narcisa, and others to be friendly to *ordinary* Serbs whom they did not hold responsible, although some like Sanela were not so forgiving. *The best way is to try the guilty ones, no matter which side, and then you can forget the past,* said Samir. Nor did they object to the idea of criminals on their own side being arrested. *There is no question that many of ours did things that were just as bad,* Senad told me.

It is always easier to discuss the possible criminality of your own side in the context of your side's generally acknowledged victimhood. The problem in Foca was the feeling that the Serbs' victimhood and need to defend themselves had never been understood or acknowledged. The Hague was unjust, I was told repeatedly, *because only Serbs are there and only Serbs are punished for genocide, only Muslim women were raped, and I know Serb women were raped and Serb children killed. No Muslims there, just a few for some crimes, but no one for genocide!*

Were Muslims trying to wipe out Serbs? I asked.

Probably . . . Tatiana sat twisted up in her chair, tapping her foot repeatedly against the floor in the distress this topic was causing her.

What will people think about us and our country if they see only Serbs there and no one else? If other people of other nations were there [fighting] also they should be there also!

What about Mladic and Karadzic?

It is stupid and awful to blame only one side!

All the young people in Foca, including Helena, agreed with this last sentiment. And they had another concern. They could accept that some on their own side had committed abuses, and they wanted those individual perpetrators tried, preferably by national courts rather than a biased international community. *Maybe there are some Serb criminals,* Stojan told me, *but I don't think the authorities could have ordered the crimes. The people who did it had to choose to do it. Individuals have responsibility.* But trying Mladic, Karadzic, and Milosevic would not liberate Serb society, as those at The Hague might wish.

On the contrary, trying their leaders would, symbolically, put their whole society on trial, because many of them still believed in those leaders and the project in which they had been engaged: the *patriotic defense of the Serbian people.* These young men and women astutely understood the implications of Milosevic's indictment. If Republika Srpska was not the result of a valiant struggle for liberation in which, unfortunately, some horrors and excesses had occurred, as in all wars and on all sides; if the Serbs had not endured bombing, and losses, and deprivation for something honorable and worthwhile; but if instead their Entity had been brought into being through a collective *criminal enterprise* that involved among other things "genocide; persecutions; extermination, murder, unlawful confinement, tortures; deportation; and wanton destruction," as Milosevic's indictment claimed, and if all these acts had actually been sanctioned or ordered by Milosevic, Karadzic, Mladic, and other leaders, where did that leave these young Serbs and their families, who as decent people could not condone such actions?[23] Completely homeless for a start.

No wonder they could not believe the charges and preferred not to think about the actions underlying them.

War crimes trials have a reputation for attempting to be too many things to too many people. Not only are they intended to uphold and develop international law and ensure that leaders and states are as accountable for crimes as individual criminals; the punishment they exact is intended to vaccinate society against future wrongdoing. They are a forum for victims to recount and exorcise their experiences, a history lesson, and a means of arriving at objective truth, which supposedly will assist recovery and reconciliation. How to combine these aims? In The Hague the pressure of time and the pursuit of facts—Did this gun position actually fire these mortars? Was the defendant present when this killing took place?—meant that only selected witnesses were called to recount their journeys through hell. History lectures designed to show the "context" in which the atrocities had occurred were often cut short. As the judges explained, the criminality of any particular attack upon a civilian population was not diminished by the defendants' belief that the civilians were members of an ethnic group that was responsible for starting the conflict, or that that ethnic group might have carried out similar attacks in other places or at other times.[24]

Nor do such trials end the historical debate. In Japan today there are young nationalists who argue that the version of events promoted by the war crimes trials in Japan at the end of the Second World War, the "Tokyo Trial View" of history, is wrong and undermines morale. The Japanese did not plan or wage an aggressive war in Asia; it was "a tragic and noble struggle for national survival and the liberation of Asia from Western colonialism. The Chinese and Korean Wars were regrettable errors." A hundred thousand people including babies and the elderly were not mutilated, raped, and massacred in a few weeks by Japanese soldiers in Nanking in 1937. Some soldiers acted with excessive zeal in the heat of battle and some innocent civilians got caught in the crossfire. Hiroshima, planned in cold blood, was a much greater crime. Japanese schoolbooks treat these matters with discretion, mentioning only that in "December 1937 Japanese troops occupied Nanking" with a footnote stating that reports of the killing of Chinese civilians resulted in international criticism. In contrast, Japanese junior high school students petitioned the Peace Museum in Hiroshima, which commemorates the victims of the atomic bomb, to provide an "aggressors' corner": they wanted an explanation of Japanese responsibility for the war to complement the gruesome horrors suffered by the Japanese in August 1945.[25]

These matters are debated in Japan half a century after the end of the Second World War. Is it necessary to wait that long in Bosnia? Is it possible? Narcisa felt secure for the moment, but she worried that if SFOR left, *War might start again. I think we would attack each other, goodness knows who first.* Sanela worried that the Milosevic trial was failing to teach the Serbs that the quest for a Greater Serbia was wrong, and that they might try again. Nikola thought there was bound to be a war in fifty years because the international community had interests in Bosnia, and they always intervened.

The Balkans is a barrel of gunpowder; it just looks like peace at the moment, Dusan's mother told me. *When NATO goes it will be destroyed or divided, you cannot stop people from doing what they want.* She asked if I had seen Danis Tanovic's *No Man's Land,* which had won the Oscar for best foreign-language film of 2001. In the film, three soldiers from Serb and Muslim military units are trapped in a trench in no-man's-land. One Muslim is lying on a mine, placed there while unconscious by a Serb soldier (now dead), who explained to his young colleague that when Muslims came to remove the body the mine would explode and kill them all. All three soldiers want to get out, but neither side wishes the other to leave, knowing that the other's presence is what keeps them safe. They call for help from the international community, to defuse the bomb and to rescue them all, and while waiting, argue over the causes of the war. There are flickers of a human relationship. The international community, reluctantly intervening because the media are there, cannot remove or defuse the mine. Their presence exacerbates the relationship between the soldiers and their distrust of one another ends fatally. The film ends with the surviving Muslim soldier still lying on the mine as darkness falls. *That's Bosnia,* said Dusan's mother, *a body lying on an unexploded bomb.* Tatiana liked the scene *where one is asking the other who is guilty and he says "We are guilty, because you have a gun pointed at me."* I agreed with her that responsibility established at gunpoint meant nothing, but I thought both she and Dusan's mother had missed what I saw as the central metaphor of the film: that the real danger to all the people of Bosnia came from the failure to discuss and defuse the brutal crimes that lay hidden beneath the bodies of their victims.

Could it be done? I had heard a Bosnian Serb politician on the radio calling for "a thick line" to be drawn under the past. That had also been Tito's approach, which was one reason why the new history plaque in Foca's museum singled out communism for its anti-Serb characteristics: many Serbs now felt that Tito's emphasis on "brotherhood and unity" had led to a denial or minimization of their suffering at the hands of the other ethnic groups in the Second World War, a denial that had contributed to the conflict today.

In Sarajevo a consortium of one hundred NGOs from all three ethnic groups in both Entities agreed. They had decided to establish a "truth commission." It would draw on the experiences of previous commissions such as the South African and Latin American ones, but it would not be identical. Respected citizens from all three ethnicities would travel from community to community and hold public hearings whose aim would be to allow all citizens to speak freely about their experiences as victims; and to encourage those who had acted with moral courage to help and protect their neighbors to speak up.

This was not about forgiveness and apology. *Eighty percent would say an apology was insincere because mistrust between ethnic groups is so deep,* explained Jakob Finzi, a Jewish civic leader from Sarajevo who was one of the commission's main advocates. He continued: *People are not just victims of war, they are victims of propaganda. Many don't know what happened on the other side. Unfortunately there were crimes on all three. It is clear Muslims were the greatest victims but they have to recognize their crimes against the other side. In this region everyone is ready to be a victim and no one is able to take responsibility. If we can show we are all victims, and there are some perpetrators, it will be easier to live together.* The main aim of the commission would be to establish the actual truth of events, what had happened and why. Finzi envisaged a database and eventually a joint historical commission. This was not a substitute for justice. The commission would work in cooperation with The Hague and had no power to grant amnesty for war crimes. Remarkably, the project had the support of every political party and all religious groups. It hoped to embark on hearings in the coming year. *Truth is not always healing; it can be a bitter pill, but it's better to swallow it now,* Finzi warned. The alternative was *three Bantustans or three ghettos,* a disaster for everyone.

In Foca opinions were divided. Many argued that it was better to forget crimes than to engage in endless discussion. Tatiana did not think the commission was needed, nor did she want to find anything out for herself. She had met a couple of boys from Gorazde in SFOR, and they had all agreed it was unnecessary to look at the past when you were having a good time. Most of the others in Foca felt similarly. Divac was fed up with Srebrenica. He thought it was important to find out what had happened there *because whenever you say Bosnia or Republika Srpska, people think immediately of Srebrenica.* But he was sure the commission could not work. *Serbs would never accuse another Serb in front of Muslims,* and Muslims were the same. All three sides had a *patriotic defensiveness* that made such a project impossible. It was worse now than just after the war. People in Foca had

talked more openly then; now they were secretive
other side refused to *acknowledge real facts;* but *eve*
came out and said what had happened, nothing wo

Svetlana did not agree: *Something has to happen becaus*e .
mess now. Nikola, in spite of his stated wish to *forget everything,*
wanted me to bring Finzi to Foca immediately so he could have a serious talk. He wanted *someone to make things better. People on both*
sides should make some kind of reconciliation because even small chil-
dren can now see it was a mistake. Things should not be forgotten, they
should be discussed in a way that leads to conclusions. Remembering
was useful if it achieved something. Forgetting appeared to be his response to powerlessness.

Nikola's view was the one that prevailed in Gorazde, although
Elvira told me there was no substitute for the law and she did not
need reconciliation with anyone and was not looking for it. Nina
agreed with Finzi that it could make people angrier but that it was
still good for the truth to come out. They would need outsiders to
help them be honest. Gorazde young people believed a scrupulous
examination of the past was the one action that would allow them to
forget, something they were as keen to do as young people in Foca. *If*
you decide to forget about something, Narcisa said, *in ten or fifteen*
years it comes to the surface. This would not be good. No one thinks the
same, so we need to talk and then forget.

I stayed in the Drina valley as autumn came. In my last week Braco, a
former Muslim policeman from Gorazde who now worked for the
Organization for Security and Co-operation in Europe (OSCE) in
Foca on education, took me to a small village called Popov Most. We
drove together up the valley, switchbacking through steep meadows
and orchards, as the weather fluttered between storm and sun, to arrive at a large, communist-era primary school building. The obliga-
tory mural of a partisan hero still decorated the wall, although a
shrapnel scar had disfigured his face. The building looked empty and

deserted, but Braco took me around to the back. One section had been renovated, and inside one sparsely furnished classroom five small Bosnian Muslims who had returned to the village were going to school with six small Bosnian Serbs. They were just assembling, and all was not completely well. One Muslim child had come in with his father, who wanted to report that his son was getting beaten up by two of the Serb boys. The three antagonists eyed one another angrily and sat as far apart as possible.

We left the children together and discussed the problem in the corridor. The father was adamant that it was nothing ethnic. His house had been burned down in 1992, but he had been back happily for two years. *Why not come back? It is my home.* He got along fine with everyone, indeed it was Serb neighbors who had told him what was happening to his son, because the children in question bullied everyone—their father was a well-known radical. He just wanted it stopped. The schoolteacher was reassuring. He would call all the parents to a meeting to discuss all the children's behavior and it would be resolved.

The teacher was a serious and soft-spoken Serb who had lived in Sarajevo. He thought the school was going well. Some of the Serb parents had refused to let their children go to school with Muslim children at first, but now they accepted it. They all learned Cyrillic and Latin, he taught the Serbian curriculum, but he adapted it. There were sections on "the Battle of Kosovo" and "slavery under the Turks" which he thought were inappropriate, so he ditched them. The main problem was that a neighbor had hijacked their water supply so the children had to pee in the schoolyard, and also they needed books. The OSCE had promised, but none had yet appeared.

Back inside the classroom things had settled down, and I was given permission to speak to the children. Yes, they all liked the school, and they enjoyed all the classes except math, and they wanted a toilet. *What's the capital of Bosnia-Herzegovina?* I asked. *Banja Luka,* said half of them cheerfully; *Sarajevo*, said three others somewhat shyly. The teacher smiled. *They still have to learn these things*, he said; and all the children politely stood up together to say goodbye.

I spent my last morning in Foca visiting the museum with Ana. It had been built as a hotel by the Austro-Hungarians and had the best location in the city. Today it had glass missing from the front doors, cracked plaster, and cobwebs. All the downstairs rooms were locked. Two women came down to greet us. They were extremely apologetic. They were fighting with the municipality, which had taken over the building at the beginning of the war; for now their twelve thousand objects were confined to a handful of rooms upstairs.

The municipality even destroyed a plaque on the wall which stated that President Tito lived here in 1942, said one of the women, who seemed to be a curator.

Why did they do that?

Because they thought history began in 1992.

She was happy to show me everything. She unlocked the rooms dedicated to the partisan war, unchanged since Ana's childhood. We looked at large maps of shifting front lines and photos of the Central Committee (*all famous, all dead*, Ana commented), homemade partisan boots, and a Remington typewriter used for issuing directives. Then we were taken to the room where the curator kept her mobile exhibition: "A History of Foca from Prehistory to Today." There were Turkish pipes, a Roman vase, an Austro-Hungarian cupboard and gilded mirror, a German 1944 banknote exhorting the local population to "Come to our side before it is too late. Save your life, then liquidate your commissars and then come. This banknote guarantees a hundred people freedom, life, and bread."

There were domestic objects that looked Ottoman. *Are these Muslim?* I asked.

No, that is the most common mistake. These things were in Serb, Croat, and Muslim houses.

So people in this town had a common culture?

Only in part, because they did not wear the same clothes, but material objects were the same.

She showed me a display of postcards of schoolchildren in a variety of ethnic dress, and all the different cultural associations that had existed in the 1930s. There were photos of nineteenth-century Foca, a graceful, multi-spired town, in its fork of the river. *This is only part of what we have. There is no room to display it all.*

You have no pictures of the Aladza mosque? I asked. She became slightly flustered. She said she would look.

Meanwhile I wanted to see the memorial room for the current war. She seemed curiously reluctant, but unlocked the door, revealing blown-up photos of burned and horribly disfigured dead children from Josanice. The curator shook her head. Ana translated the history lesson from the plaques on the wall. As she did so the curator, increasingly distressed, kept interrupting. She told me repeatedly that it was not the view of the people who worked there, it was just one man's opinion. If you asked her for an explanation of why neighbor ran from neighbor she would not be able to give one. She was not sure if anything written there was true. Her personal opinion was that it was a mistake to write any historical explanations at present. It needed time for the truth to come out.

We went into the next room and looked at photos of the 647 men and boys who had died for Srbinje. Then we headed down the uncarpeted stairs. The other woman caught us before we left and pressed something into our hands. It was two small guidebooks to "Foca." The covers showed an unrecognizably smart museum, behind which was the spire of an intact mosque and the clock tower. There were also two postcards of the Aladza mosque, serene in winter sunlight. Someone had cared enough to preserve them.

Epilogue: Letters from Iraq and Sierra Leone

Sulaymaniyah, Iraq—August 2003

I've been sent north from Baghdad to look into the mental health needs of internally displaced persons (IDPs). Northern Iraq is awash with them—850,000 or more. Some have been uprooted repeatedly, beginning in the 1970s when Saddam burned villages on the Iranian and Turkish borders and forcibly relocated Kurds into military-run collective towns; then in the Arabization campaigns that drove them out of Kirkuk and Mosul and Baghdad; in the Anfal campaign of 1988 at the end of the Iran-Iraq war, when probably 100,000 were killed, many by chemical weapons; in the first Gulf war when, betrayed by the West, they fled to the mountains; and in the internal fights between Kurdish factions in the mid-1990s. One in six people live in collective towns, one-fifth of them in destitution. There are also substantial numbers of IDPs still living in camps and public buildings. We received a U.S. government report that described a grim and desperate situation, so we came.

Each site seems more unbearable than the one before. I lie in my stuffy hotel room wondering whether it is worse to live for three years in a boiling-hot tent in "Takya transit camp" in a barren wasteland, with scorpions and snakes to contend with, and no work of any description; or to spend fifteen years in former police barracks in single rooms housing families of twelve, sleeping on a concrete floor where unspeakable horrors were once perpetrated by Saddam's security forces. The Police Machinery Building is in the middle of an industrial site where the noise from the factory keeps residents awake all night. The only way for pupils to get to school is to cross a highway on which four children have been seriously injured and two killed.

There is work near the barracks. Some men do casual labor and most boys over ten years old sell pencils or gum on the street. They do badly in school partly because they are exhausted and partly because it is hard to study in a room shared with eight others and used for everything. When I ask the boys what they do to make themselves feel better when they feel really low, the only thing they can come up with is sitting by the highway and watching the cars. In Takya, the desert camp, one girl says that all she longs for is cool water to bathe her face when she returns from collecting wood for fuel. She has never been to school and collects wood for four hours every day. She does not understand why the mobile clinic that visits once a week can have a fan and a fridge but none of the eighty families who live in the camp can.

On another site, an old army barracks in the middle of nowhere, the children have some space to play, but it is dangerous, rough, garbage-strewn ground with open streams of sewage and with unexploded ordnance still around. According to the children the worst thing on this site is the "fights." Most of the men have jobs in the Peshmerga, the Kurdish army, earning a meaningless salary but keeping their weapons. There are frequent quarrels over water and other issues. Some children saw one man shoot another dead last year. They cannot forget it and fear it could happen again.

The children get into fights as well. The schoolteachers tell me that violent methods of parental discipline such as beating children with belts or sticks or placing a heated knife against the skin are common.

One man banged his son's head against a wall because he failed sixth grade. Boys at the Police Machinery Building tell me they often hear one boy scream at night because his father takes a belt to him. A slow-speaking, thickset fourteen-year-old, he dropped out of school in second grade and has worked carrying stones at the cement factory ever since. He gets upset with the boys for mentioning his father's treatment of him. *You're embarrassing me. It's none of your business. Nobody beats you if you aren't doing anything.*

This is inhuman and it has gone on for thirteen years. We are stuck between the earth and the sky and no one cares, the Anjoman at the Police Machinery Building tells me. They at least have someone in authority, although "Anjoman" usually means a committee, not a single person. Many camps are so demoralized there is no leadership at all. *There's no law here,* says an old man at the army barracks. *No one is in charge, people are very poor, and we are completely dependent. The government doesn't help. One official said "Let everything collapse so people go home." He said "Sell your houses" but he has to be joking. How can we go home when our houses are worth 2,000 [Kurdish dinars] at most and a house in Kirkuk 80,000? We don't need blankets or water; we just want help to get home.*

These are the people who have fallen between the cracks, the truly dispossessed, many of whom have been in one camp or another since the 1980s, and who are too poor and vulnerable just to pick up and go home. There are probably around 13,000 of them living in these circumstances, scattered through Iraq's three northernmost governorates. In some ways this latest war has been a disaster for them, even though many of the families have stuck photos of George W. Bush up on the barracks wall and tell me with delight how much they admire Tony Blair. Before the war the UN had extensive plans for income regeneration, improved schools and play spaces, water and sewage systems, and actual rehousing. Since the war all plans but those for the most minimal water and sanitation services have been suspended indefinitely because the local authorities are determined that these IDPs should not be "made too comfortable" as this would be a "disincentive" to going home. But the means and assistance necessary for going home have so far not been provided by anyone. The UN is on its way out, since the Oil for Food funding ends in November 2003; the Coalition Provisional Authority has not fully arrived and its plans are unclear. The local Kurdish authorities treat this group as a political football, on the one hand stressing their plight as a means to push return, on the other arguing that assistance is not the local authorities' responsibility.

The local communities have become increasingly hostile to the displaced people, calling them "scroungers" and "invaders." One local representative of an international organization told me her employers did not provide certain services for this group because *those people remain there just to benefit themselves. They just want an easy life.* She had never visited the sites herself.

A fourteen-year-old who had lost his leg in a traffic accident when crossing the road told me he had tried to attend the local youth club. *I wanted to do English and computers,* he said. *They told me they had no space, but then they let in others after me.* The able boys had had the same treatment. *People look at us like scum and it makes me feel like scum,* another boy said. The children at the Takya camp were often stoned by town children on the way to school, and were told by the teacher that they were lucky she was willing to teach them.

I have worked out my own way of conducting a rapid assessment on these sites. First I look for a person or persons in authority—a schoolteacher, an Anjoman, or just a responsible family—and sit with them to try to get the basic facts on water, food, shelter, education, health problems. I am always made welcome, seated on thin cotton mattresses, offered water and tea. Inevitably more and more people, adults and children, come quietly into the room to contribute to the discussion. Then I ask if I can talk to a small group of children alone: between six and ten boys and girls separately. This is generally easy when teachers are present, as they see the point of getting the children's views on things.

In the Takya camp there was no teacher and the adults found my request disturbing. They were worried that the children would get the facts wrong or would not want to talk, but courteous as ever they acceded to the strange request of a foreigner whom they had made a guest. A family allowed me to use one of their "rooms." This was risky for them because, they told me, other families would think they were getting something and be jealous. So I went out repeatedly to explain to the families crowded around the tent that I was not "taking names," I was simply learning from the children how they lived. "Taking names" is enormously significant. Having your name taken means someone is going to help you. So few outsiders visit these sites that people would clutch at me and beg me to write down their names without the slightest clue who I was or why I was there.

Singling out ten children was another problem. On every site scores of others would press in at the windows or push at the door or find some way to creep into the space. Contrary to their parents' worries, they were all desperate to talk. As soon as the girls in the Takya camp sat down they all started talking at once: *We don't need anything, we just need our homes . . . We are burning . . . We don't have any freedom here . . . There's nowhere to save the food, no fridges . . . It's burning inside our tents . . . Nobody cares about us.* Even smaller girls in the camp lead restricted lives after school, remaining at home in the stifling tents, as there is nowhere for them to play.

When I asked the girls what frightened or upset them most it was *Scorpions and snakes . . . I have to wake two or three times a night to check if there are scorpions, then I can sleep.* Every child had been bitten by a scorpion. And there were other worries: *Insects get in your ears . . . We don't have a dentist: all my teeth hurt . . . People in Takya town make fun of us . . . I'm scared of the dark in case someone kidnaps us . . . The Islamic army said they were coming to butcher people; I didn't sleep all night . . . They were trying to put explosives here to blow up the camp so we were very scared.*

This mention of war was unusual. For the most part in the eleven sites I visited, children made little reference to the wars that had displaced them. Their worries and fears centered on the everyday hazards and discomforts of their current lives: fights, discrimination, beatings, land mines, snakes and scorpions, heat, dust, noise, dirt, dangerous roads, sickness, the absence of space to study, and, universally, the lack of space to play.

In all the sites I asked the children what their hopes were for their own futures and was amazed that in spite of their circumstances they did not lack ambition. All of them wanted to be doctors, lawyers, teachers, or engineers. There were slightly more would-be teachers among the girls, and the girls' reasoning was different from the boys'. They wanted to be doctors to *help poor people,* whereas the boys told me simply *Doctors have a better life, make good money.*

But in the boys' group in the Takya camp, the first to speak was a fifteen-year-old who had dropped out of school and now collected garbage three hours a day for $2.50 per month. He said *I would like to die. I don't have anything to do when I'm not working. My life is too hard, I just want to die. I have thought of it [suicide] a couple of times. I don't do it because it would upset my parents and I know they need me.*

For a moment, as we absorbed his seriousness and his misery, no one said a word. Then another boy spoke up: *We are all very sad here.* We had a long discussion about this. They said they wanted someone to help them. *There is no one we can talk to. We keep it to ourselves.*

I always worry that assessments suck information out of people and give nothing in return. Yet it was extraordinary how much the children liked these simple discussion groups. In every camp they would happily have continued to talk about themselves for as long as I allowed, and they thanked me for giving them the chance, even though I gave them nothing. In one camp they broke into applause and asked when we could meet again.

The hardest thing was the apathy and hopelessness among the adults. One boy told me *My dad has heart problems because he is so sad.* After fifteen years none of them thought it was possible for them to change anything. When they heard I was going to see the minister in charge of IDPs, the schoolteacher's family at the Police Machinery Building begged me to mention the dangers of crossing the road to school and their repeated requests for a bridge.

The Minister for Human Rights and Deportees told me that nothing had as yet been decided regarding these IDPs. *The trouble is people don't want to give up their comfortable lives in town where they can earn money, go to school, have TV and satellite dishes, and return to the relative hardship of the village. Most of these families have two houses. Father lives in the village, mother in the city.*

I asked the minister if he had hard evidence for this. The majority of the IDPs I had met were desperate to return to their former lives in Kirkuk. *Would we stay here if we had any money?* a boy at the Police Machinery Building had asked me. They all wanted to leave, but not to go back to the piles of rubble that were all that remained of their old homes. The minister told me he had no evidence, but he believed what he said. I asked if he had visited the Police Machinery Building. *Where is that?* he asked.

I explained where the camp nearest to his office was, and I passed on the families' request that he urgently address the issue of getting their children safely to primary school. Perhaps the authorities could construct a footbridge over the highway, or at least hire a very assertive crossing guard. He thought he might be able to do something at least for a couple of hours a day. He would send a delegation to investigate.

Kailahun, Sierra Leone—November 2003

I finished my assessment in northern Iraq and submitted a proposal to train local social workers and place one in every camp to help the community organize and to assist the most vulnerable families. While the proposal sat in the donor's in-box, security in Iraq continued to deteriorate, and my agency decided I could be more useful in

West Africa. It took fourteen hours to get from Freetown to this small devastated town, on a road that was large parts swamp and river.

I spent this morning with two groups—ten thirteen-year-old girls and ten boys. Most of them came back only two years ago when the rebel forces withdrew. Half the boys had been abducted and made to fight with the rebels, from ages as young as five. All but one of the children had lost at least one parent. Half of them had lost both. Living with foster parents is not easy. One girl told me her foster mother makes her a servant and beats her for the slightest thing, although she treats her own children well. Yet in spite of these overwhelming events what stays in my mind is the children's friendliness, energy, and laughter, and yet again their eagerness to talk.

In the afternoon a noisy, bright group of teenagers running the local children's club, all speaking at once, told me the foster child problem is so common that they have written a play about it to educate their town. The heroine is an orphan girl who lives with foster parents and is never allowed to go to school, never gets enough food, has to do all the chores, and is often beaten. Then she is forced into early marriage and dies in childbirth. In spite of all this, the children's optimism shines through: the play is called "All Is Not Lost."

Chronology

1908   Austria-Hungary annexes Bosnia-Herzegovina

1914   Gavrilo Princip, a Bosnian Serb student, assassinates Austria's Archduke Franz Ferdinand in Sarajevo

First World War begins

1918   Kingdom of Serbs, Croats, and Slovenes founded, incorporating Bosnia-Herzegovina (BIH)

1929   Renamed Kingdom of Yugoslavia

1939   BIH divided between Croatia and Serbia

1941–1945   The Second World War

BIH incorporated into the quisling Independent State of Croatia

The Drina valley changes hands repeatedly, coming under Fascist, Partisan, and Chetnik control

1945   BIH becomes one of six republics within Tito's highly centralized Socialist Federation of Yugoslavia (with Serbia, Croatia, Slovenia, Macedonia, and Montenegro)

1974   New decentralizing constitution attempts to counter Serb hegemony with strong federal institutions and regional autonomy for Serbia's provinces of Vojvodina and Kosovo

The chronology is drawn from the following sources: I. Lovrenovic, *Bosnia: A Cultural History* (London, 2002); Joe Sacco, *Safe Area Gorazde: The War in Eastern Bosnia, 1992–95* (Seattle, 2000); L. Silber and A. Little, *The Death of Yugoslavia* (London, 1995); The Bosnian Institute's *Bosnia Report* (London); and interviews in Foca and Gorazde.

Each of the six republics and two autonomous provinces has its own parliament and a representative on the federal presidency

1980   Tito dies

1981   Unrest in Kosovo: Albanian demonstrations in favor of granting Kosovo republic status are suppressed by federal army

1983   Communist authorities in BIH sentence Bosnian Muslim activist Alija Izetbegovic to fourteen years for counterrevolution, conspiring to create a "Muslim state," and calling for multiparty democracy (he serves five years)

1984   Winter Olympics held in Sarajevo

1985   Serbian Academy of Arts and Sciences declares that under communism, Serbian sacrifices in the Second World War have been rewarded with economic and political discrimination and with genocide in Kosovo, and recommends territorial unification of the Serbs as the solution to these problems: "The full national integrity of the Serbian People, regardless of which republic or province it inhabits, is its historic and democratic right"

1987   April: Serbian Communist Party official Slobodan Milosevic begins his rise to power as "defender of Serbs" in Kosovo

        September: Milosevic takes full control of the Communist League of Serbia

1988   June: The bones of Prince Lazar, the canonized Serbian ruler killed in the Battle of Kosovo in 1389, are displayed at large gatherings in Serbia and Bosnia encouraging Serbs to "return to their religious and national roots"

        October: Provincial government of Vojvodina is deposed and replaced by Milosevic loyalists

1989   January: The government of Montenegro is deposed and replaced by Milosevic loyalists

        February: Albanian miners strike, demanding respect for Kosovo's autonomy

March: New Serbian constitution revokes Kosovo's and Vojvodina's autonomy but retains their representatives in the federal presidency (Milosevic now controls 4 of the 8 federal presidency votes)

June: On 600th anniversary of the battle of Kosovo, Milosevic tells more than a million Serbs at the battle site: "Serbs through two world wars . . . liberated themselves and when they could they also helped others to liberate themselves . . . Six centuries later we are again in battles and quarrels. They are not armed battles though such things should not be excluded yet"

Croatian Democratic Union (HDZ) is founded in Croatia with Franjo Tudjman as president of party

December: Milosevic is elected president of Serbia

1990   January: Fourteenth Extraordinary Congress of the Communist League of Yugoslavia rejects proposals for a more decentralized Yugoslav Federation

Slovene and Croatian delegations walk out, ending the conference and Yugoslavia's Communist Party

February: Serb Democratic Party (SDS) is founded in Croatia

Milosevic declares a state of emergency in Kosovo

May: In Zagreb, football riots between Belgrade Red Star and Zagreb Dynamo supporters

Croatia's first democratic elections: HDZ wins a majority and Tudjman is elected president of the republic

Yugoslav People's Army (JNA) orders all territorial defense units in Yugoslavia to disarm except those in municipalities with Serb majorities

Party for Democratic Action (SDA) founded in Sarajevo, with Izetbegovic as president of party

July: Kosovo assembly declares Kosovo an equal and independent republic within the Yugoslav Federation

Serbian assembly annuls Kosovo assembly and government, takes over its powers

Serb Democratic Party (SDS) founded in Sarajevo, with Radovan Karadzic as president of party

August: In Croatia, Serb nationalists, supported by the JNA, clash with Croatian police

November/December: First democratic elections in BIH: SDA (26.6%), SDS (23.5%), HDZ (14.4%) form coalition government, with Izetbegovic (SDA) as president of presidency, Momcilo Krajisnik (SDS) as president of assembly, and Jure Pelivan (HDZ) as president of government

December: Communists retain control of Serbia and Montenegro in multiparty elections

1991   February: Serb minority in Croatia form Serb autonomous regions of Krajina, committed to remaining within Yugoslavia "with Serbs from all other nations, including BIH, that accept a common state"

March: Serb autonomous regions of Krajina declare independence

Milosevic and Tudjman secretly propose to divide BIH between Serbia and Croatia

June: Council for National Defense of Muslim Nation founded in Sarajevo, with Patriotic League as military wing

Slovenia declares independence and leaves Yugoslav Federation after ten-day war

Croatia declares independence

July: War between Croatia and Serbian autonomous regions, which are supported by JNA. Non-Serb recruits and officers start to leave JNA. War lasts six months, involves ethnic cleansing and attacks on civilians, and displaces 500,000 Croats and 250,000 Serbs

Serb irregular forces and JNA occupy one-third of Croatian territory

SDA and SDS hold nationalist rallies in Foca, attended by respective political leaders

Foca Trans bus company strike ends with formation of ethnically divided bus companies in Foca

September: Serb autonomous regions begin to be declared in BIH

UN imposes arms embargo on all of former Yugoslavia, thus allowing JNA to retain military superiority

October: JNA shells Dubrovnik and other Croatian towns

BIH assembly declares BIH a "sovereign and indivisible state of equal nations"

Karadzic warns that Muslim nation could "disappear" if BIH seeks independence

Assembly of Serbian Nation founded in BIH

European Community (EC) proposal that Yugoslavia become a community of sovereign states with joint institutions, protection of minorities, and possibility of dual citizenship is rejected by Serbia and Montenegro

November: SDS-organized Serb-only referendum in BIH; Serbs who vote support remaining in Yugoslavia

December: EC accepts Badinter Arbitration commission findings that Yugoslavia is in dissolution, invites the republics to request international recognition

Serbia and Montenegro reject commission findings

Serbian autonomous regions in BIH, including most of Sarajevo, declared to be Serbian Republic of Bosnia-Herzegovina with Radovan Karadzic as president

Serbs and Muslims in Bosnia arm themselves; Serbs get more and heavier weapons from JNA and territorial defense forces

1992   January: Ceasefire in Croatia; UN troops deployed in Serb-controlled areas, JNA troops pull back into BIH

SDS proclaims Republic of Serbian Nation in BIH; Karadzic declares: "united Bosnia-Herzegovina no longer exists"

EU recognizes Slovenia and Croatia

February 29/March 1: Referendum in BIH; 64% vote for independence

March 3: BIH government declares independence; Serb paramilitary units attack in some areas of BIH

April 3: Serb paramilitaries and JNA occupy Bijeljina; 500 Muslims killed, the rest driven out

April 4: Bosnian presidency orders general mobilization; SDS sets up barricades in Sarajevo

April 6: EU and USA recognize Bosnia-Herzegovina; Serb snipers kill four antiwar protesters outside BIH parliament

April 7–17: In Foca, Muslim militia defeated by local Serb forces and paramilitaries from Serbia; attacks on non-Serb civilians in town and nearby villages continue throughout the year

April 10: Zvornik occupied by Serb forces

April 13: Visegrad occupied by Serb forces

May: Gorazde attacked by Serb forces, beginning four-year siege of city

May 12: Sixteenth Assembly of the Serbian People in BIH; Karadzic announces six strategic objectives, including eradication of the Drina River as a border between Serbian states; General Ratko Mladic of JNA warns that attempting to separate Serbs from non-Serbs and have the non-Serbs simply leave the territory would not be possible and would amount to genocide

May 15: UN Security Council resolution 752 calls for withdrawal of JNA from BIH

Bosnian Serb Army (VRS) formed, with Mladic as commanding officer

May 20: Armed Forces of Republic of Bosnia-Herzegovina (ARB-H) formed

May 27: VRS shells civilians in bread queue in Sarajevo: 20 dead, 100 injured

May 30: UN Security Council imposes sanctions on Yugoslavia for failing to respect resolution 752

June: UN approves humanitarian airlift into Sarajevo; VRS hands over airport to UN

July: Western media report widespread atrocities against non-Serb civilians in BIH, including forced deportations and organized killings within camps

August: Serb Republic of Bosnia-Herzegovina renamed Republika Srpska (RS)

September: Forces from Gorazde push back VRS troops, enlarging besieged area; mule train over mountains keeps enclave supplied

UN authorizes UN Protection Forces for Bosnia

October: 7th Muslim brigade of ARB-H formed in Zenica, declaring its aim to be a "fight for the faith"; volunteers from Arab countries terrorize local Serbs, Croats, and Muslims

1993   January: Vance-Owen plan proposes ethnic cantonization of Bosnia

February: Fighting between ARB-H and Bosnian Croat forces (HVO); attacks on Muslim and Croat civilians

March: First airdrops of food supplies on Gorazde

May: UN declares Sarajevo, Zepa, Tuzla, Gorazde, and Bihac to be "Safe Areas"

VRS offensive takes remaining Bosnian government territory in Drina valley, tightens siege on Gorazde, closing mountain route to Sarajevo

Muslim soldiers massacre 65 Serb civilians in village of Josanice, near Foca

UN founds International Tribunal for War Crimes Committed on the Territory of the Former Yugoslavia (ICTY), with headquarters in The Hague

June: UN authorizes use of force to protect Safe Areas

1994   February: Shell from Serb position kills 68 people in Sarajevo market

ARB-H and HVO agree to a ceasefire

Serb forces begin to withdraw heavy weapons from around Sarajevo after NATO ultimatum

April: VRS intensifies shelling of Gorazde and advances to town center on right bank of Drina

NATO bombs Serb positions around Gorazde

VRS takes 150 UN personnel hostage; British jet is shot down

VRS shelling continues as international community disputes use of air strikes; 313 killed and more than 1,000 wounded in Gorazde in less than three weeks

April 24: VRS retreats three kilometers from Gorazde center, agrees to demilitarization of Gorazde area and UN-monitored ceasefire

1995   May: VRS shells Sarajevo marketplace and Tuzla, killing 71 civilians

After NATO ultimatum to stop shelling Sarajevo, VRS takes 350 peacekeepers hostage and uses them as human shields at military targets

July: VRS occupies Srebrenica: deports 25,000 Muslim civilians and executes 7,000–8,000 men and boys

London conference warns that VRS attack on Gorazde will be met with substantive and decisive airpower; UN withdraws monitors from enclave

VRS occupies Zepa, expels and kills non-Serbs

July, Karadzic and Mladic indicted for genocide, crimes against humanity, and violations of the laws or customs of war

August: Croatian army retakes most of Croatian territory (Operation Storm); mass exodus of Serbs, atrocities against those remaining

Croatian army and ARB-H lift siege of Bihac

VRS shells kill 41 civilians in Sarajevo market

NATO begins air strikes on VRS positions

September: Croat ARB-H forces advance to within 25 kilometers of Banja Luka; local Serbs flee to Serbia

October: Ceasefire supervised by NATO

November: Negotiations begin in Dayton, Ohio

December 14: Dayton Peace Accord signed in Paris; BIH divided into two Entities, Republika Srpska and the Federation of Bosnia-Herzegovina

1996   First violence against Serbian security forces by newly formed Kosovo Liberation Army (KLA)

June: Karadzic forced to resign presidency of SDS; Biljana Plavsic becomes president

November: Opposition alliance (Zajedno) wins elections in Serbia; Milosevic annuls results and holds new elections

Massive street protests begin, continue until original results reinstated in February 1997

1997   July: Milosevic elected president of Yugoslavia

November: Gorazde declares itself an open city committed to facilitating the return of Serb citizens, in return for increased international aid

1998   January: With Plavsic's support, moderate Milorad Dodik becomes prime minister of RS and transfers administrative authority from Karadzic stronghold of Pale to Banja Luka

February/March: Serbian security forces massacre civilians in Drenica area of Kosovo

March: In Foca, Dragoljub Kunarac hands himself over to ICTY, charged with rape as a crime against humanity

July: KLA steps up offensive against Serb forces, which respond with brutal counterinsurgency campaign

Milorad Krnojelac, primary school headmaster and former warden of KP Dom prison in Foca, arrested and sent to The Hague

October: Bosnian elections return nationalist parties in both Entities

Holbrooke Agreement with Milosevic arranges ceasefire in Kosovo, averts air strikes, and permits international civilian monitors in province

1999   January: Massacre of 45 Albanian men at Racak, Kosovo

March: NATO bombs Serb targets in Kosovo and Serbia, including Belgrade; Serbian security forces expel 800,000 Albanians from Kosovo

May: Milosevic indicted for genocide in Kosovo

June: Milosevic agrees to withdrawal of Serbian forces and UN administration of Kosovo; NATO air strikes cease

December: Franjo Tudjman dies

2000   January/February: In Croatia, HDZ loses parliamentary elections, moderate Stipe Mesic elected president of Croatia

April: Biljana Plavsic indicted for genocide and crimes against humanity

July: Constitutional court of Bosnia and Herzegovina rules that both Entities in BIH should amend their constitutions to ensure the full equality of the three "constituent peoples" throughout the country

October: BIH elections return moderates to power in the Federation and nationalist hard-liners in RS

October: Vojislav Kostunica elected president of Yugoslavia; Milosevic first refuses to accept the result but steps down after popular demonstrations supported by the army and police

December: BIH and Federal Republic of Yugoslavia establish diplomatic relations

Milosevic is arrested on charges of corruption and theft in Serbia

Milosevic handed over to the ICTY and sent to The Hague

2001   February: ICTY sentences three men from Foca for mass rape as a crime against humanity

April/May: In Banja Luka, foreign visitors and hundreds of Muslim returnees, attending the laying of foundation stone for the reconstruction of the Ferhat-Pasha mosque, are trapped in Islamic center by several thousand Serbs; riots leave 30 injured, one dead

August: Bosnian Serb General Krstic found guilty of genocide for his role in the massacre of over 7,000 Muslims at Srebrenica in 1995, sentenced to 46 years in prison

Three high-ranking Bosnian army officers indicted for alleged crimes committed in central Bosnia in 1993–1994

September: Milosevic indicted for war crimes and crimes against humanity in Croatia

October: Izetbegovic resigns as leader of SDA

November: Milosevic indicted for genocide in BIH between 1992 and 1995

December: In RS, SDS bans indicted war criminals from membership, including party founders Karadzic and Krajisnik

2002   January: Bosnian authorities hand over six suspected al-Qaeda members to the United States

February/March: NATO fails in two attempts to capture Karadzic

March: Yugoslavian president Kostunica, Serbian prime minister Zoran Djindjic, Montenegrin president Milo Djukanovic, and EU foreign policy chief Javier Solana sign an "agreement in principle" to replace Federal Republic of Yugoslavia with a new union called "Serbia and Montenegro"

Krnojelac sentenced to seven years for aiding and abetting crimes against humanity at the KP Dom in Foca

No Man's Land (Nicija Zemlja), written and directed by Sarajevo native Danis Tanovic, wins Oscar for best foreign-language film

April: Dutch government resigns after publication of official government report on the role of Dutch peacekeeping forces in Srebrenica massacre

October: BIH elections marked by low turnout and success of nationalist parties in both Entities; votes of non-Serb returnees entitle Federation parties to 17% of seats in RS assembly

Bosnian Serb company found guilty of exporting military hardware to Iraq in violation of the UN arms embargo

December: Biljana Plavsic pleads guilty to crimes against humanity

2003   February: the term "Yugoslavia" is dropped in favor of "Serbia and Montenegro" and disappears from the map of Europe

Notes

Introduction

1. Kofi Annan, *Report of the Secretary General pursuant to the General Assembly Resolution 53/35* (New York, 1998), para. 503.

2. ICTY, Sentencing Hearing Transcript, Biljana Plavsic, case no. IT-00-40-I (The Hague, 2003), 611–612. All documents from the International War Crimes Tribunal at The Hague are available online at *www.un.org/icty.*

1. Fighting Begins

1. The four Cs (Cyrillic for S), displayed around a cross, stand for the phrase "only unity can save the Serbs."

2. Alija Izetbegovic was president of Bosnia-Herzegovina at that time.

3. The word "Balija" probably comes from the Turkish term used to describe someone living on the edge of a town. In the past Muslim villagers sometimes used it about themselves; it is now a term of abuse used by non-Muslims about Muslims. Many Serbs connect it with "Ballist," the name of the nationalist Albanian organization whose members Serbs regarded as collaborators with the Nazis in the Second World War.

2. The War Goes On

1. "Brotherhood and Unity": the slogan introduced by Tito after the Second World War to encourage loyalty to a unified Yugoslav state. For some the phrase later came to symbolize an attempt to submerge ethnic distinctness.

4. Why Did We Fight?

1. Norman Cigar, *Genocide in Bosnia: The Policy of "Ethnic Cleansing"* (College Station, Tex., 1995), 121.

2. Noel Malcolm, *Bosnia: A Short History* (London, 1996). Ivan Lovrenovic, *Bosnia: A Cultural History* (London, 2002). Intermarriage: Tone Bringa, *Being Muslim the Bosnian Way: Identity and Community in a Central Bosnian Village* (Princeton, 1995), 156.

3. Josip Zupanov, "Research Shows Beyond Doubt, Intolerance and Media Propaganda Did Not Cause the War" (1995), in Mark Thompson, ed., *Forging War: The Media in Serbia, Croatia, and Bosnia Hercegovina* (Luton, 1999), 317.

4. Cigar, *Genocide in Bosnia,* 122.

5. *Merhaba:* an informal nonreligious greeting of Turkish origin, meaning "you are among friends"; used primarily by Muslim men and older people. Bringa, *Being Muslim the Bosnian Way,* 56.

5. What Became of Our Neighbors?

1. Human Rights Watch, Bosnia and Herzegovina, *"A Closed, Dark Place": Past and Present Human Rights Abuses in Foca* (New York, 1998).

2. Ibid., 11.

3. Ibid., 12, 15, 16.

4. ICTY, Indictment, Gagovic and others, Foca case nos. IT-96-23, IT-96-23/1 (The Hague, 1996), paragraphs 6.2–6.5.

5. Human Rights Watch, *"A Closed, Dark Place,"* 15–16.

6. Helsinki Watch, *War Crimes in Bosnia-Hercegovina,* vol. 2 (New York, 1993), 254–255.

7. International Crisis Group Report, *War Criminals in Bosnia's Republika Srpska: Who Are the People in Your Neighbourhood?* (Brussels, 2000).

8. Helsinki Watch, *War Crimes,* 355, 272–273.

9. Human Rights Watch, *"A Closed, Dark Place,"* 25.

10. Mark Thompson, ed., *Forging War: The Media in Serbia, Croatia, and Bosnia Hercegovina* (Luton, 1999), 89–96.

11. Helsinki Watch, *War Crimes,* 7.

12. J. Sacco, *Safe Area Gorazde: The War in Eastern Bosnia* (Seattle, 2000), 155–160.

13. Laura Silber and Allan Little, *The Death of Yugoslavia* (London, 1995), 215.

14. Zlatko Dizdarevic, *Sarajevo: A War Journal* (New York, 1994), cited in Thompson, *Forging War,* 230. Thompson, *Forging War,* 230–231.

6. What Country Is This?

1. Many young people in Foca thought of the newly formed Federal Republic of Yugoslavia (Serbia and Montenegro) as exclusively Serb. According to the 1991 census, however, 10 percent of Serbia's population was not Serb, and in the autonomous provinces of Vojvodina and Kosovo this rose to 45 percent and 90 percent respectively.

2. Lawrence Weschler, "Letter from Republika Srpska: High Noon at Twin Peaks," *New Yorker,* Aug. 18, 1997, 33.

3. Jonathan Steele, "The Phantom Voters of Eastern Bosnia" (War Report, Oct. 1997).

4. Brcko had had a majority Muslim population before the war and had been taken by Bosnian Serbs. They did not wish to relinquish control of the town because of its strategic position in the corridor of land connecting eastern and northern RS. In 1999 a final agreement established a special demilitarized district for the entire Brcko prewar district under the exclusive sovereignty of BIH, belonging simultaneously to both Entities with a unified multi-ethnic government. Brcko District Office of the Higher Representative, History and Mandate of the OHR North/Brcko (2001).

7. Where Do They Come From?

1. All textbook quotations come from books in use in Foca and Gorazde schools in 1997–98. These texts were revised in 2000 and there has since been work on a unified curriculum for Bosnia-Herzegovina, although national history curricula will remain separate.

2. In Andric's novel *The Bridge over the Drina,* a story is told that a mason walled up infant twins in the central pier to ensure the successful completion of the bridge.

3. Dusan's father echoed Serb intellectuals like Miroljub Jevtic who stressed the historical treachery of Bosnian Muslims in the popular press. "Those who accepted Islam accepted the conquerors de facto as their brothers, and the crimes of the latter as their own. That means their own hands

are also covered with the blood of their own ancestors, the former Bosnian non-Muslim population." "Rezervisti alahove vojske" (The Reservists of Allah's army), *Duga*, Dec. 9–22, 1989, cited in Norman Cigar, *Genocide in Bosnia: The Policy of "Ethnic Cleansing"* (College Station, Tex., 1995), 29.

4. Gavrilo Princip was a Bosnian Serb nationalist whose assassination of Austrian Archduke Franz Ferdinand in Sarajevo in 1914 was one factor contributing to the outbreak of the First World War.

5. Noel Malcolm, *Bosnia: A Short History* (London, 1996), 51–81. Cigar, *Genocide in Bosnia*, 14–15.

6. Bogoljub Kocovic, *The Victims of World War II in Yugoslavia* (London, 1985), 102, 174, 182, cited in Cigar, *Genocide in Bosnia*, 9. Malcolm, *Bosnia*, 192.

7. Malcolm, *Bosnia*, 174–192. It was only by considering the Second World War that I could make sense of the frequent Serbian references to a German-Vatican-Islamic conspiracy against them—although this historical underpinning fell apart when the CIA was also included.

8. Ibid., 177.

9. Bajram: the day of ending the Ramadan fast and the most important festival in the Bosnian Muslim calendar, celebrated by all the Muslims I knew, religious or not, with visits and food.

10. Tone Bringa, *Being Muslim the Bosnian Way: Identity and Community in a Central Bosnian Village* (Princeton, 1995), 83. I am indebted to Bringa, whose detailed analysis of Bosnian Muslim life in central Bosnia before the war has increased my understanding of this aspect of Muslim identity.

11. Ivan Lovrenovic, *Bosnia: A Cultural History* (London, 2002), 177.

12. This practice had been common in the past and still existed in some rural areas. Bringa, *Being Muslim the Bosnian Way.*

13. Lovrenovic, *Bosnia*, 209.

14. The group based in Zenica was not made up of "Arabians," as Fikreta calls them, but of young Muslims who identified with particular reformist tendencies in the wider Islamic world. Their presence helped to sustain Serbian fears of an Islamic "threat," but their non-Bosnian form of worship was rejected by all the families I interviewed.

15. Maja Povrzanovic has described a similar process of war-induced ethnic recognition and crystallization in Croatia in "Children, War and Nation: Croatia 1991–4," *Childhood* (1997): 81–102.

16. Vesna Pesic, "The War for Ethnic States," in *The Road to War in Serbia: Trauma and Catharsis,* ed. N. Popov (Budapest, 2000), 34–38. Petar Njegos,

The Mountain Wreath of P. P. Nyegosh, Prince-Bishop of Montenegro 1830–1851, trans. J. Wiles (London, 1930), 209.

17. Henri Tajfel, *Human Groups and Social Categories* (Cambridge, 1981), 255.

18. Miroslav Radovanovic, "O Potrebi donosenja nacionalnog programa" (On the Need to Draft a National Program), *Glas Crkve* 4 (1991); Bozidar Mijac, "Mir, da, ali kakav?" (Peace yes, but what kind of Peace?), *Pravoslavlje,* Mar. 15, 1992, both cited in Cigar, *Genocide in Bosnia,* 31–32.

19. Piete Kuhr, *There We'll Meet Again: The First World War Diary of a Young German Girl* (Gloucester, 1998), 1, 4–5, 13.

20. M. and C. W. Sherif, *Groups in Harmony and Tension* (New York, 1953).

21. Tajfel, *Human Groups,* 269–287. Once separated: Muzafer Sherif, O. J. Harvey, B. Jack White, William R. Hood, and Carolyn W. Sherif, *Intergroup Conflict and Cooperation: The Robbers Cave Experiment* (Norman, Okla., 1961). For a summary of these experiments see Donelson R. Forsyth, *Group Dynamics* (Belmont, Calif., 1999), 377–389.

22. Patrick Quinn, "Offer to End Sanctions Fails to Sway Serbs on Peace Plan," *Washington Times,* July 15, 1994, cited in Cigar, *Genocide in Bosnia,* 63.

23. David K. Shipler, *Arab and Jew: Wounded Spirits in a Promised Land* (Harmondsworth, 1986), 183, 195.

24. As Arab children in Israel learned from Arabic-language books following an Israeli curriculum, these images were mostly found on the West Bank and in books smuggled from there. Ibid., 199, 201.

25. Kuhr, *There We'll Meet Again,* 314.

8. War and Well-being

1. Frank Bodman, "War Conditions and the Mental Health of the Child," *British Medical Journal,* Oct. 4, 1941.

2. Anna Freud and Dorothy Burlingham, *Infants without Families: Reports on the Hampstead Nurseries, 1939–1945* (New York, 1973), 169, 172–173, 178, 193–207, 195. Freud acknowledged that her nursery had a selected population: children who did well when evacuated would stay in the country; the less successful evacuees were more likely to return to London and appear at the nursery. Her point is that these unhappy evacuees were more disturbed than children who had remained in London during the Blitz.

3. Charlotte J. Carey-Trefzer, "The Results of a Clinical Study of War

Damaged Children Who Attended the Child Guidance Clinic, the Hospital for Sick Children, Great Ormond Street, London," *Journal of Mental Science* (1949).

4. Dirk Van der Heide, in *Children in the Holocaust and World War II: Their Secret Diaries,* ed. Laurel Holliday (New York, 1995), 35–40, 52, 53.

5. Psychological genocide: R. M. Fields, *A Society on the Run: A Psychology of Northern Ireland* (Harmondsworth, 1973). Lost generation: H. A. Lyons, "Violence in Belfast: A Review of the Psychological Effects," *Community Health* (1973). Delinquency rates: K. Heskin, *Children and Young People in Northern Ireland: A Research Review* (Shepton Mallet, 1980).

6. E. P. Benedek, "Children and Psychic Trauma: A Brief Review of Contemporary Thinking," in S. Eth and R. S. Pynoos, eds., *Post-Traumatic Stress Disorder in Children* (Washington, 1985), 4, 5.

7. On the emergence of PTSD see Allan Young, *The Harmony of Illusions: Inventing Post-Traumatic Stress Disorder* (Princeton, 1995); Ben Shephard, *A War of Nerves* (London, 2000).

8. Wilbur J. Scott, *The Politics of Readjustment: Vietnam Veterans since the War* (New York, 1993), cited in Shephard, *War of Nerves.* Dickens: Allan Beveridge, "On the Origins of Post Traumatic Stress Disorder," in *Trauma: A Developmental Approach,* ed. Dora Black et al. (London, 1997), 4. Shell Shock: Shephard, *War of Nerves,* 357–359.

9. P. Hodgkinson, "Technological Disaster-Survival and Bereavement," *Social Science and Medicine* (1989), cited in Shephard, *War of Nerves,* 386. Social movement: B. Raphael, L. Meldrum, and A. McFarlane, "Does Debriefing after Psychological Trauma Work?" *British Medical Journal* (1995).

10. UNICEF, *The State of the World's Children* (Oxford, 1996).

11. F. Arbuthnot, "Sanctions Are Making It Harder to Forget the Trauma of War," *Guardian,* Dec. 30, 1994.

12. See Lynne Jones, "On a Front Line," *British Medical Journal* 310 (1995): 1052–54. Counseling programs: Lynne Jones, "The Question of Political Neutrality When Doing Psychosocial Work with Survivors of Political Violence," *International Review of Psychiatry* 10 (1998): 239–247.

13. Repackaging: A. Young, "An Alternative History of Traumatic Stress," in *The International Handbook of Human Response to Trauma,* ed. A. Shalev, R. Yehuda, and A. Macfarlane (New York, 2000), 51–68. Neglect of other problems: D. Silove, S. Ekblad, and R. Mollica, "The Rights of the Severely Mentally Ill in Post-Conflict Societies," *Lancet* 355 (2000): 1548–49.

14. A. Argenti-Pillen, "The Discourse on Trauma in Non-Western Cul-

tural Contexts," in *International Handbook of Human Response to Trauma,* 87–102. Vietnam veterans: Shephard, *War of Nerves,* 392–396.

15. D. Summerfield, "A Critique of Seven Assumptions behind Psychological Trauma Programs in War-Affected Areas," *Social Science and Medicine* 48 (1999): 1449–62.

16. A. Kleinman, "Anthropology and Psychiatry: The Role of Culture in Cross Cultural Research on Illness," *British Journal of Psychiatry* 151 (1987): 447–454.

17. S. Weine, D. F. Becker, T. H. McGlashan, D. Vojvoda, S. Hartman, and J. P. Robbins, "Adolescent Survivors of 'Ethnic Cleansing': Observations on the First Year in America," *Journal of the American Academy of Child and Adolescent Psychiatry* 34 (1995): 1153–58.

18. A. A. M. Thabet, Y. Abed, and P. Vostanis, "Emotional Problems in Palestinian Children Living in a War Zone: A Cross-Sectional Study," *Lancet* 359 (2002): 1801–04. On the earlier Intifada: A. Thabet and P. Vostanis, "Post-Traumatic Stress Reactions in Children of War: A Longitudinal Study," *Child Abuse and Neglect* 24 (2000): 291–298.

19. E. Cairns and A. Dawes, "Children: Ethnic and Political Violence: A Commentary," *Child Development* 67 (1996): 129–139.

20. P. Smith, S. Perrin, W. Yule, and S. Rabe-Hesketh, "War Exposure and Maternal Reactions in the Psychological Adjustment of Children from Bosnia-Hercegovina," *Journal of Child Psychology and Psychiatry* 42 (2001): 395–404.

21. See, e.g., James Garbarino and Kathleen Kostelny, "The Effects of Political Violence on Palestinian Children's Behavior Problems: A Risk Accumulation Model," *Child Development* 67 (1996): 33–45; M. S. Macksoud and J. L. Aber, "The War Experiences and Psychosocial Development of Children in Lebanon," *Child Development* 67 (1996): 70–88; P. S. Jensen and J. Shaw, "Children as Victims of War: Current Knowledge and Future Research Needs," *Journal of the American Academy of Child and Adolescent Psychiatry* 32 (1993): 697–708.

9. Day after Day

1. Diary of Krystyna Stankiewicz, Department of Documents, Imperial War Museum, 83/10/1, 23, 193, 267.

2. *I Was There,* Diary of R. J. Street, Department of Documents, Imperial War Museum, 82/24/1, 10, 17.

3. Lynne Jones and Kostas Kafetsios, "Assessing Adolescent Mental Health in War Affected Societies: The Significance of Symptoms," *Child Abuse and Neglect* 26 (2002): 1059–80.

4. Lynne Jones and Kostas Kafetsios, "Exposure to Political Violence and Psychological Well-being in Bosnian Adolescents: A Mixed Method Approach," *Clinical Child Psychology and Psychiatry* (forthcoming).

5. A. Dyregrov and M. Raundalen, "The Impact of the Gulf War on the Children of Iraq," presented at International Society for Traumatic Stress Studies World Conference, Amsterdam, 1992.

10. Making Sense of Madness

1. Ina Konstantinova, in *Children in the Holocaust and World War II: Their Secret Diaries,* ed. Laurel Holliday (New York, 1995), 256.

2. Yitskhok Rudashevski, in *Children in the Holocaust and World War II,* 161, 172.

3. Avner Ziv and Ruth Israeli, "Effects of Bombardment on the Manifest Anxiety Level of Children Living in Kibbutzim," *Journal of Consulting and Clinical Psychology* 40 (1973): 287–291.

4. G. Straker, M. F. M. Mendelsohn, and P. Tudin, "Violent Political Contexts and the Emotional Concerns of Township Youth," *Child Development* 67 (1996): 46–54.

5. S. Qouta, R. L. Punamaki, and E. E. Sarraj, "The Relations between Traumatic Experiences, Activity, and Cognitive and Emotional Responses among Palestinian Children," *International Journal of Psychology* 309 (1995): 289–304. Developmental age: K. Kostelny and J. Garbarino, "Coping with the Consequences of Living in Danger: The Case of Palestinian Children and Youth," *International Journal of Behavioral Development* 17 (1994): 595–611.

6. Vuk Draskovic's 1982 novel portrays Serbs as long-suffering, heroic, and virtuous (particularly the Chetniks in the Second World War), and Muslims as treacherous murderers who turn on the Serbs throughout history without understanding that they are betraying the nation from which they are descended.

7. S. J. Dollinger, "The Need for Meaning Following Disaster: Attributions and Emotional Upset," *Personality and Social Psychology Bulletin* 12 (1986): 300–310.

8. R. D. Goldstein, N. S. Wampler, and P. H. Wise, "War Experiences and Distress Symptoms of Bosnian Children," *Pediatrics* 100 (1997): 873–879.

9. R. S. Pynoos and S. Eth, "Witness to Violence: The Child Interview," *Journal of the American Academy of Child and Adolescent Psychiatry* 25 (1986): 306–319.

10. Z. Solomon, Y. Neria, and E. Witztum, "Debriefing with Service Personnel in War and Peace Roles: Experience and Outcomes," in *Psychological Debriefing: Theory, Practice and Evidence*, ed. B. Raphael and J. Wilson (Cambridge, 2000), 161–173. For example, the New York Police Department received this form of assistance after September 11, 2001. Members of the department told me that some found it extremely helpful but others perceived it as an unhelpful imposition.

11. Mixed results: P. Stallard, "Debriefing Adolescents after Critical Life Events," ibid., 213–244. Ineffective or harmful: B. Raphael, L. Meldrum, and A. McFarlane, "Does Debriefing after Psychological Trauma Work?" *British Medical Journal* 310 (1995): 1479–80; J. Kenardy, "The Current Status of Psychological Debriefing," ibid. 321 (2000): 1032–33. S. Wessely, S. Rose, and J. Bisson, "A Systematic Review of Brief Psychological Interventions ('Debriefing') for the Treatment of Immediate Trauma-Related Symptoms and the Prevention of Post Traumatic Stress Disorder," Cochrane Library, Cochrane Collaboration (Oxford: Update Software, 1999).

12. Hanna Kaminer and Peretz Lavie, "Sleep and Dreams in Well-Adjusted and Less Adjusted Holocaust Survivors," in *Handbook of Bereavement: Theory, Research and Intervention*, ed. M. S. Stroebe, W. Stroebe, and R. O. Hansson (Cambridge, 1993), 331–345.

13. Carola Eyber and Alastair Ager, "Conselho: Psychological Healing in Displaced Communities in Angola," *Lancet* (2002), 871. Muslim culture: Tone Bringa, *Being Muslim the Bosnian Way: Identity and Community in a Central Bosnian Village* (Princeton, 1995), 184–196.

14. Lynne Jones, "Notes for Thinking about Attachment, Grief and Loss in Societies Subject to Political Violence," in *International Child Health Care*, ed. D. Southall, B. Coulta, C. Ronald, and S. Parke (London, 2002).

15. M. Weisenberg, J. Schwarzwald, M. Waysman, Z. Solomon, and A. Klingman, "Coping of School Age Children in the Sealed Room during Scud Missile Bombardment and Postwar Stress Reactions," *Journal of Consulting and Clinical Psychology* 61 (1993): 462–467.

16. Anne Marie Oliver and Paul Steinberg, cited in R. J. Apfel and B. Simon, "Mitigating Discontents with Children in War: An Ongoing Psy-

choanalytic Inquiry," in *Cultures under Siege: Collective Violence and Trauma*, ed. A. C. G. M. Robben and M. M. Suarez-Orozco (Cambridge, 2000), 102–130.

11. Crimes and Punishments

1. Briefing note, UNHCR, Gorazde and Visegrad office, Jan. 2002.

2. International Crisis Group, *The "Constituent Peoples" Decision in Bosnia and Herzegovina* (Sarajevo, 2002).

3. ICTY, Case information sheet, Krajisnik, case no. IT-00-39 (2002).

4. ICTY, Judgment, Prosecutor v. Radislav Krstic, Srebrenica-Drina Corps case no. IT-98-33 (2001), paragraphs 73–84.

5. ICTY, Transcript, Prosecutor v. Dragoljub Kunarac, Radomir Kovac, and Zoran Vukovic, Foca case nos. IT-96-23-T, IT-96-23/1-T (2002).

6. A recent change in the property laws had made this much easier: returnees only had to wait six months rather than two years before selling their houses.

7. International Crisis Group, *The Continuing Challenge of Refugee Return in Bosnia and Herzegovina* (Sarajevo, 2002).

8. UNICEF, *The State of the World's Children* (New York, 1994).

9. I used the Heinz dilemma to assess moral reasoning. L. Kohlberg, *The Psychology of Moral Development: The Nature and Validity of Moral Stages* (San Francisco, 1984).

10. Serbs told me that the three fingers signify the eternal unity of Kosovo, Vojvodina, and Serbia, and thus the unity of all Serbs together.

11. I am grateful to Patrik Svensonn, then first secretary at the Swedish embassy in BIH, for his first-hand account of events.

12. Stanley Cohen, *States of Denial: Knowing about Atrocities and Suffering* (Cambridge, 2001), 7–9.

13. ICTY, Appeals Judgment, Prosecutor v. Kunarac, Kovac, and Vukovic, Foca case nos. IT-96-23-PT, IT-96-23/1-PT (2002).

14. ICTY, Transcript, Prosecutor v. Milorad Krnojelac, Foca case no. IT-97-25-T (2001), 7554ff.

15. Martha Gellhorn, *The Face of War* (London, 1998), 230–231.

16. Dan Bar-On, *Legacy of Silence: Encounters with Children of the Third Reich* (Cambridge, 1991), 329, 33.

17. Ian Buruma, *Wages of Guilt: Memories of War in Germany and Japan* (London, 1995), 49.

18. An Interim Agreement to accommodae the specific needs and rights of returnee children had been signed by ministers of education from both Entities in March 2002. An earlier agreement in May 2000 had stipulated the removal of "objectionable material" and the introduction of "shared core elements" to encourage a sense of common identity and citizenship in Bosnia-Herzegovina, but these changes had not yet been fully implemented and were too late for my respondents.

19. Milanka Saponja-Hadzic, "Kostunica Remarks Frighten Bosnia," *Balkan Crisis Report* 368, Sept. 18, 2002.

20. It seems this was not an idle boast; see Nicholas Wood and Ian Traynor, "FRY Arms for Saddam," *Guardian,* Nov. 25, 2002. I knew nothing at that time of a connection in arms dealing between Bosnian Serbs, Yugoslavia, and Iraq.

21. ICTY, Transcript, Prosecutor v. Radislav Krstic, Srebrenica-Drina Corps case no. IT-98-33 (The Hague, 2001), 9836, 9837.

22. ICTY, Judgment, Prosecutor v. Krstic, Srebrenica-Drina Corps case no. IT-98-33.

23. ICTY, Indictment, Prosecutor v. Slobodan Milosevic, Bosnia case no. IT-01-51-1 (2001).

24. Elizabeth Neuffer, *The Key to My Neighbor's House: Seeking Justice in Bosnia and Rwanda* (New York, 2001). Judges explained: ICTY, Appeals Judgment, Prosecutor v. Kunarac, Kovac, and Vukovic.

25. Buruma, *Wages of Guilt,* 161, 119, 114, 107.

Acknowledgments

My thanks to the William T. Grant foundation for the funding to conduct the research that lies at the heart of this book, to Peter Filkins for permission to quote his translation of Ingeborg Bachmann's poem "Every Day," and to the *British Medical Journal* for permission to quote Frank Bodman's 1941 paper on the war experiences of children.

This book was a long time in the making. I would never have begun if Professor Ian Goodyer of the Department of Developmental Psychiatry, Cambridge University, had not allowed me to pursue such a lengthy and unorthodox path during my child psychiatry training, encouraging me to return to Bosnia after the war to do the research. Professor Martin Richards and all the members and staff of the Centre for Family Research, also at Cambridge University, have provided academic guidance and friendship for almost a decade. I am particularly grateful to Sally Roberts and Gill Brown for endless and unfailing administrative support.

The idea grew out of conversations with Bosnian children during the war in Sarajevo in 1994 and 1995, and I am grateful to the support and friendship of so many. In particular Goran and Amela Simic, and all the local and international staff of Catholic Relief Services at that time. Narcisa and Semir Beslija have continued to provide me with a home from home in their beautiful city, ten years on.

British Ambassador Robert Barnett did much to make life easier during the war, and his successors Ambassadors Brian Hopkinson and Charles Crawford and the staff at British Embassy and British Council in Sarajevo continued to facilitate my work throughout my time in Bosnia.

Staff in UNHCR offices in Sarajevo, Banja Luka, and Gorazde and the OSCE office in Foca were always helpful in providing information and easing access to different parts of the country, both during and after the war. I would particularly like to thank Kris Janowski, Matthew Newton, Dejan Balic, Elisabeth Tomasinec, Aida Lakovic, Nerfisa Medosevic, and Amer Sijercic. Patrik Svensonn, first of UN Civil Affairs in Gorazde and later at the Swedish Embassy, was an invaluable source of advice. Local staff of MSF Gorazde 1996 gave me my first introduction to the Drina valley. Edin Culov was another source of introductions, contacts, and thoughtful interpretations of events. There were also many friends in Foca who prefer to remain anonymous. They know who they are.

Mirsada, Miralem, Rijad, and Nermana Adzovic gave me a home and an office and made me part of their family in Gorazde.

I am completely indebted to all my translators, especially Lejla Sudic-Hendo, Edita Beslija, Biljana Trebinjac, Vedrana Vukovic, Jasmin Kuljuh, and Ana Elez-Radcliffe, who did so much more than just translate. Their understanding and enthusiasm for the project, their empathy and sensitivity with the children, their administrative and diplomatic skills made my fieldwork possible. Their friendship is one of the things that made it so enjoyable.

The staff of the document collection of the Imperial War Museum gave suggestions as to manuscripts worth reading as well as providing working space in one of the loveliest libraries in London. I am grateful for their permission to quote from the diaries of Krystyna Stankiewicz and R. J. Street.

Many thanks to Noel Malcolm, Brendan Simms, Quintin Hoare, Vanda Vucicevic, and all the staff at the Bosnian Institute for patience with historical and factual queries and suggestions as to source material. Any inaccuracies remain my responsibility. Other helpful early readers were Mark Cousins, Dave Hansen, Nicholas Humphrey, Gill Moreton, Ben Shephard, Cornelia Sorabji, Jon Swain, and Richard Vogler.

My gratitude also to my mother for providing a quiet sanctuary in Fornalutx in which to complete the book; to my agent Katinka Matson for believing in this project through thick and thin; to my first editor, Erika Goldman; to my editor at Harvard, Elizabeth Knoll; and for such scrupulous and patient manuscript editing from Camille Smith. Elizabeth and Camille somehow stay in touch wherever I am working.

Finally I would like to thank the headmasters and teaching staff and psychologists of all the schools in which I worked in both Foca and Gorazde, for allowing me into their classrooms and for sharing their thoughts and opinions. My deepest thanks go to my respondents and their families, children at the outset, young adults now, who welcomed me into their homes and lives and gave me so much of their time. I hope they will find their thoughts and feelings about this period accurately reflected even when our interpretations of events differ. One idea that some of us discussed was for the respondents from the two cities to meet. That has yet to happen. My hope is that this book may be one step along the path to mutual understanding.

Index